MW01600553

The Name of Jesus Christ
As
Immanuel
Books I and II

The Complete Series
From the Original Manuscripts Notes

James G. Johnson

First Edition Printed May 2015 in the United States of America
Copyrighted © 1995
Bishop James A. Johnson, D.D., M.Th., Author
Lady Juana J. Johnson, Editor-in-Chief
Rev. Lawrence E. Brown Jr., Manuscript Editor

Foreword

I do not have the wisdom, language, or experience to adequately express my appreciation for you writing this book, *The Name of Jesus Christ as Immanuel*. To say that you simply "wrote a book" is an understatement. You poured yourself into this work. It is the achievement of three lifetimes. I am blessed and highly favored to have had the privilege of reading your work. It is stupendous, colossal, and vitally significant to this generation and to the generations to come. It is a work that must be published over and over again. It is a work that must be introduced to the world of theology, religion, and secularism, to both scholars and ordinary saints everywhere. For someone I know to have received this level of revelation and understanding takes my breath away and puts me doubly in awe of God. I cannot tell you how moved I am to have read this. At times, in the beginning, it was overwhelming; I literally had to put it down and walk away, not wanting to pick it back up. It was too heavy to carry. I felt Immanuel as close as you described Him in these pages. But duty required me to return to assisting my husband with the edits and when I did again I couldn't stop. This work has revolutionized my thinking, my understanding, my prayer life, my accountability in terms of faith and my trust in Immanuel. I was preaching the other day and it started coming out of me, not deliberately, but from the impact from being exposed to your thoughts. I thought, "I cannot do this. I cannot preach or teach this yet. This is Bishop Johnson's work. This is his book. It must be presented by him first." Nevertheless, it came out. I honestly have no words to describe the impact. I think my husband's words say it best: "As Luther is to 'The just shall live by faith,' as Haywood is to the 'Oneness of the Godhead,' as Wesley is to the 'Doctrine of free will and Arminianism,' Bishop James A. Johnson is to the Gospel of 'Jesus Christ as Immanuel.'

I also deeply appreciate Lady Juana J. Johnson for having the heart, the unselfishness, the love, and the trust to ask me if I thought my husband would help with this project on the night you both came to his elevation to the Bishopric with Bible Way. My heart is forever connected with both of you because of this work.

Thank you for this invaluable contribution at this crucial time in Church History.

Lady Tanya C. Brown

Introduction

In this book, Bishop James A. Johnson shares a divinely-enlightened perspective of the Name of Jesus Christ as Immanuel, as it was given by God to the prophet Isaiah in Isaiah 7:14. For many years, he has shared this thesis with many audiences while preaching and teaching God's word. He presented this thesis at the 1991 Hampton University Ministerial Conference. The presentation was phenomenal to say the least. The hundreds of theological scholar who were there were unanimously convinced that this was truly a sound and enlightening perspective. Thankfully now in this book we have this thesis in written form.

Bishop Johnson is considered by many scholars to be one of the most knowledgeable Bible teachers among us today. He is especially acquainted with the Gospel of Jesus Christ and is a sound teacher of the Apostles' Doctrine. There are few among us who have his keen insight and depth of understanding concerning the person of Jesus Christ. He is akin to a walking commentary, holding volumes of insight into the word of God concerning our Lord and Savior Jesus Christ. Having access to his teachings is a great privilege that provides the reader with an abundantly rich venue from which to receive impartation.

In this book, Dr. Johnson commits to us an abundant treasure of knowledge which is vested by God in Immanuel. He points out commonly-overlooked perspectives of the Gospel that were planted by God in the name Immanuel; the main revelation of this book concerns the way in which God spelled out in the name Immanuel all that Jesus was and did. He shows the significance of this revelation in this book. Throughout the chapters, He takes the word-name Imm/anu/el and shows how the entire spectrum of the Gospel of Jesus Christ, from His incarnation in Bethlehem, to His enthronement on high, is spelled out in the meanings of the three syllables that constitute the word Imm/anu/el. He analyzes every side of the name, from bottom to top, from the 'I' at the beginning of the name to the 'L' at the end of it and finds that God put His final and complete revelation of Himself in that single word.

Page by page, this anointed and enlightened author takes the three sub-words [syllables-Imm-anu-El] in the name Immanuel as it is in the original text 'with-us God' and from its meaning, exposes and proves that all of the main points of the Gospel are planned by God in Immanuel. By this it can be seen that Immanuel's name confirms the Gospel and the Gospel confirms the name Immanuel. From the abundance of insight about Immanuel that God revealed to him, Dr. Johnson produced this book.

While I read and researched this book as manuscript editor, to see if anyone else had discovered the same things about Immanuel that are shared by Dr. Johnson in this thesis, I was truly amazed to find that there was not another book or author that treated the name of Immanuel so thoroughly as has Dr. Johnson. Also during my research, it was interesting to find that the Hebrew scholars who translated Isaiah 7:14 in the *Tanakh Scriptures Text* agreed with Dr. Johnson's discovery about the linguistic order of the syllables in the word Imm/anu/El.

In Book II, the author continues his discussion of Immanuel by pointing out those extraordinary things that were done by God *In Immanuel Only.* In Book II, along with many other very interesting revelations, he presents an insightful discussion of how Jesus-Immanuel was the only one who went to Hell and, in so doing, satisfied the heart of God.

Although both Books affirm the general thesis of the series, in Book I, He breaks down the word Immanuel into its divinely- given syllable sequence and explains the meaning of the name and how God's plan in Immanuel is fulfilled in Jesus Christ.

Book II continues to affirm the general thesis with the theme *In Immanuel Only*, which is explained in its introduction.

Thankfully, we now have both books in this complete series of the works of Bishop James A. Johnson on the *Name of Jesus Christ as Immanuel.*

About the Author

Bishop James A. Johnson, also known as Dr. Johnson, holds a Bachelor's Degree in Christian Education, a Master's Degree in Theology, and Doctorates in Divinity, Theology, Philosophy, and Christian Education. He is a Member of the Board of directors of the Urshan Seminary in St. Louis, Missouri. He is the pastor of the Bethesda Temple Church of the Apostolic Faith in St. Louis, Missouri, where he has served for more than sixty-five years. He is also the founder of The Bethesda Temple Bible Institute [BTBI].

Bishop Johnson is the former Presiding Bishop of the Pentecostal Assemblies of the World, Inc., and he was the 1991 speaker for the prestigious Hampton University Ministerial Conference in Boston, Massachusetts.

President Bill Clinton chose to attend his church for Sunday morning service when he visited St. Louis once in the 1990s.

Bishop Johnson is considered a father in the Gospel by many people. He is known for his clear and thorough insight into the word of God and for his ability to explain it well. Although he is well versed in the entire Bible, his specialty is the Gospel, in particular, the person of Jesus Christ, and he has devoted himself to studying the Gospel of Jesus Christ.

In this book, Dr. Johnson shares what he has found in his study of Jesus Christ as Immanuel. Over a period of years, piece by piece, God revealed to him all of the concepts about Immanuel that he shares herein. Through the years, He became more and more enlightened about the unending close relationship God intended to have with man through Jesus Christ as Immanuel.

His lifelong commitment to the topic of the name of Jesus Christ as Immanuel qualifies him as a premier ambassador of the subject. His nearly seventy years of faithful stewardship to the Gospel, his proven ability to articulate what God did via Jesus Christ as Immanuel, and the soundness of his teachings on the topic make him a specialist in this study and an invaluable resource for this area of theology.

Bishop Johnson was the presenter at the Hampton University Ministerial Conference when he presented this thesis in a powerful sermon format, where he illuminated the theological community as he shared the insight God showed to him about Immanuel.

Countless numbers of pastors, bishops, presiding bishops, Bible college teachers and saints claim him as a mentor. Because of his seniority in the ranks of the leading fathers in the Gospel [sixty-five years], his fatherly wisdom, his genuine spirit of concern for the body of Christ—that we all cleave to the faith of the apostles—and his commitment to the Apostles' Doctrine, he has become known as a modern day Apostolic Father.

He has been so enthralled by the revelations given to him about The Name of Jesus Christ as Immanuel that for many years, the license plate on his car spelled an acronym for Immanuel.

As Luther is to the doctrine, "The just shall live by Faith," as Haywood is to "the Oneness of the Godhead," as Wesley is to "the doctrine of 'Free Will' and Arminianism," so is Bishop James A. Johnson to the understanding of the Name of Jesus Christ as Immanuel. We are blessed to have this revelation from God, through him, in these pages.

Author's Acknowledgements
And
Impartation

I thank God for salvation and for His marvelous grace and favor, which He has bestowed upon me in drawing me close to Him to speak to me as He did on the morning of October 14th, 1990, when He began to unfold to me His purpose and His plan for us [mankind] in Jesus Christ as Immanuel.

I thank Him for continuing to unfold aspects of this revelation to me over time and in various settings. From that day to now, He has fed my mind on various occasions by showing me the different aspects of the Gospel that are fulfilled in Jesus Christ as Immanuel.

Because God imparted to me the rich truths about His name as Immanuel freely, I am obliged as a messenger of the Lord (a preacher) to impart those same things to the entire body of Christ: that is, those wonderful things about Jesus Christ as Immanuel that I share in this book.

I also heartedly thank my wife, Lady Juana J. Johnson, for her genuine interest and determination to see my work(s) in print. I appreciate how she saw to this as if it were her own personal work. I can say that she came to the Kingdom for such a time as this. She sought the appropriate venues and resources to help get the job done. She worked with me and the manuscript editor to take my set of manuscript notes and from them produced this book.

As we moved through the different stages of the publication process, at points when things were progressing towards the completion of the work, when we could see it forming and coming to pass, she rejoiced personally for my work's success. Prayerfully and passionately, she worked to see this book completed and in the hands of the saints.

I also thank Reverend Lawrence E. Brown, Jr., 'my son in the Gospel,' who worked with us as manuscript editor. He also was determined to see his father in-the-Gospel's work published. (He said) it was like a calling from God to see to it that this great thesis be published among the saints with the greatest fidelity to ensure that it would be purely a James Johnson work. He took the challenge and worked diligently to assist my wife and me in bringing this to pass.

I also thank his wife, Lady Tanya C. Brown, for her assistance and encouragement and all that she did to support her husband's efforts towards the project. At certain stages in the process, when we saw it coming to pass, she rejoiced with us too. I am grateful for everything she did to assist her husband in seeing this first edition published.

I am also thankful to and appreciative of the many pastors, Bible teachers and saints who have shown genuine interest in this work. I am grateful to those of you who have prayed for this venue of impartation and have waited with anticipation for its completion and publication. Your interest in it has been truly inspiring to me. Your frequent encouragement and enquiries about its completion date helped motivate me and those who worked with me on this project to bring it to this point.

As I have received from the Lord, so do I impart this book to those of you who are in the theological community, ministers of every ecclesiastical rank, and to all of my sons and daughters in the Gospel, as a literary gift which contains the impartation of the revelation of the Name of Jesus Christ as Immanuel.

Thanks to all of you for your interest and reception.

God Bless you all in the Name of Jesus-Immanuel.

James G. Johnson

Bishop James A. Johnson, Author

Table of Contents: Books I and II

Editor's Preface, Book I

I thank God and Bishop James A. Johnson for offering me the privilege to work as Manuscript Editor on this most precious project.

I have felt a sense of awe from the beginning of the project until now—publication of the first edition.

With great honor and fear, I have tried diligently to structure and transfer all of the information from the original manuscript notes into the chapters in this book. In transferring the contents of the notes, I sought to keep the exact contextual meanings that are in the manuscript notes in each chapter of the book.

In the transfer process, I was careful to preserve the integrity of all of the divinely-inspired thoughts of this great man of God. It was my goal to maintain nearly all of the words and paragraphs exactly as they were presented in the original manuscript notes. In transforming the manuscript into a book, I strove to deliver to the readers an absolutely authentic work of Bishop James A. Johnson.

This required placing the manuscript's thoughts together into chapters so that a particular concept flowed well as the content came from the author's mind. Nearly everything in the manuscript notes is in this book. Even those essays that, due to lack of space, were not transformed into chapters yet are in The "Appendix of Essays" at the end of the book. Passages from some notes are used in more than one chapter because they relate to more than one topic. Thus, it is not a mistake that a note is mentioned more than once.

Caveat: In an effort to keep the original context and thoughts just as they are presented by the Bishop in the notes, I minimized editorial remarks on the subject matter in the chapters. However, any editorial comments are in italics. I also limited the use of transition statements to only those that were absolutely necessary for clarity.

This book is composed of a number of essays and expositions on the subject: *Name of Jesus Christ as Immanuel* that were divinely-imparted to the author over the years.

The passages in this book are in the author's exact words. The information from the manuscript notes are presented in the book exactly as in the notes and are written in calibri font. Thus, the author's exact words appear in calibri font throughout the book.

What I have done in constructing the chapters is to gather all of the essays on the same theme or topic into chapters of like themes.

To show the exact location of the passages in the original manuscript notes, I used MS (manuscript search) reference numbers that tell the exact location in the manuscript notes where the materials are found.

I use the MS reference numbers as a system to verify that the book adheres to the author's original passages. The reference numbers (MS) ensure that all passages in the book can be traced back to the original notes by page and line. The manuscript search numbers identify the page number of the manuscript on which a passage is found. It tells in what quarter of the page {a, b, c, d} the passage is found and the line of the quarter page. Example: MS124,a,3 is manuscript note page 124, in the first top quarter of the page(a) on line 3 in that quarter of the page.

All MS numbers are listed in the **Manuscript Page Index** in the back of the book.

Passages in handwriting fonts are passages or comments hand-written in the notes by the author himself in the already typed manuscript binder. This was for an even more personal effect for his sons and daughters in the Gospel who shall have this for years to come.

I also researched other authors. As I researched many other author's writings on Immanuel to see what makes this work significant. I found three things; (1) That no one else commonly known in the theological community, among writers had presented this breakdown of the name Immanuel. (2) That the meaning of the name Immanuel in the English and Latin interpretations was different from the meaning the author teaches in the book (3) That Erudite Hebrew scholars who know Hebrew language very well that the original text was given in, agree with Dr. Johnson's interpretation of the name Immanuel. It is an awesome revelation.

In the production process, I held sessions with the author; working closely with Bishop James A. Johnson and the Editor–in-Chief his wife, Lady Juana J. Johnson. In those sessions, we worked together adopting chapter topics and presenting the explanations of the concepts which were in the manuscript notes to get the most clarity of thought flow. Even today we are still discovering ways and things that can be done to make this work more powerful. And that will always be. Bishop Johnson is such a perfectionist when it comes to writing and speaking he would have held this work back until it was as perfect as other commentaries that took more than one hundred years of revisions and new editions to get there.

However, thankfully on May 6, 2015 during the week of his sixty-fifth pastoral anniversary, he released this book to be published, trusting us and God that it would be presented right.

The core of the revelation given to the author that comprises an abundance of insight on the topic; The Name of Jesus Christ as Immanuel is in here. This thesis that cannot be found in any other book, is vested in this book and is hereby being made available to the entire body of Christ. The essence and particulars of the thesis are well explained and broken down by the author in this book. The Name of Jesus Christ as Immanuel is thoroughly elaborated. We have worked and prayed that we successfully deliver this work with the highest degree of authenticity.

As the editors of Matthew Henry, Adam Clark and other commentary writers were trusted guardians of those works and strove for perfection in their presentation. They worked for more than one hundred years and are still preserving, perfecting, and presenting the works of those authors; we are committed to the same for this work.

This is a dynamic work that will constantly be perfected. All experienced authors and editors of commentaries and like-books, know well that there must be new editions, revised editions and the ongoing renewal of the presentation of a work for generations to come.

This book is also presented as an heirloom and a keepsake for those who want to have a piece of Apostolic Faith Heritage. It is a precious impartation from one of the greatest modern apostolic fathers that God gave to us. It is already signed by him for all who shall have it and be blessed by it.

Lawrence Brown, Jr., Manuscript Editor

Author's Preface

Receiving the Revelation

On the morning of Sunday, October 14, 1990, the Lord spoke to me and said, "Where there are no words, there is nothing to think. Take for instance the word Immanuel." *Then he caused me to notice the Latin and the English interpretations of the name Immanuel*; in Latin *it is* "*Nobis (cum) Deus.*" In English, *it is* "God (with) us." *However*, in Hebrew, *Immanuel is* "WithusGod," as given in Isaiah 7:14.

God said, "The Latin and *the* English are accurate, but not precise, but the way I gave it (*the syllables in the name Immanuel*) to the prophet Isaiah—that is precise."

Words are thoughts embodied—where there are no words, there are no thoughts expressed.

I then took note that there is no syllable between "anu" and "El" in the name Imm/anuel. *Hence*, there is no room for decisive or broken thought, nothing that indicates a separation between us and God. Here the English is not as precise as the Hebrew. Although it is accurate in meaning, it is not as finely tuned.

"With us God," *as in the original Hebrew of Isaiah 7:14*, would be (is) more precise—then there *(is)* would be no preposition (adv. conj.) between.

*In the original Hebrew syllable arrangement, El is the last syllable in the name Immanu**El**. As I progressed in this study, and as you will read in this book, I saw that* in Imm/Anu/**El**, God places Himself last to thereby join immediately with us.

He made Himself least, little beyond all others in size or degree: smallest; slightest; fewest. *Least is* the superlative of little. God makes Himself last and least in Immanuel. *How?* In Immanuel, El, God in His almightiness makes Himself last in the Name via making Himself least of all men in the cross. *On the* cross, God in Christ became lower than any man had ever been before God. It was the bottom (*Profundis Immensis*) of the bottom in humility, humiliation and judgment. **It was the lowest hell, the darkest, deepest death. He made His grave with the wicked in**

His death. In Imm an uel, as only El the Almighty could do, He conjoins the superlative ("His name shall be great") of little and the unimaginable superlative of great—Jesus Christ—*and* hereby proves that he is the greatest.

Later, by serendipity, I discovered on January 2nd, 1991, as I searched in a "Black's Law Dictionary" for the meaning of "Q.V." *I read the Latin phrase:* "*Quoties in verbis nulla est ambiguitas, ibi nulla expositio contra verba fienda est.*" This translates as: "*When in the words there is no ambiguity, then no exposition contrary to the words is to be made.*"

This caused me to notice that the English interpretation of Immanuel is **God/with/us,** *having the word with between God and us, is different from the original Hebrew of Isaiah 7:14.* The original Hebrew interpretation is **with/usGod,** "With us God," which (is) more precise—there *is* no preposition (adv. conj.) between *us* and *God. Seeing this is the key revelation [concept] of this thesis.*

As it is established in this book, it is evident that God arranged the syllables in the name Immanuel purposely **to show the unique and eternal union between God and man in Jesus Christ our Lord, the Son of God, as revealed to the prophet Isaiah In the name of Immanuel.**

Therefore, the thesis of this two book Series is:

To show the unique and eternal union between God and man in Jesus Christ our Lord, the Son of God, as revealed to the prophet Isaiah In the name of Immanuel.

Author, Bishop James A. Johnson

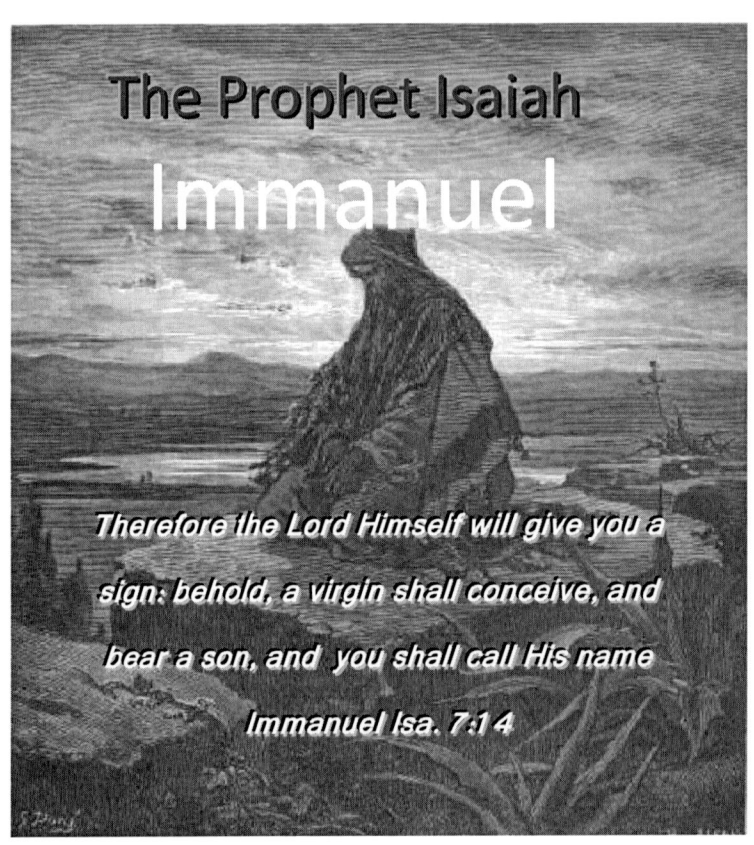

The Prophet Isaiah

Immanuel

Therefore the Lord Himself will give you a sign: behold, a virgin shall conceive, and bear a son, and you shall call His name Immanuel Isa. 7:14

Thesis Statement:
To show the unique and eternal union between God and man in Jesus Christ our Lord, the Son of God, as revealed to the prophet Isaiah In the name of Immanuel.

Chapter 1

THE DIVINE MESSAGE IN THE NAME IMM/ANUEL

As I explained in the preface of this book how God revealed to me the significance of the divinely sequenced syllable arrangement in the name Imm/anu/el, in this chapter I share the meaning of the divine positioning. That is the message God was giving in the sequence of the syllables in Imm/anu/El.

Starting in this chapter and continuing throughout the entire book, I explain the relationships of God to man shown in the sequence of the word parts in the name Immanuel.

God gave us His name in Imm-Anu-El, syllabylized and tripartite so as to aid our faith and understanding of His plan in Immanuel. The positioning of the word parts in the name Immanuel are significant and specific to what God planned Immanuel to be. Therefore, in this chapter I explain the relational and spiritual meanings of the arrangement of the word parts that make the name Imm/anu/El. I answer the question; "What did God intend in the name Immanuel by placing the syllables [word parts] together in their order?" We can see man's close relationship to God in Immanuel. In the succeeding chapters, it is explained how this closeness to God is demonstrated by Immanuel's cross, in Christ's descent into hell, and ultimately when Jesus and the church are glorified together in an eternal and inseparable union forever. All of this is smelled out in the syllable sequence of the name Imm/anu/El.

As you read and study this book you will understand how in the name Immanuel with its precise word part order, spells the entire spectrum of the gospel. It spells the incarnation—virgin birth, Jesus 'suffering on the cross, His decent into Hell for us, His resurrection from the dead for us and with us, and His final glorification of the saints.

In all of this we can see the unique and eternal union between God and man as revealed to the prophet Isaiah in the name Immanuel.

Linguistic Analysis of Immanuel as a three Partite Name / Word

Immanuel is a three part [name] word. It is comprised of a preposition, a pronoun and a noun of which all of them are significant to understanding the divine message in the name Immanuel:

1. Imm, preposition (with); language
2. Anu, us; man
    Objective case of pronoun "we"
3. El, God, noun
    I.   The language of man is a tool of man and is less than man (Imm)
    II. Man is more than language but less than God (Anu)
    III. God is more than man and language together (El)

Imm/anu/El

In the linguistic arrangement *of Imm/anu/El*, God places what is least first and that (He who*) [El, God]* which is greatest last, with he {man} *[anu-man]* who is more and less in the middle.

1. Language is in the **ante** position [with a word in language]
2. Man is **inter**position [anu-man]
3. God who is most is **post**position. [El-God]

So God caused the word to move in syllabic sequence from least to greatest, from last to first. God preceded man and man preceded language of speech. The order was   first God then man, then the language of man. But In Immanuel, God does most unseemly things.

He shows us in Immanuel that "my thoughts are not your thoughts and my ways are not your ways.

In Immanuel, El creates a man without a man. He caused a King to be born in a stable and laid in a manger. He sent an all-riches one to become the poorest of all (nowhere to lay His head). The King of Heaven to become homeless "out of the ivory palaces into a world of woe." The King of Heaven became a servant of men. Eternal life took on a birthday. The greatest became the least. God became man. The eternal <u>One</u> <u>died</u> on a cross, etc., etc., etc.

Comparing the Latin and the English Interpretations of Immanuel to the Original Hebrew Interpretation

The fact that the most commonly accepted interpretations of the name Immanuel are different from its original Hebrew interpretation must be mention at this point. The original Hebrew meaning of the name Immanuel was given to Isaiah in Isaiah 7:14 which is withusGod having nothing between the words 'us' and 'God'. But the Latin and the English [the most commonly accepted interpretation] are different from the original Hebrew in as much as they both have a word between us and God.

The Latin and the English have words between God and man but in the Hebrew there is nothing. In the Hebrew man and God are inseparably close.

In the Latin cum is interposed   *Nobis (cum) Deus*
In the English "with" is interposed.   God (with) us
In the Hebrew "Imm" is anteposed.   WithusGod
Please notice that In the Hebrew, no word, hence no-thought, nothing is interposed between anu and El, i.e. us and God.

In the Hebrew, we have the thought which is God's thought as Alpha, the original as it was given in the original prophesy concerning Immanuel. The English, the Latin are attempted copies. They are translations *where* a measure of the original intent or force is "lost in the translation.

This is a perfect example of what mean when He said God said; "My thoughts are not your thoughts; my ways are not your ways." Isaiah 55:8

In all things Divine pertaining to man, God is first, original. He always thinks, plans, speaks or acts before us. We think, or attempt to think His thoughts or speak His words AFTER Him. However, in the name Immanuel He places Himself last in the spelling. This we will explain in a few more minutes of reading.

In Immanuel, Anu and El are juxtaposition [side by side] with each other. In the linguistic arrangement, God has placed no word, hence no thought of His between the two - NEITHER should we! Stare Decisis!! Stare Decisis!! Stare Decisis [let it be as it is]!!

In Jesus Christ, both men and God are together and it cannot and will not ever be otherwise. A man cannot be in Christ and not in God as he cannot be in St. Louis, Columbia, Kansas City or Jefferson City, and not be in Missouri - or in God and not in Christ. Jefferson City is the capital of Missouri. A man can't be in Washington, D.C. and outside the U.S., etc., etc.

The Divinely Given Linguistic Arrangement of the Name Immanuel is telling of the Intended Closeness of God to Man in Imm/anuEl:

Notice that in the name Immanuel God is last ImmanuEL. That is not an accident. God placed Himself there on purpose. The name Immanuel needs all of its parts for its meaning to be complete. We cannot just have part of the name. We cannot just have Immanu which means 'with us' with out the most significant and most necessary part [El-God]. It is the God[El] part of the word on the end of it that makes the word powerful and complete ImmanuEL.

The preposition *[with]* and the pronoun *[us]* are upheld by the Name *[El],* the being of God. The Life of El is breathed into the name Imm/anu/el. In fact **With us** is without form and void but for El. Only by the life of El does "Immanu" become a living soul.

God did in Immanuel just as He did in the making of Adam [man]. He formed Adam then breathed life into him. The form needed the breath of God to become a living soul so does the name Immanuel need its life source [El-God]. El makes "Immanu" His own living and unique "soul." As in the formation of Adam, he does not become a living soul, i.e. an active creature, without breath; so linguistically, Immanu is a 'form only' until El "breathes" His unique Life into it by His presence - but His presence giving the term Life is last in the word form as Adam's breath, which was the foundation of his life came last -

16

after his formation. <u>So the last syllable in the term Immanu/El is the foundation of His total being.</u> **Immanuel** cannot exist without El. Adam could not exist without the breath of life. Thus, God is in Immanu/el and that is truly marvelous. The miracle of God being in man will be further expounded in the coming chapter on the virgin birth.

El, Last and the Foundation of Immanuel

God, who is absolutely free, and has always been, could have breathed Adam's breath first and built his body around his breath - as He is going to do qua, with our pre-perfected spirits at the time of the rapture. He gave us the Spirit manufactured first, in as much as we now have the Holy Ghost, then the body will be made/glorified at His coming to envelope it. But in Adam's case , He made Adam first and gave him the breath of life last. Being God, and doing things after the counsel of His own will, He who is the breath of Life of Immanuel, names Himself last. Yet He is the foundation of His saving name- comprehended in Jesus Christ. Unless El, God (be here) there is no *Jesus Christ!* Here God must be! Here God IS! God made Adam's body first a perfect body, then gave him perfect life to complete a perfect being.

The Church, the Bride Receives its Life before its Glorification

Now in the church age, we have "come to the spirits of just men made perfect." After our spiritual perfection, God is going to clothe us with a new body, a house from heaven, a building not made with hands.

In the perfection of the church, God reversed the order He used in Adam's formation. ***"God does what He wills in the Army of heaven and among the inhabitants of the earth. None can stay His hand or say unto Him what doest thou [Dan 4:35].***

The life of the first man's being came last. The life of the second man's name came last. The Life of the second man's bride [the church receive the Holy Ghost] comes first. The Spirit that raised Jesus from the dead and which will raise us up and quicken us already indwells us.

El, the Essential Foundation is Last

Note : Men in erecting buildings put in the foundation first . God in making man put his foundation in last, i.e. his breath. The foundation of the church is Jesus Christ, Immanuel. The essence of the glory in the name is the last part, El. This is juxtaposed [next] to us. *El's name* being thusly juxtaposed, it will remain there throughout the endless ages of eternity. God's name will eternally be Immanuel, Jesus, which means, by **Jesus Christ and in Jesus Christ, God and men will be** everlastingly together.

In the New Testament God is Nameless without us!

As El is added to Immanu, anu is also necessary for Immanuel to be complete. That is 'man', 'us', 'we' must be in Immanuel and not only there but immediately next to El in the name. And this has great implications for the inseparable union with God in Immanuel.

In Immanuel, God speaks clearly to us, "in Jesus Christ, there is nothing, absolutely nothing between you and me, nothing between us.

Song: *"What a fellowship! What a joy divine! Leaning on the everlasting arms"*

There is Nothing Between us and God in Immanuel

"Of language and light"
"Of language and fellowship"
"Of language and rest"
"No syllables between"
"No harmless preposition between"
"No word between"
"No thought between"
"No thing between"

The significance of the divine positioning of the word parts in the name Immanuel is that it reveals the inseparable relationship of God with man in Imm/anuel.

Observing the Divine Linguistic arrangement, comparing the English, Latin and Hebrew interpretations of Immanuel we can see the unique and eternal union between God and man via Immanuel.

The Word Arrangement Relative to the Relationship of God with Man in Immanuel

As we look at the word-name Immanuel we see that God is with us, He is next to us. He is last. He is juxtaposed with us. These are all true in the linguistic word arrangement. But, what is not true is that there is anything between us and God. Immanuel being immeasurably close to us is referred to in this book as His with-us-ness and later in this book we will refer to that as Immanuel's "withness". All of these relational positions and what they mean will be discussed in the next three chapters of this book.

In Immanuel, God is Eternally juxtaposed to Man[Us]

In Immanuel, we didn't choose God. He chose us. He elected to move near to us in juxtaposition. So while we didn't move and God moved too close to us to measure, this created God with us and simultaneously us with God. So due to God's own volition and action, we are **"next-syllable neighbors** [anuEl]- and there is no punctuation between. God's most excellent and final name is not without US.

All of El's Jehovistic titles [names of God in the OT] excluded us nominatively while *they* included us purposefully. But in Immanuel we [**anu**] are included in the name and the purpose Imm/**anu**/El

Significance of El being Next to—With Man in Immanuel

The unique and ultimate use of a preposition in man's language for the ultimate interpretation concerning the ultimate relationship respecting the absolute God is the word "with".

In Immanuel: A simple word of language one syllable, "with" makes man's in the lowly being (See Isaiah 40) that he is, being with God is glorified by Him who is infinite in glory. Man connected with God glorifies and elevates him.

In Immanuel, the being of God and the actions of God are united to man in this being and action God names Himself [He exposes His intent]. Hence God's ultimate being and action toward man is Immanuel.

In Immanuel, God acts towards man exclusive of man's condition and without reserving Himself. In Immanuel, God empties Himself towards man in His "withness", though man is emptied man. (A creature of vanity) *In Immanuel God is with man as omnem plentitudinen [the abundance of all that man needs]*

Thought Embedded in the Word Immanuel

As I shared in the preface of this book, "words are thoughts embodied - where there are no words, there are no thoughts expressed". For example in the word Immanuel there is No syllable between anu and El. Hence, there is no room for decisive or broken thought. Thus, in the word part arrangement of the word-name 'Immanuel' there is nothing which indicates a separation between us and God.

This concept is the core of this thesis and is developed more clearly in the succeeding chapters of this book.

From what we have learned in this chapter, we can see that in the name Immanu/El God is both next to man and last. In the next chapter the significance of El being last in the name Immanuel is explained.

Erudite Jewish Scholars Confirm this Thesis

While observing the word parts in the name Imm/anu/el should be sufficient proof of this revelation and understanding, this revelation has been confirmed by certain erudite Jewish scholars. The New Jewish Publication Society of America translates the word Immanuel in Isaiah 7:14 to mean 'with us is God'. This is the translation in the JPS Tanakli Hebrew text. A number of translations including but not limited to the King James Version [English], the Vulgate [Latin], the standard English, the Artscroll Tanach, the Stone Edition and the JPS Tanakli translation, translate the name Immanuel as God with us [English] or us with God [Latin]. Different from those was the JPS Tanakli translation which translates Immanuel to mean 'with us is God" which nearly matches the syllable pattern God revealed to the author Dr. Johnson. It should not be surprising that both the Tanakli's translation and the one revealed to the author nearly match as far as syllable sequencing is concerned, because both the Tanakli's and the author's translation are based on the original Hebrew text of Isaiah 7:14. (Editor's note).

Conclusion: In the name Immanuel as given by God to the prophet Isaiah God purposefully order the syllables to describe how God is with man in Immanuel. The syllables anu and El are precisely next to each other showing that In Immanuel God is inseparably close to man. This close relationship as described by God in the name Immanuel is demonstrated by Jesus closeness to us via His incarnation, suffering on the Cross and His/our glorification and eternal union. Thus, God gave us His name in Imm-Anu-El, syllabified and tripartite so as to aid our faith and understanding. How can we have Jesus with any part of Immanuel divested?

Chapter 2

WHY IS GOD [EL] LAST, IN THE NAME IMMANU/EL?

Why is God [**El**] last in the name Immanu/El? in our thinking, El [God] should be first and foremost in everything. That is a very reverent thought, but in God's positioning Himself last in the name Immanu/El, He had something very special in mind. In this case His thought is not our thought. As I studied the implications of the syllable arrangement in the name Imm/anu/El God revealed some very significant and powerful reasons why He placed His name on the end of the word.

The significance of El being last in the name Immanuel is that it shows His relationship to man as being final and complete—the greater part is last, the best and most necessary; and for other divine reasons that are discussed in this chapter. In here, I explain how El's being last in Immanuel tells us that He is the final manifestation of God, His final word to us, His final revelation to us, His final expression, His final and immutable decision to be ever with us and for us. It shows the finality and lowliness of the Cross by which He finally validates His promise to never leave or forsake us.

This positioning [El being last] is indicative of the fact that everything concludes in Immanuel. And all things pertaining to Gods dealings with man finally culminate in Him. These reasons and more for El being last in Immanuel are expounded in this chapter.

Why is God Last in the Name Immanuel?

His Plan for Our Eternal Salvation is Final
God being last in the name ImmanuEl shows us that we do not have to worry that there is something coming after Jesus to change God's plan as some men do in business deals. We can rest in Him, believe in Him, rejoice in the final plan of eternal life for us—it is final. He comes on the end as a rear reward to make sure nothing changes His plan for an eternal inseparable union between Him and man.

Immanuel the Final Manifestation of God
Immanuel is God's final man and the final manifestation of God. There is no "Post-Jesus" or "Post-Christ to Jesus Christ." Immanuel is truly Alpha and Omega. The human family is ultimately concluded in Him in every way—right and wrong!

In Imm/Anu/El, God places Himself last to thereby join immediately with us. Least little beyond all others in size or degree; smallest; slightest; fewest—infrequently coupled with last superlative of little.

El placing Himself Last in the Name Immanuel has great significance for us pertaining to the things of Our Salvation
El being last in the name Immanuel, assures us that all things wrought for us in Immanuel are final:
The rapture of the church
The atonement of the Cross
Our eternal life
There will never be another fall—our redemption is final. The case about our sins can never be reopened

or brought up against us. The atonement for sin is final.

Immanuel, God's Final, All-Transcending Word to Man

Immanuel, the Eternal Name, permeated with eternity (eternal blessings). It is the epitome, the ultimate in Divine language. It is God's final name! It is God's final word! Immanuel is God's final, all-transcending word to man. It is the composite of all that God has been, is, or ever will be to man.

Having taken on the name Immanuel, Jesus Christ, to be against us, would be a mighty work for God Himself to undo all that He, by His own power, has done already through Christ—even as is significant in His name Immanuel. It is done by His and only His might. It is God's final word to be with us. No more is to be said.

Immanuel, God's Final and Ultimate Work On the Calvary

In the New Testament, the names Jesus and Immanuel are never found in an adjectival construction in a sentence (e.g., wonderful, great, glorious, etc.) for all these things in the nature of the case were in them. There is no adjective powerful enough to modify them. The Father's Name, in Holy Scripture, is never as hallowed as it is in Jesus/Immanuel.

On the Cross, Immanuel was with us in the ultimate darkness of time and eternity; therefore, there is no question that He will be with believers during earth's little trials and sorrows. Calvary was Immanuel's "high water mark"; all else is "downhill" for Him. His promise, "I will never leave you nor forsake you" was ultimately and finally sealed for us by Immanuel on the Cross.

0, what a rest Sweet Rest Immanuel, God's final word, God's final work. Immanuel, God's ultimate word, God's ultimate work.

EL's Final Commitment, He will Never be Negdanuel to His Believing Children!!

Immanuel-Jesus, the highest, greatest, strongest, grandest, wisest, loveliest, richest, etc. etc. word in the Bible. He who stands in juxtaposition to us, being with us, is opposed to or against everything that is against us. Hence, Paul's gloriously exclaimed gospel in Romans 8!! Who shall separate us? With God for us, who can separate us?

Immanuel will never be Negdanuel [God against us] to His believing children ! God's final word to His believing children is His final word Immanuel!! He'll speak no more!!

Immanuel, Terminating Revelation of God

Immanuel is God's "unbordered" name. Immanuel is, at the same time, where El, God terminates the further revelation of His wisdom and power to man—and the past revelation.

Immanuel is the embodiment of all of God's word to man - and the final word. He is called in Revelation 19:13, "the word of God" (19:11 -16) and "KING of KINGS and LORD of LORDS."

We cannot trace God acting even in eternity past before Him or in eternity to come after Him. Immanuel is the First and the Last.

Note: Bishop Hancock said, *"Jesus as the first thing God made."*

Immanuel, God's Ultimate and Complete Word

Immanuel, God's ultimate statement of His Goodness, Godhood, His might, His glory, His love, His majesty, His creativeness. When He said, "Immanuel", He said it all in composite form. He spoke eternity. He spoke time.

He spoke love. He spoke hate. He spoke life. He spoke death. He spoke victory. He spoke light. He spoke darkness. He spoke weakness. He spoke resurrection. He spoke Hell. He spoke heaven. He spoke this world. He spoke the world to come (the world that is). He spoke brokenness. He spoke wholeness. He spoke of victims and the vanquished and victors. He spoke victimization. He spoke conquest and quietness, etc., etc., etc. Immanuel speaks of finiteness and infinity. It speaks of mystery and revelation; majesty and poverty (nakedness), hiddenness and openness. Humanity and deity and unity. It speaks of immeasurable wisdom and power. It speaks of Christ! Is Immanuel God's ultimate, last, final word? Yes, it is!!!

Immanuel, God's Last (Final) Name

All of God's previous names were evolutionary in character; i.e. they named God and gave room for man to look for more of the revelation of God's "Godness". When God uttered and became Immanuel, this was His last utterance. There is nothing which will ever supersede Immanuel, Apart from Jesus Christ, El (God) has no more revelation of Himself to man. Christ is all! All of God's names prior to Immanuel; i.e., Jesus Christ, were relatively inclusive, but in Jesus, Christ is the absolute, the total, the final inclusion of all that God ever has intended or will ever intend to be for man. Note Martin Baber on "I Am That I Am"—I shall be then as then you shall find me—but in Immanuel, El is "I shall be everywhere as everywhere they (all of them) shall find me—and always (or...always find me...) even unto eternity.

His eternal Name does not depart in His judgment. In His judgment, He stains His raiment, but doesn't mar its beauty. The stain is there, but the whiteness is ever present. God having named Himself will not rename or unname Himself—nor can we rename or unname Him—no matter what He does, when He does it, or how He does it. Jesus, Immanuel is El's (God's) final name.

Immanuel, God's Ultimate and Final Expression

Immanuel, The Ultimate and Final expression, manifestation from God to man of God's (El's) absolute freedom! Through Immanuel, God expresses the highest degree of His eternal freedom! Daniel said, "He does what He wills in the army of heaven and among the inhabitants of the earth. None can stay His hand or say unto Him, what doest thou?" Immanuel will never be Negdanuel [God against us] to His believing children! God's final word to His believing children is His final word—Immanuel!! He'll speak no more!!

Immanuel Last and Lowest on the Cross

God makes Himself last and least in Immanuel. In Immanuel, El (God) in His almightiness makes Himself last in the Name [Immanu/**el**] via making Himself least of all men in the Cross.

On the Cross, God in Christ became lower than any man had ever been before God. It was the bottom (Profundis Immensis—i.e., measureless depths) of the bottom in humility, humiliation, and judgment. It was the lowest hell, the darkest, deepest death. He made His grave with the wicked in His death.

In Immanuel, as only El the Almighty could do, He conjoins the superlative of little [least of all men] and the unimaginable superlative of the greatest of all men—Jesus Christ.

Hermeneutical Principle of Least-First Greatest-Last
It is the observed pattern of instances throughout the scriptures where God puts the least in first and the greater-most significant in last. examples:
(a)As explained in chapter one, God formed Adam's body first, then breathed life into him last.
(b)The lesser revelations of God in the O. T. came before, the greatest revelation "Immanuel" in the N.T..
(c) The lesser of the great names of God are introduced first in the Old Testement and the greatest of all of God's names "Immanuel" came last in the New Testament.
(d) The lesser of the syllables[word parts] in imm/anu/El the "with" **"Imm"**, **"anu"** man, are sequenced before the greatest syllable [word part] **"El"** God. Immanuel.

Conclusion: Immanuel is God's final name and the final manifestation of God. There is no "Post-Jesus" or "Post Christ to Jesus Christ." Immanuel is truly Alpha and Omega. The human family is ultimately concluded in Him in every way, right and wrong!

Chapter 3

SIDE BY SIDE WITH JESUS
THE "ANUEL" RELATIONSHIP

This chapter continues the discussion from chapters one and two, concernig divine intent in the positioning of the word parts in the name Imm/anu/el. Herein I expand on the concept that the divinely sequenced positioning of the word parts in the name Imm-anu-El is most significant, particularly the 'side-by-side' positioning of man with El in Imm/**anuEl**. As you read, you will see that in Immanuel, God intends to have a close, inseparable relationship with man/men, something of which He had been deprived since the fall. God, who was separated from us in Adam, has now in Immanuel drawn near to us. *"God was in Christ [Immanuel] reconciling the word unto Himself" I Corinthians 5:19.*

Prior to Immanuel, and since the fall of Adam, there was a wedge between God and man. But now because of Immanuel, the wedge of separation is gone and we now have access to God's abundance of wonderful things, which we shall discuss later in this chapter. Now in Immanuel, God has access to us to bless us. When I speak of our access to God's abundance via Immanuel, I speak of the access that was previously hindered by the gulf of separation between God and man since man's falling away It is this gulf that wedged Him from us, blocking man's (Adam's) access to God until Immanuel came.

But now, in Immanuel, we have access to an

immeasurable closeness to God. This closeness in this chapter is referred to by such terms of El's "juxtaposition", "withness", "closeness", "being next to us", "being side-by-side with us", "no separation", "being in union with" and " being immeasurably close to". As already explained in chapter one of this book, the us [anu] and God [El] in the name Immanuel are purposely side-by-side and show an inseprable union God and man, having nothing between them. In the last chapter I explained the significance El being last in the name Immanuel.

This chapter explains the significance of El [God]being indivisably next to anu [man]in Imm/**anuel**. In here, I share the relational blessings and benefits of God being joined together with man in Immanuel.

The Blessings and Great Benefits of the Union of God and Man are Realized in the Juxtaposition of God to Man in Immanuel

Here the '**anu/El**' union is defined and explained in terms of juxtaposition and "withness" ["*Withness" is a word coined for this thesis that describes the 'anu/El' relationship, saying that El is with us in Immanuel.*] Using the term juxtaposition, I explain what it means to the born-again saint to be next to God in Immanuel. I also explain what "withness" is and the significance of "withness" in the **anu/El** relationship.

Meaning of the Word Juxtaposition

1. Positioning things side by side or close together. Juxtaposition: comparing-contrasting things side by side, for example: The things of God and the things of man are contrasted in Immanuel:

Sin/righteousness, Hell/Heaven, cross/crown

 Being in juxtaposition-with-us, Immanuel addresses our *inanis et vacua* with His allness of plentitude. That is to say our emptiness and voidness is addressed by His abundance and suficantcy. Through the presence of Jesus in the Holy Spirit, He (Immanuel, Jesus) metes every one of our spiritual needs. In other words, being next to God, He rubs off on us, He fulfills us, He completes us, He helps us, He delivers us, He upholds us. Whatever damage we have from the fall, He comes to repair it. He is fully aware of and fully able and fully willing to mete our every need.

Being Juxtaposed to Us, Immanuel Addresses Our *Inanis et Vacua* with His Allness of Plentitude

Our disquietness	His peace
Our darkness (ignorance)	His wisdom
Our ignorance	His light
Our sins	His righteousness
Our infirmities	His strength
Our death	His life
Our mortality	His immortality

etc., etc., etc., (and others; and the like; and so forth; and the rest). Immanuel, God of the eternal, et cetera. Whatever our condition, God is immeasurably close to it to change it. Bishop K. F. Smith said *"tuck your head and run real close to the Lord"*

In Immanuel, God Acts Towards Man Exclusive of Man's Condition and without Reserving Himself

In Immanuel, God empties Himself towards man in His withness, [*withness— term for God's union with man*] though man is emptied man(A creature of vanity). In Immanuel, God is with man as *omnem plentitudinem*. In Immanuel, God is ready to supply anything we need to be close to Him. He is determined that nothing will hinder His union and relationship to man. He is ready and able to do everything to make it work.

He Answers all Possible Hindrances:
1. Distance between our humanity and God 's Divinity.
Ans. "I'll become both human and divine to effect a union(union via incarnation).
2. Time and eternity
Ans. "I'll put eternity in your spirit" (union via new birth, new creation).
3. Space (Earth and Heaven—"I'll close it").
Ans. "I'll come where you are so I can bring you where I am" (union via transportation).
4. Righteousness and sin
Ans. "I'll be [made] sin for you to destroy its existence" (union through substitution). "No syllables between" (union via super metamorphosis).
5. Life and death
Ans. "I'll abolish it" (union via abolition).
6. Mortality and immortality
Ans. "I'll change you and make you immortal"
"That He might bring us to God!! (no 'fringes,' so thorough, so perfect, so final in action)
"Between us and God, not even a harmless preposition"

In Jesus Christ, man finds union, fellowship, absolute, superlative. This is the reason for the sublimity of the "who shall separate me" Romans 8.

We are made nigh by His blood, the blood of Christ. Nothing could ever have brought us closer (or so close). Eph 2:13

7. Of man's darkness (ignorance) and God's absolute light ("We shall see Him as He is [then like God]"). "I am come a light in the world (of man's darkness) (to man's), that he that follows me should not walk in darkness but should have the light of life" (union through [via] light [dispelling darkness]).

8. Our poverty—God's riches "Though He was rich, yet He became poor for our sakes, that we though His poverty might be rich" (union via enrichment).

Romans 8:32, "He that spared not His own Son, but delivered Him up .... how shall He not with Him also freely give us all things?"

Often, in this world, what separates us is monetary status; i.e., poverty-riches. Deprivation is the gulf. "The bridge between black and white is green." Enough wealth can change a man's (or lack of it) association. Hence in Immanuel, Jesus by His blood and grace changes our "economic level."

Romans Chapter 8 Describes El's Commitment to be Juxtaposed [in Union] to Us In Immanuel

Romans 8 treats on "the Immutability [unchanging relative to His commitment to be with us] of Immanuel". "The Perfection and the Immutability of Immanuel"... which results in the case that nothing CAN SEPARATE!

The person of Immanuel sanctifies (exalts, if the case be so), all that flows from Him. Anything from Him by which He favors man is in the nature of the case; inherently high, incomparable, glorious, etc., etc.,- etc., etc.

Being Juxtaposed to God in Immanuel Can Only Help us— and Not Harm Us

For believers: Nothing poor can flow from this Rich Being. Nothing low can flow from this High Being. Nothing weak can flow from this Strong Being.

Nothing foolish can flow from this Wise Being. Naught of death can flow from Him who is life eternal.

We must remember He was "With Us God." Two unequal, disparate entities, inextricably joined; joined for the transfer of God's Godness to us—not our humanity to God.

He needed nothing from us to assist, to help enrich His Godness. It was our fallen humanity which needed everything from "good sense" (wisdom) to immortality. *We* were fallen not God. He was always the same. He was problem-free but master. We were problem-laden and problem-victimized. He came to be with us.

Behold this glory! We didn't – and couldn't—go to be with Him. So He came where we were, that someday, we could be like Him and be where He is.

God's Commitment to an Inseparable Union with Us is Described by St. Paul in Romans 8: 35-39

Who shall separate us from the love of Christ? Shall tribulation, or distress, or persecution, or famine, or nakedness, or peril, or sword?

As it is written, for thy sake we are killed all the day long; we are accounted as sheep for the slaughter.

Nay, in all these things we are more than conquerors through him that loved us. For I am persuaded, that neither death, nor life, nor angels, nor principalities, nor powers, nor things present, nor things to come, nor height, nor depth, nor any other creature, shall be able to separate us from the love of God, which is in Christ Jesus our Lord. Romans 8: 35-39

In Immanuel, every aspect of God's action (speaking) is supra-superlative so that El Himself thereby will affect a supra-superlative union between Himself and man.

Juxtaposition-Withness of El

Withness is a word coined for this thesis that describes the 'anu/El' relationship, saying that El is with us in Immanu/el.

What is the Difference Between 'the Withness' of El in Immanu/El and Any Other Withness?

What is the significance of this withness?

Does the withness of El make a difference, other than any other withness? If there is a difference, what is the difference?

The difference is the difference that only El intended. Could any man intend in place of El? Could any man circumscribe El's intent or action? Could any man confine or define it?

Do we get a glimpse of the purposes of El's intent in such terms as justification, peace, righteousness, reconciliation, communion, fellowship (power), and immortality? These things do make a difference! They are things from God in Immanuel that have no equivalent in the "withness" of any other being. These terms are indicators of His unmeasured nearness. His name through faith in His name has made this man whole. What a name! Acts 3:16. Song: In The Name of Jesus...We Have the Victory.

In Immanuel, salvation for man means deliverance and endowment. No one else but Jesus can save us. Bringing out and bringing in; severance and enrichment; detachment and enlargement, disassociation and union." He has brought us out of darkness and into His marvelous light." "He shall save His people from their sins... (who washed us from our sins and made us kings and priests). Herein is the manifestation of God's wisdom and Right-the exercise of it. In Immanuel, God commits Himself to the exercise of His power and wisdom unmeasured, for salvation is His purpose for time and eternity. <u>His withness is for salvation, and His salvation necessitates His prudence, wisdom, and power.</u> And no one else or nothing else can save us. So what difference does El's "withness" make? The difference is deliverance, absolute and eternal. None but Immanuel could effect this.

> In Immanuel, we are close to God or with God because God in Christ made the move and came indivisibly close to us. We are not close to God in Christ because we moved close to Him, but rather because He moved close to us. El in Immanuel moved close to us though we were and are unlike Him in mind and in body. When that which is perfect is come (mind and body) we will be near Him and like Him. Now we are near and unlike,

Bishop K. F Smith said concerning Jesus' closeness and our need to take advantage of it, "tuck your head and run real close to the Lord".

He is Able to Deal with Sin and Its Damage to Us

One definition of juxtaposition is being side by side to compare and contrast. This is what happened when Jesus and His holiness is positioned next to us and our unholiness. Our unholiness really shows clearly. He shows us up. He magnifies our state of sinfulness. But He does not do so without having the magnification and abundance of grace to deal with every point of our sin and the damage [injury] it caused. There is no saint who has been filled with the Holy Ghost who has had or has a problem in this area who Jesus does not have the sufficiency of grace to cleanse and help them overcome. God knew who we were and what we were when He moved next door to us in Immanuel.

The Side by Side Positioning of the God of Light with the Darkness and Sin of Man

In Immanuel's Juxtaposition with us, Jesus is God's Magnifier of the affect of sin and death and, too, the multiplier of grace and life in response to the multiplication and magnification of sin and death. In Immanuel, Jesus Christ is God's exponent for sin and death, righteousness and life. Sin is made exceeding, sinful; i.e., sinful beyond the power of law to magnify it. Death becomes judgmentally exceeding deathful. Righteousness is made exceeding righteousness beyond the self of law- and yet by the law - "cursed is everyone that hangs on a tree." Life is made "more abundantly." Only in Immanuel do God and man experience absolute union via absolute disunion. *Where sin abound grace did much more abound.*

Abounding Grace in El's Withness

Adam's broken fellowship and Adam's dismissal from Eden only presaged the absolute brokenness which God affected between Himself and man in Immanuel.

Eden's cleavage was El's "trial run;" Heaven's "preliminary." What was absolutely broken was absolutely bonded between El and Anu in Immanuel. In Immanuel, and only in Him, *is our* brokenness and absolute bonding. Like in the book of

Philemon—"separated to be received forever"[v 15].

One of the Main things El Deals with in Jesus-Immanuel is the Effect and Damage of Abounding of Sin against Us
"Where sin abounded, grace did much more abound."
For every point on sin's circle of damage, injury, etc., El has placed a point on the outer concentric circle of His grace to respond, counteract, address, save from, (to) it. Hallelujah!!

According to I Corinthians 1:24, Christ, Immanuel is juxtaposed to us,' bringing the wisdom and power of God next to us. What a blessing for the born-again believers to have Immanuel in the Holy Ghost. That means that we have the mighty God in us, and nothing can separate us from His love. Not even sin and death, for He in Immanuel has dealt with both of them by His abounding grace!!

Jesus the Divine Exponent of Divine Things

El is exponentially with us in Immanuel
Exponent
Algebra — a small number written above and to the right of a symbol or quantity to show how many times the symbol or quantity is to be used as a factor i.e. multiplied by itself.
Example: $2^2 = 2 \times 2$; $a^3 = a \times a \times a$

$a^2 = a \times a$

$2^4 = 2 \times 2 \times 2 \times 2$

$2^3 a^2 = 2 \times 2 \times 2 \times a \times a$

"All of the promises of God are "yes" and "amen" in Jesus Christ", Immanuel.
Immanuel is "with us God" "If God be for us who can be against us?
Immanuel is God's final testimony of favor towards mankind.

Jesus is God's exponent for sin and death and righteousness and life
Romans 8:1-5 *"that the righteousness of the Law might be fulfilled in us..."*. MS page 44

No Point of Damage goes Unanswered. Neither is Anything not Dealt with by Jesus Christ as Immanuel

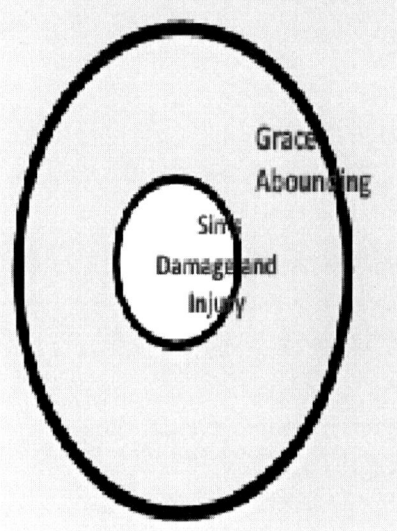

Grace Abounding

Sin's Damage and Injury

In Immanuel, God Addresses every Point of Damage from the Fall and Adam's Disunion from God. In Immanuel, Every Point of Injury is Dealt with, where Sin Abounds Grace did much more Abound. MS58

On the concentric circles in the figure to the left. There is an inner circle and an outer circle. The line of each circle is made up of millions of dots which are side by side making the line of the circle. The dots that make the circles are called points.

The inner concentric circle represent points of sin's damage and injury. The outer circle represents the points & places to respond to sins points of damage and injury (abounding grace).

Romans 5:20 Where sin abounded grace did much more abound.

In Immanuel, We are Close to God Himself

In Immanuel, we do not have God's representative, God's emissary, God's ambassador, not even one plenipotentiary [empowered representative], not what represents God, not God's created things, but we are in juxtaposition to God Himself; e.g., "The Spirit helpeth our infirmities;" i.e., God Himself. "I will not leave you comfortless. I will come to you."

"And God (Himself) shall wipe away their tears." See Revelation 7 and Revelation 21:3:4, God (Immanuel) has taken out of our hands (Isaiah 54) the cup of trembling, yet He has not left us "empty-handed," He has given us in its place "a well of living water," "rivers of living water" "Where sin abounded, grace did much more abound (all by Immanuel who made us nigh to God; i.e., in juxtaposition to God, without a quiet, harmless syllable between.

Abundance of Spiritual Things in Immanuel
Song:
1. Is not this the land o f Beulah, blessed, blessed?
  And of light?
2. I've believed the true report .
3. 0 sweet rest ("the joy of His presence , a perfect sweet rest .. .).
"...out darkness into His marvelous light"

In, by Immanuel we are brought into a realm of special things, beauty, glory, light, grandeur, miracles, power, "special diet [feeding on the word of God , sermons, Bible classes]," royal finery, etc., etc., We are brought into indivisible proximity to God, the King. What a holy, happy place!!!

What Being Juxtaposed to Immanuel Means

In Immanuel is man's ultimate relationship with God. It is the highest, most beneficial, closest, longest lasting, richest, most glorious. etc. etc. that man could ever have with God or any other.

In Immanuel, man finds incomparable, incomprehensible union. Eternal union beyond all that man is capable of imagining in the term"union". God is the super association of the universe. It is union Indescribable. El being in an indescribable union with us means indescribable blessings and glory for mankind. Hallelujah! In the natural consequence of the case, Immanuel evokes Hallelujah. The Mighty words with the "God Suffix"[*Hallelu/**jah**, jah means God*]. Imm/anu/El

In Immanuel, God Moved Next to Us

In Imm/anu/el, there is not even a syllable between man (anu) and God (El). On Calvary, man in absolute sinfulness (He was made sin for us), and God in absolute righteousness, as they only could be, in Immanuel, there is no other place-no other way! And in this meeting, there is an absolute resolution of their estrangement. Here was reconciliation! "Where we're nearest, we're farthest away." And so it could only be! Man's absolute sinfulness, God's absolute holiness. All that man was, and all that God is, became juxtaposed in Immanuel, but the last word of meeting was not man, but El(God). So the last word of the word is, El(God), Imm/anu/**El.**

The person of Immanuel sanctifies (exalts, if the case be so), all that flows from Him. Anything from Him by which He favors man is in the nature of the case; inherently high, incomparable, gloriousetc., etc.,- etc.

We are Juxtaposed to the Greatest, Most Loving Jesus-Immanuel, Who is for Us

Immanuel—the highest, greatest, strongest, grandest, wisest, loveliest, richest word in the Bible. He who stands in juxtaposition to us, being with us, is opposed to or against everything that is against us. Hence, Paul's gloriously exclaimed gospel in Romans 8!! Who shall separate us...? If God be for us, who...?

Immanuel will never be Negdanuel [God against us] to His believing children!! God's final word to His believing children is His final word - Immanuel!! He'll speak no more!!

We are in Juxtaposition to the Almighty One

El, the Self-Existent, Eternal One, Immortal, Invisible
El, the only wise.
El, One of unlimited might.
El, He who is absolutely free.
El, Possessor of heaven and earth.

1. He, who is unlimited in might, can empower, strengthen, uphold me.
2. He, who is absolutely free, can surely free me from any oppression or bondage.
3. He, who is possessor of all, can certainly enrich me, bless me.
4. He, who is only wise, can surely dispel my darkness, enlighten my mind, make me wise.

5. He, who is self-existent and eternal life itself, can surely give me life everlasting.

0, Immanuel, greatest, most glorious of all, Hallelujah!

...and to think, He is along side me, too close to measure! "Thou art with me."

In Psalm 23, David referred to his Shepherd being with him—but in Immanuel our Shepherd is with us after the power of an endless life, by His own blood, by a new covenant, by a new and living way. Note: in Jesus Christ God has MADE 'unto' us, wisdom, righteousness, sanctification and redemption ('unto', denoting motion towards and reaching).

Conclusion: Being juxtaposed to God in Immanuel is a place of immeasurable closeness. We are closely positioned for transformation and access to God's plentitude of salvational blessings. It is us being side by side with the Eternal One as described by God in the name Imm/**anu**/El. It is a closeness that positions us to take in His wisdom and to be conformed to His image. It is like the Garden of Eden where God can walk in our lives and commune with us, bless us, and transform us. It is having access to God in the sense that there are no walls of separation. Thus, the side-by-side positioning of us and God in the name Immanuel fulfills El's divine intent for an eternally inseparable union between God and man.

Old Testament Names of God

God	Elohim (Mighty One)	Genesis 1:1
God	El (Might, Power)	Genesis 14:18
God	Eloah (Mighty One)	Nehemiah 9:17
God	Elah (Aramaic form)	Daniel 2:18
Yahweh (Jehovah), God, Lord	YHWH (Yahweh)	Genesis 2:4; 15:2; Ex 6:3
Lord	YH (Yah) (Yahweh)	Psalm 68:4
Lord	Adon (Lord, Ruler)	Joshua 3:11
Lord	Adonai (Lords, Rulers)	Genesis 15:2
I Am That I Am	Eheyeh asher Eheyeh	Exodus 3:14
I Am	Eheyeh	Exodus 3:14; Isa 40-55
Most High God	El-Elyon (Supreme Might)	Genesis 14:18
The God of Sight	El-Roiy	Genesis 16:13
Almighty God	El-Shaddai (Might of the Powerful Ones)	Genesis 17:1
Everlasting God	El-Olam	Genesis 21:33
YHWH of Hosts	YHWH-sabaoth (Lord of Armies)	1 Samuel 1:3
YHWH will provide	YHWH-jireh: Will see or Provide	Genesis 22:14

I, YHWH, am your healer.	YHWH-rapha: Heals	Exodus 15:26
YHWH is my banner	YHWH-nissi: Our banner or Victory	Exodus 17:15
YHWH who sanctifies you	YHWH-m'kaddesh: Sanctifies	Exodus 31:13
YHWH is peace	YHWH-shalom: Peace	Judges 6:24
YHWH is my shepherd	YHWH-raah: My shepherd	Psalm 23:1
YHWH, our maker	YHWH-hoseenu: Creator	Psalm 95:6
YHWH, our righteousness	YHWH-tsidkenu: Righteousness	Jeremiah 23:6

These were names which God was known by in Old Testament, and there were many others too. They described the character of God revealed in different situations throughout the Old Testament.

However, if you study each of the Old Testament names and the instances where they were introduced, you will find that none of them promised salvation, eternal life or redemption. Neither did they describe God being joined together with man; i.e., God becoming a man or Him humbling Himself to die on a cross.

Immanuel is the only name given in the Old Testament where these salvational things are promised.

The name Immanuel, which was given historically in the Old Testament in Isaiah 7:14, is fulfilled in the New Testament in the person and works of Jesus Christ. It is the only name wherein God becomes a man and dies for our sins on the cross and ultimately brings man to everlasting life with Him in a unique and eternal union. This is discussed in more detail in the next chapter *" Immanuel, God's Greatest Name"*.

Chapter 4
IMMANUEL, GOD'S [EL'S] GREATEST NAME
God's Most Complete Revelation of Himself

In this chapter, I compare the other 'Old Testament names of God' with 'Immanuel'. I set forth that only in Immanuel is the full revelation of God to man revealed. Immanuel is not just another Old Testament name in which God describes His character and actions using finite verbs and adjectives, but rather it is the infinite name of God that cannot be completely described by the tools of language [verbs and adjectives]. God incrementally revealed certain aspects of His own person and power in the different names He gave Himself throughout the Old Testament. But in Immanuel is the complete revelation.

While God revealed Himself incrementally and progressively throughout the Old Testament using finite verbs and adjectives to describe Himself, He was "all along the way" all and more than those partial revelation-names described Him to be. Because in those names He had not yet revealed Himself fully. El's full revelation of Himself was forth—coming as it was revealed to the prophet Isaiah, in Isaiah 7:14, through which He would finally be made known in His most complete revelation of Himself in the name Immanuel.

In the different names God called Himself; from Elohim to YHWH, from Adonai to El-Olam, from YHWH to His Jehovistic titles, and the phrase names He was referred to; "God of Abraham" to "The Holy One" He was all that those names meant and immeasurably more than all of their meanings put together. Each of His Old Testament names were merely suited particularly for the instance in which they were used.

They described His might, His holiness, His power, His authority and His Lordship etc. etc.

However, in none of those Old Testament names did God describe Himself so completely like He does in the name Immanuel. Hence, Immanuel is God's greatest name. None of the Old Testament names had God in union man in them. None of them had the saving blood of Immanuel's Cross in them. None of them included the eternal life of man. None of them described a close relationship of God with man. None of them described man being filled with the Holy Ghost. None of them was God's final name. None of them were boundless.

In the Old Testament there was no other name that described God and man, inseparably joined together in one body, as it was so in Immanuel.

No other name under heaven could save us, other than Jesus-Immanuel.

Here, I discuss the name Immanuel, which is the Old Testament name for God-incarnated, God as a man. However, the fulfillment of this Hebraic Old Testament name "*Imm/anu/El*" is in the New Testament. It is fulfilled in the life, the birth, the works, and the very being of Jesus Christ as Immanuel. Jesus Christ is the fulfillment and the person of Immanuel. So in this book, we study the Name of Jesus Christ as Immanuel. Jesus Christ is the fulfillment of Immanuel. Jesus is Immanuel No other Old Testament name describes what Jesus is but the name Immanuel. No other name describes Jesus so completely like in the name Immanuel.

Immanuel, God's Greatest Name

Immanuel God's Name with US in It

All of El's Jehovistic titles excluded us nominatively while they included us purposefully. In Immanuel, we are included in the purpose by being included in the Name itself.

Jehovah-Shalom	Peace
Jehovah-Roah	Shepherd
Jehovah-Rapha	That healeth thee
Jehovah-Shammah	There, present
Jehovah-Roi	King
Jehovah-Tsidkenu	Righteousness
Jehovah-Nissi	Banner
Jehovah-Mekaddiekhim	Sanctifier

These are names in which El is hyphenated in meaning. In El Shaddai, He is apart from us yet ministering to us as the breasted One[nurturing]. In El Elyon, He is Most High. In Elohim, He is alone, yet all powerful. etc., etc., etc. In Immanuel, however, all of the foregoing relationships of El, in which He favors men, draw Him immeasurably close, and He becomes One with us: "Thou hast exalted Thy Word above all of Thy Names" (i.e., Thy Word Incarnate).

The Old Testament, from Genesis to Malachi, gives witness to El's wisdom and might. On the list above, we see verbal descriptions of the actions of God; all of these were described using verbs and or adjectives. This is because they are partial revelations. However, in Immanuel's name, no verb can contain [describe] Him, and no adjective can modify Him because His actions are not limited to time and the earthly realm, as many of the other Old Testament names related to .

In the Old Testament, we only find El's final name in prophecy [Isaiah 7:14]—not in action, not in manifestation, not in person—for in the Old Testament, there is no Cross by which El will reveal His ultimate Name.

The name Immanuel is the greatest name God had ever revealed of Himself. It is the only name with both God and us in it. It is the only name with the saving blood of the Cross in it. It is God's unique and eternal name that includes everything relational and salvational pertaining to us.

Immanuel, God's All-Inclusive Name

Immanuel is all-inclusive. It incorporates God's purpose, plan and action towards and with man from eternity past into eternity to come. It is the greatest word in the Bible!!

Immanuel Validated by the Cross

Immanuel name includes the blood of Jesus.....If not for the Cross, Immanuel is not Immanuel. If not for Immanuel, the Cross is not the Cross. (See Romans 11:6 on "Grace" and "work.") The Cross of Christ was the ultimate self-validation of God's name —the ultimate crescendo.

Hallelujah, the Cross is in His Name

There is no hallelujah like "Immanuel's Hallelujah." Hallelujah always has the same sound, no matter for what reason we utter it, but we utter it for different reasons. It is never said for so high a reason, as there is no higher idea than speaking it because we are thinking "Immanuel" (i.e., Adonai with the Cross in His name; Adonai with His own blood shed in His name). Hallelujah, Hallelujah, Hallelujah, Hallelujah, Hallelujah, Hallelujah, Hallelujah!

Immanuel, God's Greatest Name

Immanuel is Isaiah 6's "Adonai" with His own blood shed in His name. What an incomprehensible reconciliation! What a union! Adonai above and in the temple, Adonai on a Cross, and Adonai with us — all are comprehended in Immanuel.

Pre-Time Planning of the glorification and exaltation of the Saints is incorporated in Immanuel:

Immanuel is God's only name with the Gospel of Jesus Christ in it

The Gospel of Christ, from El's pre-time planning to the glorification and exaltation of the saints, is incorporated in Immanuel. The name includes God's plan for both Jesus and us before the world began. It includes:
The immaculate conception
The virgin birth
The ministry of Jesus, a sampling of His future tenderness, shepherdizing, etc., etc..
The Cross - of Jesus
The resurrection of Jesus
The glorification of Jesus
The supranomination of Jesus
The session of Jesus
The administration (post-calvarian), etc., etc., etc., etc. Our

calling, etc. (Romans 8), etc., etc., etc., etc.
Our session in the holy city in Jesus' presence on thrones
seats. I.e. Jesus from birth to enthronement. We from new birth
to enthronement. He from a virgin's womb to a throne in glory.
We from the dark night of sin to thrones, seats, in glory.

Immanuel is God's Boundless Name
Proceeds its own formation

   Immanuel, God's Name with the unending et
ceteras. Immanuel, God's name of matchless union,
matchless, incomparable glory. Immanuel, the exponent
of Hallelujah. Hallelujah reaches its highest and final
crescendo in Immanuel. All the beautiful Hallelujahs
psalms are more beautiful in Immanuel. In Immanuel, the
earth becomes Eden, and Eden becomes Paradise,
Paradise becomes the Holy City respecting Hallelujah.
Everything about God's relationship to men, as witnesses
the book of Hebrews, becomes enhanced, is elevated,
becomes better via Immanuel.

   Even Hallelujah, which was never an empty word,
becomes super- loaded via Immanuel.

   God has enshrouded His incomprehensible person and
power and work of **full redemption in His incomprehensible
Name — Immanuel.** Immanuel without either definitive locus
or time.

'Immanuel' Is El's Incomprehensible Name
*El's Name — from Unpronounceable in the Old Testament
to Incomprehensible in New Testament*

   In the Old Testament God's name was so holy they
could not say it YHVH, as a tetragrammaton, was
unpronounceable. In Immanuel, we do not have an
unpronounceable name, but rather, one so profound, real,
life giving and eternally glorious until it is
incomprehensible. God has enshrouded His

incomprehensible person and power and work of full redemption in His incomprehensible Name—Immanuel.

Immanuel is God's Name of Unlimited Grace to Match the Unlimited Verdict of Wrath

Immanuel is God's access name. It neither distinguishes [discriminates]men (black, white, young, old, etc.) nor measures God [define in a limited scope]! In this name, each is open to the other. Because God comes to man without measure, man can come to God without limits, even unto eternal life and glory in Jesus Christ.

In Immanuel, God does not limit or measure Himself in man's salvation, for His wrath [earned by the fall] directed towards man is immeasurable. Hence, the, name has neither adjectives nor adverbs — no words between Anu and El.

In Immanuel's Name, God is Last and Most Complete Revelation of Himself

In Immanuel, God breaks all His past, previous records for greatness, for wisdom, for might, prudence, judgment, etc., etc., etc. All of God's previous names were evolutionary in character, i.e. they named God and gave room for man to look for more of the revelation of God's "Godness." When God uttered and became Immanuel, this was His last utterance.

Nothing will ever supersede Immanuel. Apart from Jesus Christ, God has given no more revelation of Himself to man. **Christ is all! All of God's names prior to Immanuel were relatively inclusive, but in Jesus Christ, Immanuel is the final inclusion of all that God ever has intended or will ever intend to be to man.** Note Martin Baber on "I Am That I Am"; the saying is "I shall be then as then you shall find me," but in Immanuel, this becomes "I shall be everywhere, as everywhere they shall find me—and always they will find me, even unto eternity."

Song: *In vain we've tried a thousand ways ...*
... but what we need thru all our days...
is Jesus, just Jesus.

Immanuel the Ultimate Boundary

Beyond Immanuel, there is no revelation of His will [there is no other]. Hence, Immanuel is the ultimate boundary of man. Immanuel is the "ultima thule" [the highest that there is] of the revelation of God to man. He "predates" and transcends law in the divine economy and in the structuring of El. Immanuel was a lamb slain from the foundation of the world. The Church was chosen in Him before the world began.

This is not said of the Law, the next highest order of religion. Immanuel is in ante position in respect to the Law. Law is in interposition between. Immanuel is post position. Immanuel is Alpha & Omega!!

Immanuel, El's Verb-less Name

In Immanuel, God excludes the use of all verbs known to man because the love is basis of all of His actions toward man, and the love in which He will work for man is foreign to man (see I John). God's action in Immanuel is foreign to man and is unmeasured—it is indescribable by the tools of human language, so in El's construction of the name Immanuel He uses no native verbs. No verb known to man could adequately contain [the scope of God's actions can not fit in limited verb descriptions]God's actions toward man. The greatest action verb in the human language is "love," and God's love exceeds this word.

Immanuel, God's Greatest Name

This discussion is explaining why in the syllables of the name Immanuel God put a preposition [with] a pronoun [us], a noun [El], but no verb, Imm/anu/El.

In Immanuel, God loved man beyond language, so He did not include a verb in His name. Immanuel, then, is God acting beyond all human action. God declared He would use a preposition to describe man's relationship to Him, but no verb would be adequate to describe God's unlimited love and freedom.

Immanuel is God acting, by His own acts, in His "withness" towards man — out of and into infinity!

In John 3:16, God describes His love-action by using the language, "For God so loved the world..." in a way that we could possibly, though meagerly, conceive it. He immediately transcends the description with the mind-boggling qualifier, "that He gave His only begotten Son," which puts the action word in an incomprehensible category. This verbal description of the love of God is incomprehensible and far beyond our language and usage of verbs to explain it.

Thus, God is speaking both within our language and at the same time beyond it, which makes revelation and faith a requisite for understanding.

In Immanuel, God names Himself by a new name. Everything about Immanuel is new, from conception onward: ministry work, words, character, death, resurrection, glorification, session, supranomination, administration we can name it.

Immanuel is God's verb-less Name. No verb can contain Him! (His action) In Immanuel, God's actions towards us are absolute and tenseless, i.e. in as much as El in Immanuel is all and more than any of His prior names described God to be, He cannot be described by a verbal expression alone. His work in Immanuel is not limited to any verbal description, to any time (tense) or term describing actions limited to time [tense] or a particular scenario, or event like the O.T. Jehovistic titles described Him by His actions in certain time-bound instances. In other words, Immanuel is the full revelation of God that includes God's eternal and unbound power and actions. Such actions are out of the limits of time and place. God's actions are not limited to those we use verbs to describe.

He has acted.

He is acting.

He will act.

The roots of what He will do lie in what He has already done. He has proposed, planned and executed toward us eternally, temporally and then again eternally — all via Immanuel.

Immanuel is neither verbal nor adjectival. There is no "great Immanuel" or "wonderful Immanuel," no "great" or "wonderful Jesus" in the New Testament. Immanuel is so inherently great and wonderful, until it goes without saying, i.e. using adjectives to modify Him. Furthermore, our adjectives cannot modify Him!

The most glorious "with" ("With" and man never so glorious as in relationship to:)

The most glorious relationship

Through The King All-Glorious

("With" and man never so high as in relationship to the Most High God.)

Why a preposition but **no verb**? **Verbs** have to do with action. Action, in our terrestrial realm, has to do with energy and life - Adam's life, temporal existence, e.g. "the sun shines". In Immanuel, Adam's life will be completely abolished and displaced by God's life, mortality will be displaced by Immortality. Immanuel is ultimately about immortality. i.e. "God-likeness" for man. Immanuel is about the abolition of death and all that is kindred to it, or bespeaks it. Immanuel has to do with life beyond life, uncaused life, transcendent life, the life that God is.

No Tongues can Utter a Greater Name than Immanuel-Not Even Angel's Tongues

The angels' tongues have no words so great, for Immanuel is greater than angels' tongues (see I Corinthians 13:1-2). Nothing in angels' vocabulary compares to Him, our Lord Immanuel.

Immanuel, God's New Name

The Bible, from cover to cover, answers the question, "Who is Immanuel? Because, beyond Immanuel, we cannot know God in either direction of eternity. In Him is the total revelation of God. In Immanuel, God names Himself by a new name.

"Immanuel," El's All-Inclusive Glory Word
It Is God's Final Name

Immanuel, as God's glory word, is His most composite, complete word. It is all-inclusive. It incorporates God's purpose, plan and action towards and with man from eternity past into eternity to come.
Immanuel is the greatest word in the Bible!!
Immanuel is the most beautiful (term) (tripartite) (three-syllable word in the language of men. It is the most wisdom-laden most far-reaching word. It is God's most excellent and final word. Jesus, Immanuel is El's, God's final name.

And as was already explained in chapter 2, In Immanuel, we have the full and final revelation; In Immanuel, we are brought face to face with incalculable incomprehensible distances, respecting the heart of God in the depths of "up" and "down." Immanuel has to do with

El, God in the maximum exercise and revelation of His Prudence, Precision, Passion and Power, towards His people.

Immanuel is God's Union Name

In Immanuel, man finds incomparable, incomprehensible, eternal union. This union is beyond all that man is capable of imagining in the term "union." "God with us" or "with us God"" is the super association of the universe.

El in indescribable union with us means indescribable blessings and glory for mankind. Hallelujah! In the natural consequence of the case, Immanuel evokes Hallelujah. Mighty words with the "God Suffix."

Immanuel Incorporates All

In Immanuel, from the "I" to the "L," from the bottom to the top of the letters, the word is loaded with divineness i.e.; the divine mind, will, purpose, power, beauty, prudence, wisdom, knowledge, etc., etc., etc. . *El*" is God in being; Immanuel is God in relationship. Immanuel is the most absolute revelation of God known to man. Immanuel is God in the revelation of His absolute Godness to man. It is the all-encompassing gloriousness of God in a single word. It is the super-gloriousness of His revelation of Himself to usward. Immanuel incorporates time and eternity. It incorporates, creation because it incorporates us. It incorporates the Cross. It incorporates eternity. It incorporates the resurrection, ascension, session and the supranomination of Jesus. It includes everything salvational. It excludes nothing. It is the greatest word ever uttered.

Conclusion: Of all the Old Testament names given by God; from Elohim to YHWH, from Adonai to El-Olam, from YHWH to His Jehovistic titles, and the phrase names He was referred to; like "The God of Abraham" to "The Holy One", none of them included the salvation of man, eternal life, God with man in an immeasurably close union. None but Immanuel meant that God would be with us and never leave nor forsake us. None other than Immanuel incorporated the Cross, the resurrection, the ascension, the session and glorification of Jesus and the saints. Immanuel is God highest, most complete and final name. It is El's greatest name.

Terms used in the next chapter:
Negd-anu-El
Negd-against
Anu-us [man]
El-God
Against-us-God
El-negd-anu
El-God
Negd-against
Anu-us
God against us
These words were coined by the author and are used in the next chapter's discussion to show what it would be like if God was against us instead of for us as He is in Immanuel.

Chapter 5

*IF GOD BE **FOR US,** WHO CAN BE AGAINST US?* God is with us and for us in Immanuel; He is not against us ["Negdanuel"]

What if God was against us in Christ instead of being for us—what would that be like? That would be terrible! Thank God that is not the case. In this chapter, I share how God is truly for us in Immanuel and not against us. I present that God's wrath is restrained by the mercies that we have in Immanuel. Immanuel is our protector from the wrath of God. No wrath or judgment can be administered to us or poured out upon us except by Immanuel's consent. In Immanuel, God willed an awful, terrific force against us, then became the Defensive Wall for us against His own wrath He directs His wrath towards us, then "fielded" it in Immanuel. A main point that is made in this chapter is that in Immanuel God is a defense for us against His own wrath. He would not release His wrath of which we deserved upon us without being Immanuel first to absorb it for us. This is profoundly demonstrated in the Cross of Immanuel.

Unimpeded Access to the Abundance of God in Immanuel

In Jesus Christ, we have unimpeded, unhindered, uninhibited access to the plenteous grace and love of God, and God gives Himself the right to walk in our heart's gardens in "the cool of the day and hold with us communion sweet." God in Christ—Immanuel makes our relationship to Himself ireless; i.e. [harmless] without wrath.

God in Christ has broken down all walls between us (middle or whatever) i.e., between God and man. When we see Jesus, we see walls gone. In the church of Jesus Christ, we see the true 'city without walls' between God and man.

Imagine, If God in Immanuel was Against Us, What Would that Be Like?

What if, instead of Imm/anu/El being for us, God had been as He could have been Negdanu/El [against us God] or El nag-Anu[1] [God against us]? What if God had put all the force of Himself that He willed for us, instead against us without a wall [no barrier of protection]; without a wall; we would be like the Iraqis were during the Iraqi-Coalition war in 1991; without an air force.

In the USA Today (March 22-24, 1991), it was stated, "The United Nations today prepared to end a food embargo against Iraq after hearing the allies bombed Iraq back to the 'pre-industrial age.'" The U.N. Under-Secretary-General Martti Ahtisaari reported that the "near-apocalyptic" allied-apocalyptic assault means that Iraq needs huge quantities of food, fuel, and other emergency supplies to avert starvation and disease." Iraq asked the United Nations to halt the U.S. "continual air

---

[1] NegdanuEl and El negd-Anu are two words made by myself and a Jewish lady who happened to be a very wise Rabbi. The words were created to show how much God is for us in Immanuel and not against us. She made the word Negdanuel. Then from it, I made the word El negd Anu this one shows that if God were against us, He would have put His name [El] first in the name.

umbrella" over its territory, saying it was "terrorizing the Iraqi people."

Being left 'Wide Open,' Vulnerable to the Destruction of the Outer Forces, Mercilessly Struck without a Shield of Protection or a Defense to Help

Now, what if there were no United Nations relief effort—no Red Cross, no eye to pity, no arm to save, no missions of mercy? What could the defeated, suffering, battered Iraqis do?

Immanuel the Only One to Save Us from Wrath

We could have been saved from El's wrath by none other than Immanuel! Only by His power and knowledge, being God, could He redeem, and justify us, saving us from El's wrath.

Immanuel is God's access name. It neither distinguishes men (black, white, young, old, etc.) nor measures God! In this name, man and God are open to each other. Because God comes to man without measure, man can come to God without limits, even unto eternal life and glory, in Jesus Christ.

In Immanuel, God does not limit Himself or measure Himself to man in man's salvation, for His wrath directed towards man is immeasurable.

Hence again, the, name Immanuel has no adjective between Anu and El. Immanuel is God's "wall-less," "unwalled," measureless name! Immanuel simply constructed by God [a simple easy to say word] but it is unlimited in power and glory!

In Immanuel, God willed an awful, terrific force against us, and then became the Defensive-Wall for us against His own Wrath. He directed His Wrath towards us, then "Fielded" it in Immanuel

What if God in His unequalled [unmatched] power to mete out judgment, to satisfy His anger, wrath, Hismeasureless anger because of our sins, decided to be Negd Anu El (El Negd Anu) (against us God) without walls or barriers, unkind, wrathful, judgmental, merciless, unforgiving, cruel, death-dealing, hell-sending, unhindered, uninhibited, absolutely open, etc., etc., etc. ? Where would we be? What could we do? What would we do?

What if He would have named Himself as a wrathful God Negd Anu El, El Negd anu instead of the loving God to man without barriers [His name is what He is and He acts] as we find Him uniquely in Imm/Anu/El? (Without measure, too! No adjectives of measure; hence, God is unlimited).

What if God had been in Christ, as He had every right to be, damning the world rather than reconciling it? God, who has all power, being absolutely free, could have, had He chosen so to do, come in Christ to condemn us.

Jesus-Immanuel Came Not to Condemn

But Jesus said "I came not into the world to condemn the world". He could, in His mercy, take man's judgment to its ultimate conclusion, with all of its sorrow, pain and death but not on man, but in Himself in order to save His fallen creatures. He could have been Negdanuel, but He was not, because He would not! (In a coming day, the Lamb of God will be the Lion of the tribe of Judah world, look out!)

65

If God be For Us, Who Can be Against Us?

The Iraqi-Coalition Force War, Wrath Meted out on a Helpless Country with No Relief, No Defense

As devastating, as cruel, as crushing, as painful as

> *"For God sent not His Son into the world to*
>
> *condemn the world; but that the world*
>
> *through Him might be saved."*
>
> *18 He that believeth in Him is not 'condemned:*
>
> *but he that believeth not is condemned*

the war was on Iraq, Iraq and the rest of the world have really seen nothing yet in comparison to what is coming when the love of Jesus "goes into reverse" and the 7 seals are opened, the 7 thunders roll, and the 7 vials are poured forth upon the wicked of the earth; and when, for a short moment of time, God lets the world see that He could have been Negdanuel all along rather than being (Immanuel). This is why it is such a blessing to know that the total thrust of Jesus' first advent was salvational, not condemnatory. He came to save that which was lost.

Jesus' First Coming as Immanuel is not to Condemn, but to Save

Jesus demonstrated and said concerning His purpose for coming was not to condemn the women caught in adultery, whom He showed as He spoke. On the Cross, where He was without vengeance, He prayed for the forgiveness of those who had crucified Him.

66

1. "The Son of man came not to condemn..."
2. "Woman, where are thine accusers?"
"...neither do I condemn thee..."
3. "Father, forgive them, for they know not what they do."

Before Jesus came, conscience and Law, the two great "condemnation powers" had done their work, thoroughly. What man needed when Jesus came was relief, rescue, redemption, and righteousness. Man needed salvation, comfort, and peace with God. He needed freedom. God decided Himself not to be Negdanuel in His relationship towards us However, His supreme delight was in being Immanuel, "In the volume of the book it is written I delight to do thy will. Oh God, yea. Thy law is in my heart; said Immanuel."

Immanuel is (God with His own "Imm" [with] rather than a "Negd"[against])

In the Tribulation the World Will See that He could have been Against Us all Along
"For the great day of His wrath is come, and who shall be able to stand?" (Without Immanuel's shield, imposition, imputation)[Rev 6:17].
Who shall be able to face Negdanuel without Immanuel?
What a state, Negdanuel without Immanuel! (The great day of God's wrath is God's wrath sans [without] Immanuel; God's naked *[unrestrained]* wrath, God's arm made bare), and no Immanuel.
God's ungloved fist.

All we can expect without "Immanuel" is "Negdanuel". We can never come to "Imm El Anu"!

In the Gospel Age, God will only be Negdanuel or Elnegdanu via Immanuel so that He can truly be IMMANUEL .

If God be For Us, Who Can be Against Us?

Immanuel will turn from being 'for Man' to being against this Wicked World in the Tribulation

In the tribulation, God will be without being Immanuel (of force). Immanuel will be **latent** while Negdanuel will be **patent** in the tribulation.

In the Church Age, El in Christ is Immanuel

God will not Change; the Cross proves His Commitment to be Immanuel and not Negdanuel.

But in the Church Age of Immanuel is For Us

Now [in the Church Age—Dispensation of Grace] Immanuel is patent [active, seen and experienced by the church] and Negdanuel is latent. God's wrath is possible, but not evident.

Jehovah only vents His wrath as Negdanuel, because He Himself has become Immanuel. only by Imm!

Negd and Imm

Jehovah God would not unlash the horrific power of Elnegdanu, NegdanuEl until He was Immanuel. He would not release the fury of his being against us until in Immanuel He was with us and for us.

Jesus at Calvary, as Immanuel, was both victim and savior in order to redeem, rescue, save us. He was the man of two gates. He was opened to all the gates of hell as He bore our sins and, consequently, the full fury of God's wrath. Simultaneously, he was open to the gates of Heaven in order to sustain, bear, and endure the awful laden fury of Jehovah. "He by the grace of God tasted death for every man" He tasted, i.e. experienced, the first and second deaths for every man. Had not Heaven's gates been opened wide to Jesus (Immanuel), He could never have borne our grief of sin, deaths 1 and 2, and received our sorrows of both hells.

So, to Immanuel and because He was Immanuel, both the gates of Hell and Heaven were opened to Him. No divine "negd" with Devine "Imm"!

Only because God was <u>with us</u> in Christ could He be equally against us in Christ. What a being Immanuel was, and yet it is only because of His "Imm" that Jehovah exercises His "negd".

*This discussion continues from here in to the next chapter: "If God be **"With Us" What Can Separate Us"***

Conclusion: How shall God, who has named Himself Immanuel, now name Himself "Negdanuel" or "Elnegdanu"? Shall El reverse all that He has set forth in Christ to usward from the bowels of eternity, and via the Cross? Or i.e., validated in Calvary ?

Chapter 6

*IF GOD BE **WITH US**, WHAT CAN SEPARATE US?* Nothing can separate Us from God?

The name Immanuel means with us God and as discussed in the previous chapters of this book the name El being positioned next to us in Immanuel shows that God's plan to be with us is final. He will not change His mind about being with us. It is His last word on the matter. El being with us can be seen in His being in man [with man] on the Cross, in the grave, and His descent into Hell.

Therefore, it is also true that He will never be against us nor separate from us. In this chapter, I present God's immutable plan to be 'with us' and 'for us' in Jesus Christ as Immanuel. God, as explained by the Apostle Paul in Romans 8, is for us in Immanuel and not against us, and is determined in Immanuel that nothing shall separate us from Him. He has declared Himself to be with us in Immanuel and will never go back on His word and be against us nor separate from us.

In this chapter I, presented the **Immanuel** [withusGod] union, wherein God and man are together with nothing between. Such a relationship goes all the way into eternality. This is the essences the unique and eternal union between God and man in Immanuel.

In Immanuel there is no barrier between us and God. Here God in Christ guarantees an absolutely perfect flow of all His love and resultant Godness towards us. Here Love is flowing unhindered, uninhibited. Here is where grace abounds. It only abounds towards us by Jesus Christ. He is God's Imm anu El.

Only in Jesus Christ is the "Berlin Wall" [great wall of separation] completely broken down between, God and man, Heaven and earth. The Vail in the Temple was not rent in twain until Immanuel died.

There in the Old Testament temple set up was all its splendor and arrangement for service, but there was a Vail in it too. The way into the Holy of Holies, yet unrevealed; but when Jesus, Immanuel died the Vail was rent in twain, that separated man from God, and now by faith, we have access to Him - and (He freely to us,) all through His precious blood. "

Song
God is Great he greatly to be praised God is great
in my soul..R. C. Lawson

Since Immanuel is with Us, He is Not and will Never be Against Us

Having taken on the name Immanuel, which means with us God, for Jesus Christ, to be against us would be a mighty work for God Himself i.e. to undo all that He has done already in Christ - even as is significant in His Name Immanuel. By His might done–*can* only by His might *be* undone!

How shall God who has named Himself Immanuel now name Himself "Negdanuel" or "Elnegdanu"? Shall El reverse all that He has set forth in Christ to us ward from the bowels of eternity - and via the Cross? Or i.e. validated in Calvary ?

To cancel out His latest, most meaning - fraught Name, [His name spells I am with you] God would have to deny Himself and annul, expunge, amend, modify all that He has done from the eternal purposing, and image - producing in Christ to the crucifixion, to the resurrection, to the glorification, enthronement and supranomination of His blessed Son. This cannot occur and shall not occur because He who willed these things, and willed Immanuel at the beginning will not "unwill" or re-will them now or forevermore.

God is the Perfector and Initiator of an Inseparable Union with Us

Hence, Immanuel is God's indissoluble Name, and it inherently bespeaks an indissoluble union between God and man, God being the initiator and perfector of it all.
If God should dissolve Immanuel, then by whom would come a perfect union of God and man?

If not by Immanuel, then, by whom?
If not by His Cross, then by what?
If not from His throne, then from whence?
If God reversed Himself what of His credibility?
In Immanuel, no retraction, no amendment, no annulment – God does not will it.

All stands! Stare Decisis!! see Romans 8
Immanuel is absolute and Immutable

If El in Immanuel (be) for Us, Who (can be) Against Us?

In Romans 8, through the Apostle Paul God gives us a glimpse of the mechanics, the divine science of Immanuel; the livingness, the Anatomy of; the Architecture, the Physiology of Immanuel. Romans 8 treats on "the Immutability of Immanuel". "The Perfection and the Immutability of Immanuel"... nothing CAN SEPARATE! Unchanging withness NOTHING i.e. large or small! Immanuel terminated sin in His death and thereby offered man that which is without terminus, i.e. eternal life. He made(an end) of sin and brought in (everlasting righteousness.)

Romans 8: 34, 35

A . Christ died (for us).

B . Christ is risen (On our behalf to justify us. He is our living One who lives in us.)

C . Christ is at God's right hand, i.e. exalted and forever elevated on God's throne with unmeasured, incomprehensible power.

D . Christ intercedes for us (for our sake).

Conclusion: With that God-appointed relation, with that work in Christ by El, who can separate us, i.e. come between, create a chasm or a gulf? God in Christ has juxtaposed Himself, and by Christ, next to us, what now can interpose itself between? What can disannul the union? El did it. Who can undo it? Today we have "union-busting." *But not in our case with Immanuel.*

See Rom. 8 who shall separate me from the love of Christ? Romans 8 is Immanuel's chapter, i.e. Immanuel in His presence, His love.

Here is "El" in His inseparability from "us" because of the final work of Immanuel.

Romans 8 is the spectrum of Immanuel, seen after having passed through the "prism" of St. Paul's anointed, illumined mind and projected on to the pages of holy scripture.

Romans 8 gives clarity to the meaning of El's "withness" in His term "Immanuel."

To have faith in Jesus' Name, we must hear of it. How can we hear without a preacher? Peter and John and the Apostles had been taught by "The Name.

If God be With Us, What Can Separate Us?

God's Commitment to an Inseparable Union with us is Described in Romans 8:35-39

Who shall separate us from the love of Christ? shall tribulation, or distress, or persecution, or famine, or nakedness, or peril, or sword?
As it is written, For thy sake we are killed all the day long; we are accounted as sheep for the slaughter. Nay, in all these things we are more than conquerors through him that loved us. For I am persuaded, that neither death, nor life, nor angels, nor principalities, nor powers, nor things present, nor things to come, Nor height, nor depth, nor any other creature, shall be able to separate us from the love of God, which is in Christ Jesus our Lord.

What Can Come Between Us?

God in Christ has juxtaposed Himself by Christ next to us. What now can interpose itself between? What can disannul the union? El did it. Who can undo it? Today we have "union-busting. But in Immanuel there is no busting of our union with Him. What a unique union which is only found in Immanuel.

El being with us in Immanuel, We Go from Trembling to Treasures

By this union God (Immanuel) has taken out of our hands (Isaiah 54) the cup of trembling, yet He has not left us "empty-handed," He has given us in its place "a well of living water," "rivers of living water" "Where sin abounded grace did much more abound (all by Immanuel who made us nigh to God, i.e. in juxtaposition to God - without a quiet, harmless syllable between. [Nothing between us and God in Immanuel].

Song:

1. *Is not this the land of Beulah, blessed, blessed land of light. ?*
2. *I ' ve believed the true report*
3. *0 sweet rest ("the joy of His presence, a perfect sweet rest .. .)"...out darkness into His marvelous light"*

In Immanuel our being closely joined to El we are by this union privy to many wonderful spiritual blessing. We go from being destitute of spiritual blessing—due to the condition of the fall and the separating gulf, to having uninhibited access to God and many glorious things. We are brought into a realm of special things, beauty, glory, light, grandeur, miracles, power, "special diet,"[the word of God in preaching] royal finery [such as the comfort of God in the Holy Ghost], etc., etc., etc. We are brought into indivisible proximity to God, the King. What a holy, happy place!!! Yes! This blessed place is afforded to us because El is with us through Jesus Christ as Immanuel in these things and much more. We have the grace of God to up hold us.

We have the gifts of the Spirit to lead us. We have the fellowship of the saint to strengthen us. We have angles to minister to us. We have Christ as a mediator. We have Him as the mercy seat [high priest] in case we err. We have all these things and so much more because He is with us in Immanuel.

If God be With Us, What Can Separate Us?

The Finalness(ity) of Immanuel's Work

Whatever He removes as a barrier between God and man, He will never again reconstruct, or allow to be reconstructed. E.g.

"He will never endorse men's sins which He died for on Calvary" (Mom Johnson). He will never reinstitute (reconstruct) a vail in the temple between the holy place and the holy of holies. Having died unto sin once, He will never die again. (Endorse or promote sin. He is not the minister of sin.)

Having in hand the keys of hell and death, He will never relinquish them till all be consummated.

we have a fixed place in this union forever.

His being with Us, Goes All the Way to Eternal Life

Once New Testament believers, saints, are made immortal, and glorified, they as their Master was, will never be uncrowned, (unglorified, remortalized (an Eng. word) again. Once clothed in incorruption and immortality, they will never be unfrocked, unclothed. When mortality is swallowed up of life, it will be another of Immanuel's final and *main* acts. He is man's everlasting "Barrier-Remover." He is man's everlasting "Union-Producer." Men are trying to find and destroy the barriers to immortality.

Immanuel Is for Us and Against whatever is
Against Us—He Illuminates the Separators

According to Colossians 2:3, "All the treasures of wisdom and knowledge are hidden in Immanuel. El has accumulated, stored, His wisdom/wealth for us in Him.
He, Immanuel, who has been for us, in His Cross, blotted out what was against us even the law of commandments contained in ordinances (Ephesians 2:15). He has broken down the middle wall of partition. Thus, He is with us having no separating partition to interrupt the union. He

has slain the enmity, even the law. He has blotted out the handwriting (Colossians 2:14) and took it out of the way (way to perfect unions between God and man).

In the nature of the case of His name, Immanuel has/will remove everything that is contrary to us, against us being like God - one with Him.

The job awaiting God in Christ at the rapture of the church and the subsequent bestowal of eternal glory upon her, again is bounded only by God's infinity and none else knows this boundary.

In both directions Jesus is "the Divine exceeding"

Profundis—excelsis

Darkness—light

Abandonment—acceptance

Death—life

Etc.—etc

In all He exceeds all! Nothing is strong enough, tall enough, deep enough, dark enough to wedge the union of God with man in Immanuel.

He who stands in juxtaposition to us, being with us, is opposed to or against everything that is against us. Hence, Paul's gloriously exclaimed gospel in Romans 8!! Who shall separate us...? If God be for us, who...? Immanuel will never be Negdanuel to His believing children!! God's final word to His believing children is His final word - Immanuel!! He'll speak no more!!

God in Immanuel has Named Himself to be for Us in the name and works of Immanuel. It is clear that we don't need to Name Him. That is to say we don't need to figure out where He stands in relationship to us—with us or against us.

If God be With Us, What Can Separate Us?

How do We Interpret God's Name?

In my effort to make it very clear that in Immanuel God is for us—even the very name Immanuel spells out in its syllable sequence 'I am with you' Imm/anuEl [withusGod].

To show that God is with us in Immanuel wanted to know what word would say that God is not with us. I asked a Jewish women; a rabbi who was very familiar with the Hebrew language to compose a word that would mean God against us. She came up with the word (Elnegdanu) which means El-God negdanu-against us. This was the result of the learned Jewish woman's thought, and effort at it. It was a good attempt to assist in answering a question about God on a subject that He has answered once for all (time)[1]. Will God ever be against us?

To say that God is ever against us is to say that His name is Elnegdanu God-against-us. This is absolutely contrary to His name which He already named Himself Immanuel [withusGod]. Here in the New Testament age the name Immanuel describes God's position of being for us/with us.

Therefore, we don't have to question God's position on this. He has already proved that He is for us especially by His Cross. How do we name God in an age in which He has finally, once and for all times named Himself by His own breath?

He is with Us and for Us and Addreses Anything that is Against Us

See Isaiah 63 (I will stain all my raiment) In the tribulation, Jesus will make Himself the Lion of the tribe

---

[1] A Jewish lady Rabbi's effort to find a word that meant God against us.

Judah without losing His Immanuelness and holiness, as in the day of our salvation, He made Himself sin for us without losing His holiness.

In Immanuel, Jesus is made sin.

In Immanuel, Jesus is made the lion

In Immanuel, Jesus is made sin to make us righteous

In Immanuel, Jesus is made the Lion to apply judgment To the ungodly sinners, His enemies .

His eternal Name does not depart in His judgment. In His judgment, He stains His raiment, but doesn't mar its beauty. The stain is there but the whiteness is ever present, etc., etc., etc., etc. God having named Himself will not rename or unname Himself - nor can we rename or unname Him - no mater what He does, when He does it, or how He does it. Jesus, Immanuel is El's, God's final name and position is Immanuel—with us God.

Immanuel, God With Us

The preposition "with" includes every other preposition relative to our eternal salvation respecting God and us. In our case, in Christ, the preposition is tenseless, i.e. without tense. Immanuel was with us, e.g. in His ministry, on the Cross. Immanuel is with us as He ministers to us in every .respect in the church, as the minister of the true sanctuary.

Immanuel will be with us in the resurrection/rapture and forever thereafter. In the New Testament, God would not consider Himself with us and not for us, by us, through (to, toward) us and in us.

As God with us, He is before us, beside us, after us. E.g. after we die, He'll yet live and await the moment to resurrect, change us. Being with us, He is against all that is against us. "If God be for us, who can be against us?"

(Is time against us? Then He'll make us timeless!)

79

If God be With Us, What Can Separate Us?

On the side of; in favor of; on behalf of 'for expressing association or participation in some act, proceeding, or acting on the same side as (another lawyer) in an action at law. *In* Immanuel, God is on our side.

In the company, society, or presence of.In Immanuel, God took the humiliation of a darkened womb and the humiliation of an horrible, painful Cross.

How can a man be born when he is old? (John 3:4) Can he enter into his mother's womb a second time and be born? (And if he could, would he?) (God didn't have to and did.)
Mary, a pregnant virgin - could not have been, and was.
God, a man - did not have to be, and was.
Jesus, the Saint/Savior who was made sin and appeared as a sinner between two thieves - wanted to i.e. willed to be and was (Lo I come, it is written in the volume of the book, yea thy law is in my heart). (Didn't have a previous example and was.)

Man, the sinner made a saint - didn't plan to be, and was.
He chose to be with us based on His own counsel. He is with us indeed as He said.

Conclusion: He who stands in juxtaposition to us, being with us, is opposed to or against everything that is against us. Hence, Paul's gloriously exclaimed gospel in Romans 8!! Who shall separate us...? If God be for us, who...? Immanuel will never be Negdanuel to His believing children!! God's final word to His believing children is His final word - Immanuel!! He'll speak no more!!

Chapter 7

IMMANUEL, GOD'S MASTER PLAN
Immanuel, Tailor Made for Us

Out of El's profound love for man, in His own counsel, He made a plan to deal with the damage of the fall–the gulf and the barriers that separated God from man. The main separators were death and Hell. Even though man fell from grace, postponing God's plan for an eternal union with man, God planned that the fall would not eternally cancel His plan for the eternal union. God planned, designed and engaged in the making of Immanuel. In Immanuel, El is determined to see to it that His full redemptive plan will be accomplished.

When I say God made Immanuel, I mean He created the entire plan of salvation that is worked through Immanuel. From the bosom of the Father[El] Immanuel was planned, designed and executed. God made Him to be exactly what we needed in order for us to be saved.

In Immanuel, God Acts upon the Immeasurable Gulf between Himself and Man as God in Man via Imm/anu/el

The separation of man from God grieved God profoundly, causing Him to engage in a plan to:
(a) eliminate the barriers and the gulf that impeded uninhibited fellowship between God and man.
(b) abolish the verdict of death.
(c) shine light into darkness.
(d) bring man to the glory of an inseparable union between God and man.

Immanuel, God's Master Plan

Out of the depth of God's profound love and wisdom, God [El] made Immanuel [with-us-God]. Immanuel was God's plan for the redemption of fallen man and the earth. In Immanuel, the gulf of separation will be eliminated, death will be abolished, and the grave will no longer have an eternal claim on man.

Out of God's pursuit for an eternal union with man came Immanuel. In His counsel, His deep thought went into planning what Immanuel should be.

In Immanuel, God moved all of His "heavy" and "highly refined" salvational equipment into place for man's sake. He was determined to redeem fallen man. The purpose was to create everything for man's temporal and eternal deliverance – up to and including immortality.

In this chapter, I present the following points about El's Making of Immanuel:

(1) Immanuel incorporates the entire Plan of God for our Salvation

(2) Immanuel is Made by God to Fit us; He is Tailor-Made to be Exactly what we need Him to Be.

(3) In Immanuel, God Planned a Big Work – Salvation

(4) Immanuel was Made from the Boundless Freedom of God.

(5) The Thought of Immanuel came from the Bosom of the Father

(6) There is Nothing as Profound as Immanuel.

(7) God Made Him According to Specifications which Made Him Fit to do All that was Needed for Our Salvation.

(8) There are four profound things about Immanuel

(9) El [God] Moved to His Highest Crescendo in Making Immanuel

(11) Immanuel, God's Greatest Design

(12) No Other mind could have created Immanuel, but God's

(1) Immanuel is God's Plan for Our Salvation

In the planning and making of Immanuel, God had decided that all the fullness of the Godhead should be vested bodily in Immanuel because as Savior and administrator over His new order, Immanuel would need the wisdom and power to create and sustain the new kingdom as its administrator. In every way, Immanuel needed a special endowment in order to save mankind, create the new kingdom, and maintain it there in righteousness and true holiness. None but Immanuel could qualify.

In ministry; salvation work; and positioning, establishing, and maintaining the new order for man, Immanuel was a unique being. He was God in fact! El decided to empower Immanuel with nothing less than *omnem plentitudenesm [all that was needed]*. Nothing more was needed. Nothing else was possible. This was the superlative. There is nothing beyond God! Immanuel is strictly the being of God's (El's) deciding; Immanuel is God's own counsel (and prudence).

(2) God Made Immanuel to Fit Our Needs
God has Tailor-Made Jesus Christ in His Present All-Encompassing Gloriousness to Fit Us

God has made a perfect fit, which makes us better than we were originally [before the fall]. See Adam's and Eve's coats of skins, which were made unto them (perfect fit) in Genesis 3:21. See also I Corinthians 1:30 and 31.

(3) God Planned a Big Work [the Redemption of Man] in Immanuel

A crane standing 2 stories tall, a 10-wheel dump truck, a 5-ton bulldozer, an array of 20-foot-long, 2-foot-high steel beams on the ground – these do not indicate that a dog house is about to be erected.

The coming, living, dying and rising of Immanuel did not indicate that God was about to do a small work. Immanuel was God's "Big Work" with a colossal assignment—man's transition from corruption to incorruption, from mortality to immortality and from sin to righteousness and holiness.

He was planned by El to fulfil the whole spectrum of God's salvational scheme.

(4) Immanuel As a Manifestation of El's Boundless Freedom

God was fully free to equip Immanuel with superpowers not limited to the restraints of Adam's world. In His demonstration of power, He did things that no other being could do. These acts were done specially to prove that He was God.

Immanuel is the ultimate and final manifestation of God's absolute freedom!! Through Immanuel, God expresses the highest degree of His eternal freedom (q.v.)! Daniel said, "He does what He wills in the army of heaven and among the inhabitants of the earth. None can stay His hand or say unto Him, what doest thou?" In other words, El was free to join Himself indivisibly with mortal men (contrary to gnostic belief). Gnostics believed that god would never be near to man like He is in Immanuel.

In the making of Immanuel, El showed that He was free to make a man without the use of a man [fatherless conception] that He was free to make man by a virgin and have her still be a virgin and that He was free to bear sin and have His holiness unstained.

Immanuel, as the "Freedom of God," could turn water to wine. He could see through darkness. He could command wind and walk on water. He could make fish and bread grow in His hands. He could eat and drink with sinners – and contrary to gnostic belief, He could inhabit the flesh while doing all of these things. He could be made sin for men, die on a Cross for them and in actuality, never stop living. To live while dying to die while living, etc., etc., etc., etc.. Immanuel is El with the illimitable etc.)

God's Boundless Freedom Is Demonstrated in His Design of Immanuel

To study Immanuel is to study God in the boundless reaches of His freedom; in His height and depths, God never manifests Himself so freely as in Immanuel! (However, He was always absolutely free.) In Immanuel, God ultimately manifests His prerogative to be God, the Eternally Boundless and Free One. Only when we're glorified will we see into El's freedom, which was exercised in Immanuel. We must remember that He was "With-Us-God," two unequal, disparate entities, inextricably joined for the transfer of God's Godness to us (not our humanity to God). He needed nothing from us to assist, help enrich His Godness. Our fallen humanity needed everything from wisdom to immortality. We, not God, were fallen. He was always the same. He was problem-free and the problems' master. We were problem-laden and victimized. He came to be with us. Behold this glory! We didn't – and couldn't go to be with Him. So He came where we were, that Some day we could be like Him and be where He is.

In Immanuel, God self-exceeds the exercise of His freedom of *creatio ex nihilo* (creating something out of nothing). In *creatio* (creating), He released His word and made a universe separate from Himself. In Immanuel, He joined His own being and nature with man, "The dusty one." Then for Calvary's experience, He, in Christ, was made sin so that we might be made righteous. Then in Christ, He died – something He couldn't do by nature – all to be one with us (see Acts Chapter 20:28; I Timothy 3:16; Ephesians 1:14; and I John 3:16).

God's Ultimate Freedom in His Design and Making of Immanuel

Immanuel is the ultimate and final manifestation of God's (El's) absolute freedom!! Through Immanuel, God expresses the highest degree of His eternal freedom. God showed off His magnificence and Divine independence in making Immanuel. Daniel said, "He does what He wills in the army of heaven and among the inhabitants of the earth. None can stay His hand or say unto Him, what doest thou?" God does a strange thing.

Romans 11:33

> I John 3:23 - "And this is His commandment, that we should believe on The Name of His Son Jesus Christ, and love one another, as He gave He gave us commandment"

(5)Immanuel, Made from the Bosom of God

God opened the bosom of His heart to utter the eternal name Immanuel to the prophet Isaiah. He uttered the word Immanuel and by His power brought Him into being. All of His Godness opened His heart to man to be with him by Immanuel. The question now is: Having opened His mouth and His heart to manward, how shall He now close both His heart and mouth? (see Romans 8, "How shall He not?")

What on Earth, in time or in eternity can now close El's opened heart and mouth of El? And so the thrust of the Romans 8 Questions.

Since God's heart opened itself to man in eternity, how can anything in time close it? This is St. Paul's view in Romans 8.

In Immanuel, God had a name coming out of HIS BOSOM, and there He incorporated the ultimate manifestation of His thought, will, word, wisdom, and power. O, Immanuel, what a name! Hence, in the name of Jesus, we are allowed into the bosom of God; respecting His thought, etc., back to eternity, past and forward to eternity to come.

Immanuel is God's "unbordered" name. Immanuel is, at the same time, where El, God terminates the further revelation of His wisdom and power to manand the past revelation. Immanuel is the embodiment of all of God's word to man – and the final word. He is called in Revelation 19:13, "the word of God" (19:11 -16) and "KING of KINGS and LORD of LORDS."

We cannot trace God acting even in eternity past before Him or in eternity to come after Him. Immanuel is the First and the Last.

(6) Nothing Is as Profound as Immanuel

Immanuel is truly *De Profundis* [out of the depth of God's counsel]. Immanuel comes from out of the Father's bosom. Nothing is so profound. Nothing provides a human being with such an exalted, immeasurable range of thought. In the thought world, Immanuel is all-transcending. It eclipses all areas of human philosophy. This is because Immanuel, Jesus Christ, is God's wisdom and power.

Immanuel, then, is God's glory word – all glory *into* it (its proposal), *in* it (its production, e.g., the incarnation, the formation of the church). all-glory *of* it (what it does, its operation). all-glory *to* it (its worship).

Note: Before buildings, great or small, magnificent or mediocre, are erected, they are designed. Architects are paid well for design work, as are engineers and building scientists. The work of these people comes before the work of the builders. The actual construction is another phase.

(7) Immanuel Was Designed According to Divine Specifications

In order for Immanuel to do all that God would do in Him, he has to be designed to be born of a virgin and to be both fully a man and fully God. He had to be able to be righteous and holy enough to go to God on our behalf.

He had to be able to carry the sins of the whole world in His body. He had to be able to consciously experience the Hell of the Cross, to die both the second and the first deaths, to not see corruption and to return unchanged. He had to be able the rise from the dead and to ascend into glory in that same body that He went to Cross-Hell in. To do all of this, He must be God. He must be compatible to the Cross and the throne equally. He had to be made to descend to the lowest Hell, where only He could go, and then ascend to the highest Glory while being the same person in the same body. This creation required God.

Thus, God was both the architect and the engineer. He knew how much Jesus had to stand, how much stress He would endure, how deep He would sink, how high He needed to ascend, etc. God was also builder of every aspect of Immanuel. Hence, in every way, from design to worship, God is glorified in Immanuel.

God has enshrouded His incomprehensible person, power and work of full redemption in His incomprehensible Name—**Immanuel.** Immanuel is without both a definitive locus and time. This is why we can see God's love, character, wisdom and so much more in Immanuel.

(8) In the Making of Immanuel, We Find Four Profound Theological Factors, that Are Only in Immanuel

Four profound theological factors:
a. The Word was made flesh.
b. Jesus Christ tasted death for every man.
c. Jesus, the Son of God, is a great High Priest who is passed into the heavens.
Which is the greatest of the three? That we are made the righteousness of God in Him (our Lord Jesus Christ).
Immanuel is the Divine exponent of Psalm 23.

See I Peter 2:21-25.
²² Who did no sin, neither was guile found in his mouth.

²³ Who, when he was reviled, reviled not again; when he suffered, he threatened not; but committed himself to him that judgeth righteously.
²⁴ Who his own self bare our sins in his own body on the tree, that we, being dead to sins, should live unto righteousness: by whose stripes ye were healed.
²⁵ For ye were as sheep going astray; but are now returned unto the Shepherd and Bishop of your souls.

You were returned by the same One, by whose stripes you were healed. He healed us by His stripes. He returned us by His power.

See I Peter 3:18.

(9) God Moved to His Highest Crescendo in the Making of Immanuel

His new world in which, upon which, through which, (by which), He will declare His glory. A glorious display or manifestation presaged by Psalm 8.

Elohim's marvelous creation is in the framing of the worlds, which reaches its crescendo in Adam. However, El moved to another crescendo in the making of Immanuel and a new world by and in Him. Here is El's grandest manifestation of His might. It is not in the earliest chapters of Genesis. It is in Immanuel – God with us and unto us. In Immanuel, God intended and still intends to release mighty power, counseling, fatherhood and peace to men such as never before, for Immanuel's kingdom is El's "New Creation", Immanuel's kingdom is El's new theatre of operation.

(10) Immanuel Is El's Greatest Design

In Immanuel, God moved all of His "heavy" and "highly refined" salvational equipment into place for man's sake. The purpose was to create man's temporal and eternal deliverance – up to and including immortality. ("Imm" can also stand for "Immortality.") Immanuel's ultimate and most glorious cause was and is our immortality (see II Corinthians 5).

(11) Immanuel Is God's Architected Plan

In Immanuel, God had a name coming out of HIS BOSOM, and there He incorporated His ultimate thought, will, word, wisdom, and power. O, Immanuel, what a name! Hence, in the name of Jesus we are allowed into the bosom of God, respecting His will for all eternity, past and future. Immanuel is God's "unbordered" name. Immanuel is, at the same time, where God terminates the revelation of His wisdom and power. Immanuel is the embodiment of all of God's words to man – and His final word. He is called in Revelation 19:13, "the word of God" and "KING of KINGS and LORD of LORDS."

We cannot trace God's actions, even in eternity. Immanuel is the First and the Last.

Note: Bishop Hancock described Jesus as the first thing God made.

The world of religion, which God created in the Old Testament by speaking to the fathers through the prophets, has become a much vaster universe since Immanuel (i.e., since He spoke to us through His Son).

In Immanuel, the Sun of righteousness has risen with healing in His wings (Malachi 4:2).

In Immanuel, El moves from "brooding over" to "*Dixitque Deus*" [God's thought before speaking things into existence]. In Genesis, El's brooding was precedent or antecedent to His voice, which set the universe in motion. God's Old Testament acts related to religion were antecedent to His final voice and the final creation of Immanuel.

The brooding was God abiding in a preparatory mode. In *Dixitque*, He was acting. The Old Testament is somewhat preparatory for His *Dixitque* in Immanuel.

The Old Testament was El's "John the Baptist" for Immanuel's reign. Thus, God planned Immanuel as an architect draw out the plans for a building.

(12) No Other Mind Could have Created Immanuel, but God's

No one else could think of God dying and going to Hell. No one but God could plan for heaven to go to Hell and Hell to come to heaven as it happened in Immanuel on the Cross.

Only God could make a body, or to even think of it that can carrying the sins of the whole world in it to Calvary. Only God could be in Immanuel go to the second death [Hell on the Cross] for us, disarm it, then die the first death after having finished all He was to do in the second death. Thus, saving us from the second before going to the first. Only God could make this super being [Immanuel]. this you will see more clearly as you read chapter 13, "*Immanuel Goes to Hell*".

Conclusion: In Immanuel, God moved all of His "heavy" and "highly refined" salvational equipment into place for man's sake. He was determined to redeem fallen man. The purpose was to create everything for man's temporal and eternal deliverance – up to and including immortality in Immanuel.

Chapter 8
UNTO US IMMANUEL IS BORN

The objective of this chapter is to show that Immanuel is God's manifestation of His Godhead towards His new creation, His kingdom. Not this time, towards the universe I. e. the mountains, rivers, seas and trees, but unto Us through Jesus Christ our Lord.

UNTO US! UNTO US! UNTO US! This is the direction of El's Elohim's, Jehovah's, Adonai's glory in Immanuel - not primarily toward the already created universe. What a plan! What a purpose God had, has for us via Immanuel!

For unto us a child is born, unto us a son is given: and the government shall be upon his shoulder: and his name shall be called Wonderful, Counselor, The mighty God, The everlasting Father, The Prince of Peace. Isaiah 9:6

The Child Born is not unto the Universe this time but is unto Us-Relative to the Needs of Mankind

The child, the Son given UNTO US and Immanuel God with us all in tandem [in a cycle]*,* is a unity. One of the glories of *Isaiah* 9:6 is the UNTO US. The theme of the prophet here, does not seem to be the action of God the Creator towards His first creation, *that is* the world, apart from man, but rather the manifestation of His Godhead towards His new creation, His kingdom. Not this time, towards the mountains, rivers, seas and trees, but:

A. The government shall be *upon his shoulder, that is to say He shall be* a kingdom, *of* a new order for man—*hence unto man*

B. His name shall be called "wonderful," i.e. unto us in the kingdom, in the new order—*hence, He shall be full of wonders unto man* .

C. Is this counselor, for the universe? No, this is counseling UNTO US.

D. Mighty God with might towards the clouds, etc., etc.? No, *not for the clouds* but- rather might unto us, by the cross, the resurrection, the glorification, the session, the high priestly administration. Hence, *this is Immanuel the child unto us*

E. Everlasting Father. Not to the universe, but UNTO US.

F. Prince of Peace. Not to the heavens, but UNTO US - especially those in the kingdom, the new order.

UNTO US! UNTO US! UNTO US! This is the direction of El's Elohim's, Jehovah's, Adonai's glory in Immanuel - not primarily toward the already created universe. What a plan! What a purpose God had, has for us via Immanuel!

God Releases His Mighty Power for Us and Unto Us in Immanuel

In Immanuel, God intended and intends to release mighty power, counseling, fatherhood and peace to men - such as never before, for Immanuel's kingdom (reign) is El's "New Creation",Immanuel's kingdom is El's new theatre of operation. His new world in which, upon which, through which, (by which), He will declare His glory. A glorious display or manifestation presaged by Psalm 8.

God Moves to His highest level in the Making of Immanuel, a Level Higher than when He Created Adam and the Universe

There is a marvelous creation of Elohim in the framing of the worlds which reaches its crescendo in Adam.

However, El moved to another crescendo in the making of Immanuel and a new world by and in Him. Here in Immanuel is El's grandest manifestation of His might. It is not in the earliest chapters of Genesis. Rather It is in Immanuel, God with us and unto us foretold of in Isaiah 9:6 and fulfilled in Matthew 1:21.

Immanuel the Child Born is the Mediator of the New Order for Adam's Damaged World and the Birthing of a New and Eternal Order through the Rebirth of Man in the Church via Immanuel

The first creation and it damaged form will pass away at the coming of the New Heaven and New Earth, but the New order established by Immanuel [the church] will be eternal.

Note Brother, Apostle John in Revelation 21,
"And I saw a new heaven and a new earth for the first heaven and the first earth were passed away and there was no more sea and I John saw the holy city, the New Jerusalem, coming down out of heaven from God prepared as a bride, adorned for her husband...." John saw "a new world," but not a new church. He saw the home of Jesus', Immanuel's bride. So we see the first order passing while we see the new creation abiding eternally. God's super glory is manifested in the New Order, the new kingdom via Immanuel. He who was not only God "with us," but while being God "with us," was also "unto us." Hence, Isaiah 9:6 and Matthew 1:21 are together and speak, not a various, but a common language.

Isaiah 9:6-7

⁶ For unto us a Child is born,

Unto us a Son is given;

And the government will be upon His shoulder.

And His name will be called

Wonderful, Counselor, Mighty God,

Everlasting Father, Prince of Peace.

⁷ Of the increase of His government and peace

There will be no end,

Upon the throne of David and over His kingdom,

To order it and establish it with judgment and

justice

From that time forward, even forever.

The zeal of the LORD of hosts will perform this.

Immanuel Unto Us—a Fixed Relationship 0, what privileges are ours in Immanuel's church, since He is unto us and with us! For these privileges, see Romans 5 and Romans 8. No wonder why in Romans 8:35 St. Paul asked, who shall separate us from the love of God? Or to put it in a much lesser language form, what or who shall negate Elohim's "with" and "unto"?

Who shall separate us from the love of Christ? shall tribulation, or distress, or persecution, or famine, or nakedness, or peril, or sword? Romans 8:35

Paul is saying, to believers, "unto" and "with" are forever settled in heaven. Immanuel and all of His interpretation is eternally fixed. Immanuel will never be less *unto us*, He will not, He need not ever be more! Who can invalidate- El's "with" and "unto"?

The Angelic Message of the Birth of Immanuel Expressed His Being unto Us Again

The glory-filled voice of the angelic leader which rang out over the Judean field on that long ago night when Jesus' birth was announced to some shepherds who were keeping watch over their flock said, "Behold I bring you good tidings of great joy **which shall be to all people** (sons of Adam, the ruining one) for **UNTO YOU is born** this day in the city of David A SAVIOR which is Christ, The Lord.

96

It meant "Immanuel is here!" A defender of the weak; new rest for the weary; life water, life bread for the thirsty and hungry; wisdom for the foolish; freedom for the captives; peace with God for the condemned; restoration of friendship, fellowship for the estranged, for foreigners; companionship for the lonely, etc., etc., etc., and above all. a glorious resurrection for the dead and life eternal in a - new world in the presence of God, The Father.

Because of Immanuel the child unto us; "Beneath the cross of Jesus I fain (hurriedly) would take my stand. The shadow of a mighty rock within a weary land. A home within the wilderness. A rest upon the way. A shelter from the noontide heat, all the burden of the day."

Immanuel, 0, Immanuel, I am so glad you've come!

Conclusion Immanuel the child born is not primarily toward the already created universe. But is unto us. What a plan! What a purpose God has for us via Immanuel!

Chapter 9

IMMANUEL, HORN IN THE HOUSE OF DAVID

The objective of this chapter is to show the wisdom, the power, and the precise fulfillment of Prophecy about Jesus Christ as the Horn of the House of David.

How deep are the workings of El by Immanuel toward both Jew and Gentile, in that He was born Jewish, the Son of David and the Son of God—to bring both to God in a new relationship, so El, could be WITH both.

> *For he shall grow up before him as a tender plant, and as a root out of a dry ground: he hath no form nor comeliness; and when we shall see him, there is no beauty that we should desire him.[Isaiah 53:2]*

Immanuel, Horn in the House of David

God is only wise, and there are no exceptions to His wisdom; no qualifying words are needed to clarify His words. There are no areas in which He is not wise.

God is almighty, and there are no exclusions. He is the One who raised up for us one born of salvation in the house of His servant David.

Immanuel Was Raised by God to Be the Horn

He was raised by God to be the Horn in the house of David—to perform His mercy and fulfill His promise.

The who, God
The what, the Horn
The To Whom, for whom - Us
The where, the House of David
Thewhy, the performance of His mercy, the fulfillment of His promise
God raising Immanuel shows In Immanuel's manifestation is the:
A. T h e precision of E l ' s promise
b. The precision of the performance of the promise.
Note: What good is a promise if there be no fulfillment? A promise is only as good as its performance.
Performance is contingent upon the wisdom, ability, character, and continuity of the promise or performer.

Again we must marvel at God's wisdom, which is different from ours. He would cause a king to be born in a torn-down house: Our wisdom would dictate that the Horn must be born in a palace or place with much strength and wealth.

However, God raised up this Horn in the house of David. He was able. Behold His wisdom; He raised the Horn as a root out of a dry ground.

In raising the Horn in David's house, God performed His promise precisely, but David's house was a fallen house—a cold, negative, degenerate house. Probably, in most people's eyes, the house of David's condition at the time Jesus came was not a fit place for a Horn to be born. It was not flourishing or a fertile place to grow a horn in.

How can anything good come out of such bad conditions. Can anything good come out of Nazareth? How does one prepare a baby born in a crack house to

become president of the U.S.? When Jesus was born, "The House of David" had fallen down. "He ministered to

people" sitting in darkness and in the shadow of death. Who encouraged Jesus? Despite this, God raised Him up and made Him a saint, servant and savior in His own right.

The Horn Was Raised by El in Spite of the Deplorable Conditions of His [Immanuel's] Day

Satan would love to have seen the Horn's coming *averted but God raised Jesus, in spite of the adverse conditions, to be a* Spokesman, who *was* greater than all who had been before Him—and he did so out of a hostile environment. Just look at God!! God fulfilled His promise and showed His mighty power. Here was evidence of God's determination

to be Immanuel. God saw to it that the Horn was born and raised, even with the unwelcoming conditions of those days of Jesus' life and ministry:

A. Poor birth conditions

B. Hostile spiritual environment

C. Poor living circumstances

D. Destroyed on Calvary, yet He remained with us!

The Name of Jesus Christ as Immanuel, Book I

In Immanuel, we behold a mighty manifestation of El as He takes a speechless babe being nourished with milk from its mother's breast through a hostile environment (and the Cross) to the throne of God. That babe would form a church and reign over all as Lord and Master. Behold the Glory of God!

The glory of this is how El takes the child born of a virgin, births Him in Bethlehem (an insignificant town) and raises him in Nazareth (a ghetto-like town). Despite this, He goes on to be the messiah-king—the Horn.

Isaiah 53:1, 2

> *Who hath believed our report? and to whom is the arm of the LORD revealed?*
>
> *For he shall grow up before him as a tender plant, and as a root out of a dry ground: he hath no form nor comeliness; and when we shall see him, there is no beauty that we should desire him.*
>
> *He is despised and rejected of men; a man of sorrows, and acquainted with grief: and we hid as it were our faces from him; he was despised, and we esteemed him not* Isaiah 53:1-3

Note: The revelation of God's arm concerns a "He."

In this wonderful "He," we see the revelation of God's arm in Immanuel, as we see it nowhere else.

A tabernacle in ruins (a spiritual crack house) is fallen in: strength, faith, righteousness, wisdom, joy, peace and hope. At Jesus' coming, Israel was:

Israel at the time of Jesus' Birth

1. A crooked and perverse nation

2. A faithless generation

3. A nation whose previous leaders knew not the wisdom of God

4. A wicked-hearted people who killed prophets and stoned the messengers of God

5. A rebellious house, as Ezekiel called them (Jesus cried, "O, Jerusalem, Jerusalem.")

6. "A wicked generation, seeketh a sign"

7. A nation whose leaders (Scribes and Pharisees) were corrupt

---

He who was raised as our Horn had strength and wisdom enough not only to grow and act in sinful Israel but to save others in their houses. "From His house to our house."Look at Nazareth, where He was brought up—so full of unbelief, He could not do many mighty works there. (C.F. Isaiah 53)

The Horn of salvation was not raised "by," "with" or "through" the house (tabernacle) of David—only "IN" the house. Immanuel's rising was not "of" the house but only "in" it. His rising was in spite of the house. It was "by," "through," "with' and "of" the Holy Spirit. Immanuel was made solely by God. The Horn has risen up "IN" a fallen house.

Isaiah 53:1 asks, who has believed our report, and to whom is the arm of the Lord revealed?

Immanuel is the ultimate revelation of El's mighty arm. He is the greatest revelation of El's almightiness. It is revealed on no other scale so grand! We should notice how the prophet quickly enlightens us with the fact that the revelation of God's arm is a "He": "For He shall grow up before Him as a tender plant and as a root out of a dry ground"—see Acts 15:16.

> ***After this I will return And will rebuild the tabernacle of David, which has fallen down; I will rebuild its ruins, And I will set it up;*** *Acts 15:16*

Conclusion Jesus Immanuel was the child born to us, the son given to us, on whose shoulders the government will be.. He is to be the prince of peace and the born ruler of Israel. He is the Horn, the ruler who was born a child and who was raised by God to be the king of Israel, the king of the church and finally the king of Glory. He was born at what seems to have been the most inopportune time and in the most inopportune place—Bethlehem. In the day Immanuel Jesus, was born the Jews including those of the House of David, were in no condition to claim their rightful place as the ruling tribe of the world. They were religiously bankrupt; they were repressed and looked nothing like a kingdom established by God. That world was not welcoming to the king of glory. These conditions were described by God in Isaiah 53:1-3 as a dry ground. However, it was in that world in which Jesus was born— and in spite of those conditions.

Chapter 10

"JESUS, THE GOD–SIGN OF GOD"

In this chapter, the virgin birth of Jesus Christ is discussed in relation to Him being Immanuel. The birth of Jesus was precisely how God told Isaiah it would be:
Behold a virgin shall conceive and bear son and thou shall call his name Immanuel. Isaiah 7:14
The immaculate conception is the sign that fulfills what God said to the prophet Isaiah. The virgin birth is God coming to be with us, fulfilling the prophecy with miraculous precision.
 This is the birth of the union of El with man as already discussed in chapter one of this book.
This is the birth of the **"anu–El** union" of God and man.
This is the birth of the inseparable union.
This is the birth of the juxtaposition of God with man. This is the birth of the "withness" of El to man. It is the inception of the humiliation to exaltation process of Immanuel. This is the first sign of God moving next door to us.
Thus, in the virgin birth is the sign of Immanuel.
This sign [the virgin birth] identifies Jesus as Immanuel.

Sign of the Virgin Birth
The Sign of the virgin birth of Christ was a miraculous act, serving to demonstrate divine power and authority and to fulfill the idea of Immanuel.
The virgin birth puts the El with the anu to from **"anuEl"—"Us-God" or "Man-God." It is the essence of the with-us-God.**

In God's arrangement for Immanuel relative to His being the son of the virgin and simultaneously The Son of God, He could not be one without being the other. Not one unless the other. He had to be both to be either? He had to be both? Yes both, and only because He was both was He Imm/Anu/El."

The sign is composite. It has components. All components must be in place or it is not the God-given sign. The mother of Jesus cannot simply be a young woman of marriageable age. She must be a VIRGIN. *She must be* a virgin or *there is* no sign.

The virgin must conceive, or no sign. The virgin must bear, giving full evidence of conception, or no sign. The child born must be Imm/anu/EL or, no sign.
0, what a sign!

The Sign is Greater than all other Signs and Wonders

A sign giving witness to the wisdom, glory, majesty, power and Lordship of God (His authority). This is a sign transcending the signs in the heavens (Genesis 1; Psalm 19). The sign of God in the virgin-birth, transcends the sign of God by showing Moses' the burning bush.

This is a sign which transcend [supersedes] all of the miracles of, the wilderness; including the turning the bitter water sweet, the provision of quails on the ground, it transcends even the parting of the red sea . This sign supersedes all other miracles and wonders. It transcends Joshua's sun standing still. (God stopped the world from turning around.) David's miraculous slaying of Goliath.
It transcends Shadrach, Meschach and Abednego*'s great presence of God in their fiery furnace*. And Daniel's *deliverance from the lion's den*.

Jesus, The God-Sign of God

There Was Never the God-Sign before Immanuel

These were signs, but not God-signs, a God sign is a sign that includes the being of God Himself.

God of Abraham, Isaac, and Jacob.

God of the Hebrew Scriptures has given us a sign.

A sign: great, mighty, glorious, unique, colossal, incomparable.

Not a sign in or of the sea, wind, hail, manna, quails, fire, blood (David & Goliath), etc., but rather a God-sign of or from and about God.

God gave us His Name in Imm-Anu-El syllabylized and tripartite *Imm-with anu-us El-God* so as to aid our faith and understanding.

How can we have Jesus with any part of Immanuel divested?

The Two Parts of the Sign must Both be True

Mary, the woman who conceived and bore Jesus did not lose her virginity - part of the sign (note the scripture does not say signs, but sign).

God who began Jesus and in the process became man, flesh, did not lose His Divinity - the second part of the sign.

This sign was God's unique and incomparable sign - God's only **God-sign**. Jesus was the sign God gave us. This is a great mystery! No argument is necessary. It is a great mystery. Jesus-Immanuel, the God-Sign, is history's greatest evidence given to men of the greatness, power and glory of the God of
The Hebrew scriptures.

Components of The sign:

1: A virgin shall conceive and bear a son.

#2: The Son shall be Immanu-El.

It is impossible to find a round square hole. One can find a square hole. One can find a round hole. One cannot find one which is both.

One can find a woman who is a virgin. One can find a pregnant woman, but one cannot find a pregnant virgin; absolutely untouched by the seed of man. (I suspect that in those days(**when Mary conceived Jesus**), there were no in vitro pregnancies.)

He who is uncreated, inoriginate and ingenerate was conceived and born.
How? How? How?
"Faith walks in where reason cannot tread."

We Are to Accept It and Believe It
God has given us a sign. We can take it or leave it.
"If you believe not that I am He you shall die in your sins."
If, in our thinking, a virgin can become pregnant and have (bear) a son (**sans** the seed apart), of man's seed then it <u>is</u> reasonable absolutely!

God can become flesh, Immanuel can exist. If, in our thinking, a virgin woman cannot become pregnant and bear a son, then I can see real difficulties in our accepting the Biblical Immanuel. We find Immanuel only in the Hebrew Scriptures where we find also the God of the Hebrews.

Mary's Son and God's Son; Two parties are involved which Constitutes a single Sign

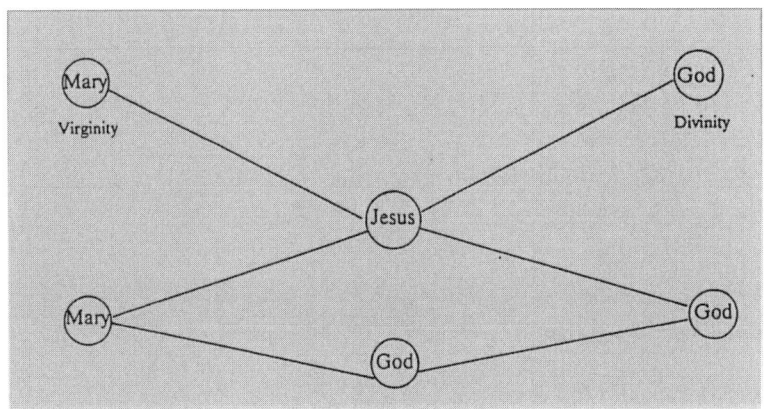

Mary and God produced Jesus. To look at Jesus, we are pointed to Mary's virginity and God's divinity.

When we look at Mary's retained virginity and at God's retained divinity, we are pointed by this mighty sign (post) [the miraculous virgin birth] to God's sovereignty over history (See Isaiah 7), *His* Lordship over man and nature, *Him being* director of times and season, *the* orderer of human affairs, Almighty God, Lord of Heaven and Earth, *etc., etc., etc.*

Mother Virgin Mary, what a name!

The man Christ Jesus, Lord of All, what a name!

I.   Mother Virgin Mary!

II. Jesus Christ, Imm/Anu/El!

A virgin conceiving and bearing a Son who is God—all this <u>A SIGN.</u>

We cannot eliminate anything from the sign and it still be the composite and complete sign God is giving

We cannot decompartmentalize here and retain the sign. We cannot divest the name of any of its parts and retain the name Imm-anu-El.

In the sign, we must retain:

A . The Virgin

B . The Conception (**Sans** the seed of man)

C . The Son Borne

D . The Whole Name of Immanuel

To divest is to weaken, to corrupt. The glory here for us is a glory of full retention.

Examples of Things that Have Missing Parts

A. What about a four-wheel car with a wheel missing - or a flat tire?

B. A bicycle with one *pedal missing* .

C. A buckle-belt with the buckle missing.

D. A cake with the *sugar* left out.

The Sign, The Name, and Salvation

The sign is as the Name; to be what God gave, it must have all its parts.

God **gave** the sign. God gave the name for our faith, understanding, life and glory. God's sign is also God's salvation - all in one!

To say "a young woman" will do, is to divest the sign of its glory.

To say Immanuel, Jesus is not God is to divest the sign of its glory.

To divest the sign of its glory is to divest ourselves of *the great* guide to God's glory.

To divest ourselves of *this great* guide to God's glory is to miss the road to eternal life.

To miss eternal life is to live in spiritual slavery, to abide in "chains" of darkness, to dwell in perpetual "night."

We need the sign which is "The Sign" of God's glory, His authority, His power!

Jesus is God's God-Sign of God.

"The whole is equal to the sum of its parts."

A massive sign!!

A massive sign!!

A massive sign!!

A massive sign!!

God <u>gave</u> the sign. Hence, it is an act of grace and consequently can only be comprehended by faith.

To human reasoning and logic, the sign of God is incomprehensible. It is only understood, like creation, by faith!

No components - no signs (sing).

No sign - no call for "behold" (no marvel)

No call to behold - no glory apparent.

No glory apparent - no worship, no lordship, then silence! Silence towards God. But here the diametrical opposite is true!

Matthew 1:21-25
King James Version (KJV)

²¹ And she shall bring forth a son, and thou shalt call his name JESUS: for he shall save his people from their sins.
²² Now all this was done, that it might be fulfilled which was spoken of the Lord by the prophet, saying,
²³ Behold, a virgin shall be with child, and shall bring forth a son, and they shall call his name

> *Emmanuel, which being interpreted is, God with us.*
> [24] *Then Joseph being raised from sleep did as the angel of the Lord had bidden him, and took unto him his wife:*
> [25] *And knew her not till she had brought forth her firstborn son: and he called his name JESUS.*

The Immaculate Conception Manifests the Might of the Mighty God

Jesus Christ is The Mighty God and the might of the Mighty God made manifest. (He manifested Himself in the flesh, via the flesh in the days of the flesh.) He was *and* is God manifest in the flesh. He was *and* is God's might manifest in what He did via the flesh. He was God continually manifesting His glory as He lived or tented in the flesh. Via the flesh, God manifested His might dually - in Mary and respecting Himself.

Jesus is not only the mighty God, but the mighty God's self-evidence of (His) the (might) of The Mighty God. It was always historically known that God was mighty, but not with this kind of or degree of evidence (i.e., the immaculate conception). It was always known that God was mighty, but this was the first time that men could look lastingly on Him, as the shepherd, and wise men and say this is He - i.e. The Lord, The King of the Jews - a baby in a natural, fleshly, mortal body. Jesus was the manifestation, the product of God's might in "a new thing" altogether. MS182 d   Jesus was conceived altogether "sans semen," "sans seed of men." " Neither naturally, in virto, or artificial insemination-"no semination" "sans semination."

Diametrical Opposite: The opposing sided of an issue.

El's Freedom to Join with Us in the Virgin Birth

El showed in Immanuel's virgin birth that He was free to join Himself indivisibly with mortal men (contrary to gnostic belief). Free to make a man without the use of a man. Free to make man by a virgin and have her a virgin. Free to bear sin and have His holiness unstained.

Immanuel and the Glory of Christmas"

Mary
The Mighty One
Men
The Conception
The Coming
The Cross
The Conclusion

Glories of Christmas

I. A woman who couldn't conceive - pregnant! (Blessed the womb that bare thee.) Delivering and giving suckle. (Blessed the paps (breasts) that gave thee suck.) - Luke 11:27
II. God who didn't need to be born - born!
III. A man who knew no sin, no guile in His mouth made sin!
IV. Men born in sin who couldn't be righteous. Innocent righteous as God is!
 V. Men, death through and through possessing eternal life, living forever, never tasting death!

Immanuel, in the Christmas Story, Look at God!

I. God gave a virgin, an untouched (i.e. by a male) woman, a baby (remained a virgin)
II. God gave Himself, who was spirit, a body (remained God) by this:
III. He made a sinless , holy undefiled man , - sin
IV. He carried ours sin in His own body and never became defiled, contaminated in spirit. Jesus was never unclean. He remained innocent, undefiled, separate from sinners, innocent.

112

He carried our sins, did away with them, and dumped them on no one. No person or place became a depository of our toxic waste. Jesus doesn't have them. We don't have them. Nobody else has them and yet they are gone!

B. A righteous man was made wickedness.

V.   Wicked men, sinners who were born in sin, were made as righteous, innocent as God, by Jesus' blood (sacrifice) and the kindness of God-God's righteousness was bestowed upon them, on them, on them. (Remained Adam's child.)

VI.   Men under sentence of death, condemned, doomed to die by divine verdict. Obtained eternal life as a gift. "The gift of God is eternal life through Jesus Christ our Lord (Immanuel). (Remain earthen vessels.)

II Corinthians 4:7 Eternal Life At Work
   "But we have this treasure in earthen vessels, that the excellency of the power of God may be of God, and not of us"
The power of God - The power of God - the power of God!
   After a similar vein, God wrought in Immanuel.
God sets His pace, example for operating in the church in Immanuel. We are miniature "Immanuels"

St. Luke 11:27
   "And it came to pass, as He spoke these things, a certain woman of the company lifted up her voice, and said unto Him, Blessed is the womb that bore thee, and the [breasts (paps) which nursed thee]. KJV "Paps which thou hast sucked."

God's (El's) Freedom in the Virgin Birth of Immanuel
   Immanuel, The Ultimate and Final expression, manifestation from God to man of God's (El's) absolute freedom!! Through Immanuel, God expresses the highest degree of His eternal

freedom **Q.V.**! Daniel said, "He does what He wills in the army of heaven and among the inhabitants of the earth. None can stay His hand or say unto Him, what doest thou?"

For example, El was free to join Himself indivisibly with mortal men (contrary to gnostic belief). He was free to make a man without the use of a man. He was free to make a man by a virgin and have her *remain* a virgin. He was free to bear sin and have His holiness unstained.

Conclusion The Sign of the virgin birth of Christ was an act of a miraculous nature, serving to demonstrate divine power or authority. It is the sign described to Isaiah that pertain to Immanuel.

Words Used in the Succeeding Chapters

De profundis-out of the depth

Profundis-the depth

Profundis immensis-the Vast fathomless depth of the Cross

Ex profundis-exiting profundis-relative to the resurrection

Gloria excelsis- glory to God in the highest

Gloriam in excelsis infinitam-glory to God in the highest-infinitely endless

Supranomination-the name above every name which Jesus-Immanuel received in His exaltation.

Adminsitration-His administration at and from His throne in His glorified state (gloriam in excelsis infinitam).

Calverian-on the Cross, pertaining to the Cross. The situation of the Cross, the lowest hell, epitome of humiliation, what happened on the Cross,

profundis-immesis, the cry my God, my God, why hast thou forsaken Me? (de profundis)

Post-Calverian-after the Cross-resurrection, ascension, glorification, enthronement, administration, gloriam in excelsis infinitam

Chapter 11

"THE NEW HALLELUJAH" IMMANUEL'S HALLELUJAH—*THE IRONY OF EL'S HUMILIATION IN IMMANUEL'S CROSS*

This chapter discusses why Immanuel's incarnation and Cross evoke a new hallelujah—In here I explain that it is because El [Adonai] has done a new thing in the coming of Immanuel. When Isaiah saw the Lord in Isaiah 6, He was Holy, high and lifted up. His glory was uncontainable, incomprehensible, and unapproachable. He evoked worship from a distance; His throne was unapproachable due to the immensity of His presence.

However, in Immanuel, this unapproachable God becomes a man. Ironically, the Lord on the high throne of Isaiah 6 comes as close as He has become in Immanuel; for Him to become one with us in the flesh is merely incomprehensible to human thought. For God to humble Himself in a human body as He does in Immanuel is a great and foreign thing. This shows God's unimaginable intent to be in an unique union with man. That is inconceivable; it is breathtaking!! However, if you look, you will see it is deeper than that!! He also bears a cursed Cross. God is going to die on a Cross for us? This evokes a new level of praise—a praise beyond the praise of the seraphim. It is a new hallelujah—a hallelujah evoked because El has amazingly created Immanuel's incarnation and Cross.

Hence, Hallelujah becomes a new word when the Lord's action becomes new, and that is when He becomes man in Immanuel.

Hallelujah's dimension becomes a "new" word when Adonai's action becomes new, that is, when He In Isaiah 6, decends to a Cross. Here we get a glimpse of God's absolute freedom. Here His glory (and presence) transcends the boundaries of both the temple and language.

This is indicative of "the extra-presence" of His presence; the cry of the cherubim signifies His transcendence over language.

Adonai revealed Himself to Isaiah under the Law, in relationship to the Temple. He was awe-inspiring, self-abasing and self-reducing in the manifestation of His splendor. This was shown when He filled the temple with the train of His royal robe, Isaiah 6.

The Temple

A temple is a means for man's ascension as he moves towards God. It is a means of descension as God moves towards man. In the book of Revelations, when Immanuel absolutely removed all division, difference and distance between God and man—even man's mortality, as death was destroyed—Apostle John saw "no temple therein, for the Lord God and the Lamb are the temple thereof." Immanuel has finalized the bridge between God and man and thereby has uniquely established a perfect and eternal union. Hallelujah!

Incomprehensible Thought-Adonai [The Lord] the King of Glory, On a Cross

In Matthew, chapter 1, Adonai exhibited a new aspect, dimension, an advanced higher ... of His power when He took on the form of man and became, for our sakes, Immanuel. When, in His eternal splendor, as the indescribable Adonai, He, El, humbled Himself, took a human body and came to be WITH us. And further, incorporate in Immanuel is the Cross.

Immanuel is God's Adonai's name with "The Cross" in it. El, Adonai is not Immanuel without the Cross. Adonai of Isaiah 6 with a Cross in His name is humanly incomprehensible. This is powerful, glorious Adonai's absolute humility.

The Incomprehensible Cross

How can He who evoked, by His glory, the trisogion of the seraphim have a name with the awful Cross in it? Only He who uniquely possessed the glory of Adonai could do this. Only He who possessed incomprehensible glory could take that glory, produce Immanuel in name and action and cause part of that action to include an incomprehensible Cross.

Adonai in Isaiah 6 is so glorious in the manifestation of His power and absoluteness, until He defies human language. He exceeds the boundaries thereof. Now - Adonai as Immanuel - He is too marvelous for words. The new Hallelujah then, is in reference to glorious, unspeakable Adonai, becoming Immanuel, God in Christ, i.e. God with us. In this divine arrangement, Adonai with us, with a Cross in His name, i.e. Immanuel, is too marvelous for words.

The New Hallelujah Because of Immanuel

Hallelujah for us, respecting Immanuel, is a word (with) new meaning. It has a new meaning like its new source, and as such, is a word beyond words. Immanuel, and consequently the

117

"new Hallelujah" are beyond words - words beyond words. There is no hallelujah like "Immanuel's **Hallelujah.".** Hallelujah 'always has the same sound, no matter for what reason we utter it, but we utter it for different ideas, causes (reasons). It is said for never so high a reason, as a result of never so high an idea as when we speak it because we are thinking "Immanuel" i.e. <u>Adonai with the Cross in His name.</u> Adonai with His own shed blood in His name. Hallelujah, **Hallelujah, Hallelujah, Hallelujah, Hallelujah, Hallelujah, Hallelujah!**

Immanuel is Isaiah 6's Adonai with His own shed blood in His name. What an incomprehensible reconciliation! What a union! Adonai above and in the temple - Adonai on a Cross - Adonai with us comprehended in Immanuel. Here we have a revelation of the "new Adonai," the "new El" and so a **"new Hallelujah."**

> *"How wonderful God's mighty plan.*
> *How grace the awful gulf did span*
> *When He took on the form of man*
> *To take our sins away*
> *Thank God for the blood*

In Isaiah 6, we see Adonai in His glorious fullness of His power. Here, He fills the whole Earth. However, In Immanuel, we do not see Adonai divesting Himself of His regal splendor, but instead we see Him manifesting another facet of Himself. Immanuel is glorious in His emptying. We see His fullness in His emptying and His humiliation.

In Adonai, we see El in His lordship of the temple and the Earth and in his kingly glory that towers above all earthly monarchs, but in Immanuel. **<u>We see Jesus</u>** in sackcloth and ashes. El gave His own blood to be with us.

The Progressive Revelation of 'El' Culminates in Jesus-Immanuel—Not in the Lord of Isaiah 6

In Adonai and Immanuel, El shows us immeasurable contrasts in the character of His power while He remains ever the same glorious Lord of all.

In holy scripture, God stages His revelation of His glory to mankind. The revelation reaches its highest peak, the ultimate place in Immanuel. Scripture takes us from Adonai in Isaiah to Immanuel in St. Matthew 1 and not vice-versa.

The Adonai of Isaiah 6, is not the final revelation of God. Immanuel is. Note: Isaiah saw Adonai, and "we see Jesus."We use the conjunction "and," for in seeing Jesus, we do not see El in the manifestation of a different power, power of a different kind, but power of the same kind in a different, and super glorious aspect.

Comparing El in Immanuel of Matthews Chapters One and Two, to El as Adonai in Isaiah Chapter Six

Isaiah 6-Adoni, El in royal spendor. In Matthew 1 & 2 Adonai, El in condescension and humiliation to be with us. Unbounded, all-glorious, absolutely free El, nevertheless, In Isaiah 6, Adonai, El is too high above man and temple to be placed except on His throne or described -   This is too marvelous for words on a throne, but where?   In Immanuel, Adonai, El is with us, yet too marvelous for words. In Isaiah 6, Adonai El is unplaced (or on His throne, but where); but in Immanuel He is in Christ. In Immanuel, Adonai's highness and Adonai's humiliation are in absolute (union) manifestation. His highness in Immanuel is manifested in His self - abasement.

"....but we see Jesus," Adonai in humiliation, power and glory. Isaiah 6 is El with an "inseparable gulf - a measureless chasm, between Himself and man.

In Immanuel, the gulf is closed and El is in immeasurable union with man. Joined without a harmless preposition between. "How wonderful God's mighty plan...."
"Dear Lord, evermore help me to see JESUS!"

Comparing Isaiah's Vision of Adonai in Isaiah Chapter Six, to John's Revelation of the Same 'Lord' in Revelation Chapter One

In Isaiah 6, God speaks and acts through intermediaries, even the prophet's purgation [purification Isaiah 6:6-7]. The declaration of God's holiness is made by the seraphim. It is seraphic.- in Isaiah 6. In Revelation 1, Immanuel speaks, lays hand upon, speaks again and commissions - and enlightens (vs. 20).

In Isaiah 6 (some) Adonai's glory is communicated by ambassadors. In Revelation 1, Immanuel who is all does all.
In Isaiah 6, Adonai is high and lifted up seated on an unreachable throne, arrayed in regal splendor. The sight is basically fearsome and one of distance, separation. "Mine eyes have seen the King, the Lord of Hosts" - at a distance. "Then flew one of the seraphim unto me" (from a distant altar?) with a live coal - and laid it on my mouth, and said, lo, this (coal*) hath touched thy lips. Also I heard the voice of the Lord ... etc., etc., etc.*

In Revelation 1, Immanuel's speech to John comes with Immanuel's right- hand laying on Him. Behold, how close the contact! A temple is a means of ascension for man as he moves towards God. It is a means of descension (condescension).
Note: In Revelation 2:1, "He holdeth (continues to hold) the seven stars in His right hand - i.e. He doesn't release them. "Who walketh in the midst [Immanuel's closeness] of the seven golden candlesticks. He holdeth ... He walketh ..." (i.e., He keeps on with no seraphim, no ambassadors, but Immanuel!)
With the same right hand with which Immanuel holds all the "Stars" of the ages, he calms the trembling hearts of saints

while He comforts, educates, and directs them. See Chapter 1:16, 17 and Chapter 2:1 N.B.

And further, Immanuel washes from sin with His own blood - not by coals from off a distant altar conveyed by seraph's hands.

Immanuel washes US FROM our sins by changing our minds concerning our sins and thus causing us to be willing to get away from them. This attitude being achieved, He then forgives us by the blood He shed. But first, He gives us a right attitude towards our transgressions. He causes us to will be parted from them.

Immanuel-Hallelujah Companion Words

The companion word to this most beautiful word [Immanuel] is **'Hallelujah'**! Immanuel is naturally followed in the nature of the case by **Hallelujah**. (Immanuel — Hallelujah) We, as God's people should be **Halleluiatic** because of Immanuel. Nothing in our lives should evoke our Hallelujahs more readily than Immanuel. In both words, while God is the cause of the entire word, He has the life of the Name at the end of each of these words ; Imm/Anu/ El and Hall/e/lu/Jah. The life of the name is the breath of it.

The Barriers, the Walls, and the Veil that Separated Man from God have been Done Away with in Jesus-Immanuel

In Immanuel, there is no barrier between us and God. Here, God in Christ guarantees an absolutely perfect flow of all His love, and the resultant Godness, towards us. Here, love is flowing unhindered. Here is where grace abounds. It only abounds toward us by Jesus Christ. He is God's Immanuel. Only in Jesus Christ is this wall completely broken down, between God and man, and between Heaven and earth. The Veil in the Temple was not rent in twain until Immanuel died.

The New Hallelujah, Immanuel's Hallelujah

There was the Temple in all its splendor and arrangement for service, but there was a Veil in it too. The way into the Holy of Holies was yet unrevealed, but when Jesus "died the Vail was rent in twain, that separated man from God, and now by faith, we have access to Him—and all through His precious blood."

The New Hallelujah

In Immanuel is man's ultimate relationship with God. It is the highest, most beneficial, closest, longest lasting richest, most glorious etc. etc. etc. that man could ever have with God or any other. This is the unique and eternal union of God with man in Immanuel.

In Immanuel man, finds incomparable union. Incomprehensible union. Eternal union. Union beyond all that man is capable of imagining in the term "union". "God with us" or "with us God" is the super association of the universe.

Indescribable El in indescribable union with us means indescribable blessings and glory for mankind. **Hallelujah!** In the natural consequence of the case Immanuel evokes **Hallelujah**. Mighty words with the "God Suffix".

Immanuel gives His own, new dimension to **Hallelujah**. The essence of **Hallelujah** changed with the coming of Immanuel. Because of Immanuel, i. e. God in His newness, in His difference, in His excellence, **Hallelujah** changes correspondingly. **Hallelujah** is a richer word now because in Immanuel El, God supplements the riches of His prior grace, etc. etc. etc.

Immanuel, God's Name with the unending et ceteras. Immanuel, God's name of matchless union, matchless, incomparable glory. Immanuel, the exponent of Hallelujah. Hallelujah reaches its highest and final crescendo in Immanuel. All the beautiful **Hallelujahs** psalms are more beautiful in Immanuel. In Immanuel, the earth becomes Eden, and Eden becomes Paradise, Paradise becomes the Holy City respecting Hallelujah.

Everything about God's relationship to men, as witnesses the book of Hebrews, becomes enhanced, is elevated, becomes better via Immanuel.

Even Hallelujah, which was never an empty word, becomes super- loaded via Immanuel.

Immanuel is God's non-temporal, non-spatial Name. I.e. it is supra- time and supra-space. It is the name in which God relates to men from Bethlehem's manger to the throne of God. It covers the whole earth, i.e. it includes men on every continent, and spans time and non-time from AD 4 to the unlimited reaches of eternity. It is the name of God in His withness to man from Judea to the far-flung islands of the sea, from the gospel age to eternity's endless ages. It includes and exceeds all time. It includes and exceeds all space. It includes all nationalities of men and all of the varieties of their mixtures. In Immanuel the human expression.

"God with us" or "with us God" ultimately only means what the heart of God meant for it to mean.

It is always, as was the case with Jonathan and David, an "arrow beyond us".

"With" in Immanuel, and "El" in Immanuel are incomprehensible terms, hence since these two terms are related to such describable, adjectival-related creatures as us, it makes the whole Name abundantly, super incomprehensible. YHVH, as a tetragrammaton, was unpronounceable. In Immanuel, we do not have an unpronounceable name, but rather, one so profound, real, life giving and eternally glorious until it is incomprehensible.

0, glorious Immanuel, Jesus Christ, our Lord! (Note the ante-inter-and postpostions of the syllables IMM — ANU — EL) God has enshrouded His incomprehensible person and power and work of full redemption in His incomprehensible Name — Immanuel. Immanuel without either definitive locus or time.

In Immanuel, none of the value of the word is derived from the community in which it was first spoken. All of its value is given to the community and the world, which it blesses. The meaning of Immanuel therefore is not a meaning of derivation,

123

but rather a value inhering in itself - and dispensed to the community. The community does not define Immanuel. Immanuel defies definition, as its interpretation indicates. Immanuel is as the beginning of the creation of the world, it precedes its formation, not succeeds it. "In the beginning God..." "In the beginning was the Word... and the Word was God."

Immanuel was spoken OF the Lord. Immanuel is God's own "pristine world". His own primordial creation.

(Immanuel is the eternal terminuses of God in both directions.)

Conclusion: Hallelujah's dimension becomes a "new" word when Adonai's action becomes new, that is when He Himself becomes man in Immanuel.

Words Used in the Next Chapter

Horn-The expression "horn of salvation," applied to Christ, means a salvation of strength, or a strong Saviour (Luke 1:69). To have the horn "exalted" denotes prosperity and triumph (Psalms 89:17 Psalms 89:24). To "lift up" the horn is to act proudly (Zechariah 1:21).

Chapter 12

IMMANUEL'S HUMILIATING CROSS

In this chapter is shown the **'anu/el union'** in its essence in the cross. The cross is the epitome of and the ultima thule of El's **withness** as described in the previous chapters of this book. The Cross is the culminating work of Jesus' Immnauelness. It seals the promise of an inseparable union between God and man. It proves with no uncertainty that God {El] intended to be with us in Immanuel. His promise 'I will never leave you nor forsake you" is shown in deed on the Cross.

On the Cross, God Almighty humbled Himself to the lowest point ever, becoming least of all on the Cross—there He was lower than any man had ever been before God. He took on the form of man to do this. There on the Cross the 'All Riches One' Who did not need this for Himself became poor so that we through His poverty might become rich. Thus, He Humbled Himself to that horrible cross.

On the Cross, Jesus was separated from God and because of His association with us He was forsaken and cried out of the depth of that hell [the Cross] Eli Eli lamsabethni which meant MY God My God why has thou forsaken me?

In this chapter on the Cross it is shown that Immanuel's being with us went as far as HIs suffering for us on the cross; which Should have been ours to bear. He became us in Immanuel and suffered as us on the Cross. Thus, the inseparable union is fully demonstrated by Immanuel's horrible Cross.

In this chapter I present (a) the humiliation of the Cross, (b) the work of Immanuel on the Cross and (c) the effect/blessings of Immanuel's cross.

Immanuel's Humiliating Cross

(a) The Humiliation of Immanuel's Cross

The Cross, the Epitome of Immanuel's Humiliation

The epitome of the humiliation of Immanuel was His Cross.

It was in the plan of El that He, first, conjoin himself with us in the incarnation and be humbled in the lowest state of the Cross. Then afterwards He would be exalted. Therefore, He descended first into the lower (man at his lowest) parts of the earth. Then He ascended into the highest heavens.

Synonyms: The Spirit of the Lord

                         The Glory of the Lord

                         The Grace of God

"He through the Spirit OFFERED Himself' - (here was Jesus' suffering) that "He by the grace of God should taste death for every man.

He[El] Sent the All Riches One and Eternal One for our Sake, to be Poor and Die

He shows us in Immanuel that "my thoughts are not your thoughts and my ways are not your ways. In Immanuel, El creates a man without a man. He caused a King to be born in a stable and laid in a manger. He sent an all-riches one to become the poorest of all (no where to lay His head).

The King of Heaven to become homeless "out of the ivory palaces into a world of woe." The King of Heaven became a servant of men. Eternal life took on a birthday. The greatest became the least. God became man.

The eternal One died on a Cross, etc., etc., etc. Here the El of Imma/
nuEl, dies on the Cross—us with us in the cross.

The Humility of the Cross—the Glory of God

The lowest point of the full process of Immanuel's humiliation
and exaltation was the Cross. The Cross was the lowest hell, the
darkest, deepest death. He made His grave with the wicked
in His death. In Immanuel, as only El the Almighty could do,
He conjoins the superlative least to that of greatest. All of
Immanuel's things are by the glory of God.

El is Last via the Cross Immanu/El

His almightiness makes Himself last in the Name Immanuel via
making Himself least of all men in the Cross. In the Cross, God in
Christ became lower than any man had ever been before God. It
was the bottom (Profundis Immensis) of the bottom in Having taken on
the name Immanuel, Jesus Christ. To be against us would be a mighty
work for God Himself i.e. to undo all that He, by power, has done.
In Imm/Anu/El, God places Himself last to thereby join immediately with
us.

Least, little beyond all others in size or degree; smallest; slightest;
fewest. His lowest state on the Cross is to be described by The
superlative of little He was extremely belittled by on the Cross. God
makes Himself last and least in Immanuel. In Immanuel, El, God in
His almightiness makes Himself last in the Name Immanuel via making
Himself least of all men in the Cross. In the Cross, God in Christ became
lower than any man had ever been before God. It was the bottom
(Profundis Immensis) of the bottom in humility, humiliation and
judgment. It was the lowest hell, the darkest, deepest death. He made
His grave with the wicked in His death. In Immanuel, as only El the
Almighty could do, He conjoins the superlative ("His name shall be
great") of little and the unimaginable superlative of great - Jesus Christ.

The Lord of Glory Descends from Glory to an Awful Cross

He took on the form of man and became, for our sakes,
Immanuel. When, in His eternal splendor, as the indescribable

Immanuel's Humiliating Cross

Adonai *Lord*, He, El, humbled Himself, took a human body and came to be WITH us[**anuEl**]. And further, incorporate in Immanuel is the Cross. Immanuel is God's Adonai's name with "The Cross" in it. El, Adonai is not Immanuel without the cross. Adonai of Isaiah 6 with a cross in His name is humanly incomprehensible.

This is powerful, glorious Adonai's absolute humility. How can He who evoked, by His glory, the trisogion (Isaiah 6:1) of the seraphim have a name with the awful Cross in it! Only He who uniquely possessed the glory of Adonai could do this.

He who possessed incomprehensible glory could take that glory and produce Immanuel in name and action and cause part of that action to include an incomprehensible Cross. Adonai in Isaiah 6 is so glorious in the manifestation of His power and absoluteness, until He defies human language. He exceeds the boundaries thereof. Now - Adonai as Immanuel - He is too marvelous for words. The new Hallelujah then, is in reference to glorious, unspeakable Adonai, becoming Immanuel, God in Christ, i.e. God with us. In this divine arrangement, Adonai with us, with a Cross in His name, i.e. Immanuel, is too marvelous for words.

(b) The Work of Immanuel's Cross

the work of Immanuel on the Cross—what happen on the cross How was Christ Immanuel on the Cross? Relative to the thesis I discussion the work of Christ on the cross in terms of the 'anuEl union' that is the union of God with man in Immanuel and Christ's being Immanuel.

On the Cross Immanuel-was Forsaken for Our Cause

Calvary, the ultimate "Inanis." (emptiness). In Genesis 1, darkness was indescribable. However, the Spirit of the Lord moved upon the face of the deep darkness. On Calvary, in Jesus' deep darkness, [His humility] He was forsaken.

The cross is indescribable in human language. However, we get a glimpse of it in the cry of Immanuel on the Cross when He said Eli, Eli, Lama Sabachthani.   This cry was out of the depth of the immensely profound suffering of the cross.

There on Immanuel's humiliating Cross was seen God's depthless hurt, depthless mercies, unbounded wisdom (in the superlative).   Immanuel's being there on the cross immeasurably separated from El on the Cross cried out, "My God, My God, why has thou forsaken me?". This was a cry de Profundis, the first words of the Latin version of Vs CXXX "Out of the depths (have I cried)".(Psalms 130).

This cry was made from Jesus who then suffer the separation of the gulf that wedged God from man since the fall. *Here Jesus as anu [anu of anuEl]* cried de profundis, a cry from the depths of sorrow, misery, degradation. (Father, why hath though forsaken me?) These were fathomless depths - only Immanuel could descend to them.   Only He could stand the pressure. No depths like Calvary!
"How wonderful God's mighty plan. How grace the awful gulf did span When He took on the form of man to take our sins away. Thank God for the blood, etc.

In Immanuel, the gulf is closed and El is in immeasurable union with man. Joined without a harmless preposition between [**anuEl**] "How wonderful God's mighty plan...."

> On Calvary, man in absolute sinfulness (He was made sin for us), and God in absolute righteousness , as they only could, in Imm Anu El - no other place - no other way! - and in this meeting an absolute resolution of their estrangement. Here was reconciliation!"Where we're nearest, we're farthest away."

Spanning the Immense Gulfs-On the Cross
Immanuel's Cross is God spanning immeasurable gulfs between God and man [anu/separation/El]. Whatever separated man from God was in the nature of the case immeasurable. E.G. sin, time, humanity, space, death. These immeasurable gulfs could not be spanned by a measured

being. Now by the blood the gulfs are spanned **anuEl** and anu [man] is in an inseparable union with El {God}

Hence, God as Immanuel acts upon immeasurable gulfs between Himself and man as God in man [the man Jesus-Immanuel]. Never before had El dealt with man's unmeasured, separating barriers as man [anu] . Only in man did He, and does He, and will He remove all barriers, walls, gulfs, etc., to the utmost

Inseparable Union Sealed on the Cross

Via His union with us on the cross He associates Himself with us in the curse of the fall: "cursed is everyone that hangs on a tree." Life is made "more abundantly." Only - in Immanuel do God and man experience absolute union via absolute disunion.

Thus In Immanuel's *humiliating Cross*, the gulf is closed and El is in immeasurable union with man **[anu].** Joined without a harmless preposition between "How wonderful God's mighty plan...."

God in Jesus Christ as Imm/anuEl became everything we needed Him to be, especially, the ultimate sacrifice on the Cross.

Absolute Sinfulness and Absolute Righteousness Met on the Cross

On Calvary, man [anu-Jesus] in absolute sinfulness (He was made sin for us), and God [El] in absolute righteousness , as they only could, in Imm Anu El - no other place - no other way! - and in this meeting an absolute resolution of their estrangement. Here was reconciliation! "Where we're nearest, we're farthest away."

This was done so that the union between Jesus and His saints, God and His saints, might be forever undissolvable. Here we have the great mystery of disunion and the great mystery of fellowship. [Romans 8]Behold what was wrought (by) what was wrought! No mountain laboring to produce a mouse.

El's Great Love Shown on the Cross

On the Cross, El engaged great love and great glory when He planned and engaged Immanuel's Cross. While it was a lowly and base event it took the high love, the high wisdom and the highest

glory of God to fulfill. While El moved down in humility by this He simultaneously moved up in love and glory because of the high calling and the very high purpose which was in the lowly Cross.

In Immanuel's Cross we can see how He moves upward in (Himself) in love, joy, etc., etc., etc., to depths of defying expression. E.g. "For the joy that was set before Him, He endured the Cross - here is an undescribable joy (beyond light-years, measureless) conjoined with matchless endurance of humiliation, sorrow, pain, darkness, etc., etc., etc. Here the word "Cross" is a metonym for everything, absolutely everything, that divine wrath could mean for time and eternity manward. Therefore. He moves to this unbounded depth only when He is with us. The only boundary of the Cross is God's own infinity. No one else can know this boundary.

Jesus Suffered an Indescribable Separation from God in His Humiliation on the Cross

See Bishop G. T. Haywood in: (How revelation)
"How wonderful God's mighty plan,
how grace the awful gulf - and
measureless - did span.
When He took on the form of man
to take our sins away. CHO:
Thank God for the blood,
Thank God for the blood,
Thank God for the blood,
That washes white as snow.

On the Cross Immanuel Spans the Immense Gulf

Immanuel's Cross is God spanning immeasurable gulfs between God and man. Whatever separated man from God was in the nature of the case immeasurable. E.G. sin, time, humanity, space, death. These immeasurable gulfs could not be spanned by a measured being.

Hence, God as Immanuel acts upon immeasurable gulfs between Himself and man as God in man. Never before had El dealt with man's unmeasured, separating barriers as man . Only in man did He, and does He, and will He remove all barriers, walls, gulfs, etc., to the utmost degree - and absolutely, until nothing remains, not even a harmless preposition of language.

Calvary, God's Darkest Night

Jesus' Eternal Moment was God's ultima Thule manufacturing event. That is, we have no revelation of anything beyond it. There is nothing we can find in Holy Scripture which transcends it. Whatever God's night is which exceeds the Cross, God doesn't want us to know it yet.

Transmitting the Curse into Universal Blessedness

He sanctified "the tree"

a . Cursed is everyone who hangs on a tree .

b . His precious blood .

How could the dying One be cursed(**), and the blood He was letting as a curse be precious? By His blood He was transmitting the curse into universal blessedness by (exhausting all) the meaning of the curse. By doing all that could in God's reckoning be done for it (in God's reckoning.)

His blood was precious because He was cursed (made a "curse) made the worst of all curses so His blood would be forever precious!

The Depth of Immanuel's Humiliation on the Cross

A. God's depthless hurt, depthless mercies, unbounded wisdom (in the superlative).

De Profundis, the first words of the Latin version of Vs CXXX (CXXIX) = "Out of the depths (have I cried).

De profundis, a cry from the depths of sorrow, misery, degradation. (Father, why hath though forsaken me?) These were fathomless depths - only Immanuel could descend to them only He could stand the pressure. No depths like Calvary!

B. Immanuel, God's fullest disclosure of Himself to man.

Immanuel "With Us God" On the Cross

Immanuel, "with us God," with us in the dual, indescribable darkness of
the cross. There was:

A.   The physical darkness ("darkness over all the earth,

from the sixth to the ninth hour, i.e. noon to 3:00 P.M.)

B.   The emotional, deep, unfathomable inner darkness
which surrounded and assailed Jesus' spirit.

C.   Jesus' aloneness (no friend, comrade, disciple shared
His execution).

He hung not between or with relatives, but between two
thieves.

D. No human really understood His plight.

E. He was uniquely God-forsaken. No person or group of
persons had experienced such abandonment by God prior
to the Cross.

Each of the above-mentioned are a part of Jesus'
"Immanuelness."

This was so that God in Christ might never forsake us. i.e. be with us
forever, eternally. Here was Immanuel in His eternal "Immanuelness."
Immanuel means The Cross! The cross means Immanuel. Here is the
believer's perfect rest - in Immanuel.

But before for the Cross, Immanuel is not Immanuel. But for
Immanuel, the Cross is not the Cross. (see Romans 11:6 on "Grace"and
work") The Cross of Christ was the ultimate self-validation of El's or
God's name the ultimate crescendo.

The Cross Says to Us, I will Never Forsake You [Eternal Union]

In the Cross, Immanuel was with us in the ultimate darkness of
time and eternity, no question that He will be with believers in
earth's little trials and sorrows. Calvary was Immanuel's "high water
mark," all else is "down hill" for Him.

"I will never leave you nor forsake you" was ultimately and
finally sealed for us by Immanuel on the Cross.

0, what a rest! "0' Sweet Rest"

Immanuel's Humiliating Cross

Immanuel, God's final word, God's final work.
Immanuel, God's ultimate word, God's ultimate work.

On Calvary, man in absolute sinfulness (He was made sin for us), and God in absolute righteousness , as they only could, in Imm Anu El - no other place - no other way! - and in this meeting an absolute resolution of their estrangement. Here was reconciliation!"Where we're nearest, we're farthest away."

Profound Things God did on Immanuel's Cross

He made a sinless , holy undefiled man,- sin
He carried our sins in His own body and never became defiled contaminated in spirit. Jesus was never unclean. He remained innocent, undefiled, separate from sinners, innocent. He carried our sins, did away with them, and dumped them on no one. No person or place became a depository of our toxic waste. Jesus doesn't have them. We don't have them. Nobody else has them and yet they are gone!
B. A righteous man was made wickedness.

Wicked men, sinners who were born in sin, were made as righteous, innocent as God, by Jesus' blood (sacrifice) and the kindness of God -God's righteousness was bestowed upon them, on them, on them. (Remained Adam's child.)

Men under sentence of death, condemned, doomed to die by divine verdict. Obtained eternal life as a gift. "The gift of God is eternal life through Jesus Christ our Lord (Immanuel).

Only in Immanuel does God's sin-laden son cry "My God, My God, why hast thou forsaken Me?—and "Into they hands I commitment my spirit" MS 59ab

(c) The Effect/Results of Immanuel's Cross

(c) The result of the 'anuEl union' on the Christ.

Berlin Wall, Separator Broke Down by the Cross

Only in Jesus Christ is the "Berlin Wall" completely broken down between God and man, Heaven and earth. The Vail in the temple was not rent in twain until Immanuel died.

There was the temple in all its splendor and arrangement for service, but there was a Vail in it too. On the Cross the veil was rent . This meant that access to God which was inhibited by the fall, was now torn wide open—giving free access to God. Bishop R. C. Lawson described this in his song 'God is Great in My Soul"

> *"When Jesus He died, the vail was rent in twain*
> *that separated man from God, and now by faith,*
> *I have access to Him, all through His precious*
> *blood.*
> *CHO: God is great, and greatly to be praised,*
> *God is great in my soul,*
> *God is great and greatly to be praised, God is*
> *great in my soul*.

The way into the Holy of Holies, yet unrevealed; but when Jesus, Immanuel, " He died the Vail was rent in twain, that separated man from God, and now by faith, we have access to Him —and (He freely to us) all through His precious blood" We are made nigh by His blood, the blood of Christ. Nothing could ever have brought us closer (or so close).

Immanuel's Humiliating Cross

We are Brought to God Righteous by the Cross

"For Christ also hath suffered once for sins, the just for the unjust, that He might bring us to God, - in what condition? Sinless, guiltless, uncondemned, holy, acceptable, innocent, *justifiable.*
How? BY HIS MERITS!! Being put to death in the flesh ... Hebrews 9:26
... He hath appeared to put away sin by the sacrifice of Himself.
Note: Jesus didn't bring us to God to be presented in the same condition we were before He suffered for our sins. Why would He bring us to God as though He had not interposed Himself? What I mean is He did something about our condition-made us righteous, then presented us acceptable unto God. Therefore He did not present us as though there had been no consummatum est (it is finished)? No closed book on our past? I Peter However, He presented us having made us righteous by His own blood.

Immanuel has Interpreted His Name for Us, On the Cross

How do we interpret God's Name when He has finally acted out its interpretation towards us in the Cross? We can call Him savior, the lover of our soul, With us God. We can call Him all that Immanuel did via the Cross.

In the Cross, Immanuel was with us in the ultimate darkness of time and eternity, no question that He will be with believers in earth's little trials and sorrows. Calvary was Immanuel's "high water mark," all else is "down hill" for Him. He proved His Immanuelness on the Cross and in His life, He meant just what He said when He said:

"I will never leave you nor forsake you was ultimately and finally sealed for us by Immanuel on the Cross**.

The Transforming Effect of the Cross

Neither Bethlehem or **Calvary** will ever again be the same because Jesus was there in both. **Calvary,** the place of the skull is different forever. Jesus was the man who made a difference everywhere He went, even the grave is not the same since Jesus went to it.

He Made Us Righteous by the Cross

God gave Himself, who was spirit, a body (remained God) by this: He made a sinless, holy undefiled man, - sin He carried ours sin in His own body and never became defiled, contaminated in spirit. Jesus was never unclean.

He remained innocent, undefiled, separate from sinners, innocent. He carried our sins, did away with them, and dumped them on no one. No person or place became a depository of our toxic waste. Jesus doesn't have them. We don't have them. Nobody else has them and yet they are gone!

A righteous man was made wickedness. Wicked men, sinners who were born in sin, were made as righteous, innocent as God, by Jesus' blood (sacrifice) and the kindness of God - God's righteousness was bestowed upon them, on them, on them.

Oh What Blessing we have by Immanuel's Coming

El's humbling himself coming to us and His Cross provided for us new rest for the weary; life water, life bread for the thirsty and hungry; wisdom for the foolish; freedom for the captives; peace with God for the condemned; restoration of friendship, fellowship for the estranged, for foreigners; companionship for the lonely, etc., etc., etc., and above all. a glorious resurrection for the dead and life eternal in a - new world in the presence of God, The Father. That is eternal life for us via the Cross. All of this via the Cross.

What Immanuel has done for us in the humility of the cross causes worship! Hence; "Beneath the Cross of Jesus I fain (hurriedly) would take my stand. The shadow of a mighty rock within a weary land. A home within the wilderness. A rest upon the way. A shelter from the noontide heat, the burden of the day." Immanuel, 0, Immanuel, I am so glad you've come!

Darkness of the Humiliation of the Cross

If were not for the Cross, Immanuel is not Immanuel. But for Immanuel, the Cross is not the Cross. (See Romans 11:6 on "Grace" and "work.") . *Though the cross was the epitome of the humiliation of*

137

Immanuel's Humiliating Cross

Immanuel it was the highest point of glory in Immanuel's work of salvation.

El's promise in Immanuel i. e. "I will never leave you nor forsake you" was ultimately and finally sealed for us by Immanuel on the Cross. The cross was the ultimate move of El for an inseparable union with man. *In Immanuel condescending to the humiliating cross, thereon,* the union of Father and Son was broken [on Calvary] so that the union of God with man could be established.

Only God Almighty Could Create and Engage the separation and Depth of the Cross.

El was the Mighty God with might unto us, by the cross, the resurrection, the glorification, the session, the high priestly administration all of this is the results of the Cross.

Conclusion: In the Cross, Immanuel was with us in the ultimate darkness of time and eternity, no question that He will be with believers in earth's little trials and sorrows. Calvary was Immanuel's "high water mark," all else is "down hill" for Him."I will never leave you nor forsake you" was ultimately and finally sealed for us by Immanuel on the Cross.

Chapter 13

IMMANUEL GOES TO HELL
Jesus-Immanuel Endured the Hell of the Cross

Eli, Eli, Lama Sabachthani—**My God, My God, why has Thou forsaken Me**? This was the cry of Jesus-Immanuel out from the depth of Hell, on the Cross (Psalm 22:1, Math 27:46, Mark 15:34). It was a cry like no other cry ever heard or that will ever be heard. It was 'out of the depth' [*de profoundis*] of the fathomless separation from God suffered by Jesus-Immanuel on the Cross.

He suffered as the only qualified sacrifice for the sins of the world. It was there that Jesus absorbed all of the pangs of that measureless nadir of Godforsaken-ness and the immense estrangement from His Father that could only be endured in the body of Jesus, the Son of God. There on the Cross, the God-man consciously and fully experienced the greatest separation and the lowest Hell that ever happened. Jesus suffered eternal Hell in a moment on the Cross.

Jesus experience fully the dimensions of Hell:

a. Conscious suffering and punishment

b. Eternal separation from God—forsaken,

c. Suffering eternal judgment

d. The second death.

On the Cross, God brought eternity into time, so that in time, on the Cross, Jesus would bear the full eternal penalty of Hell for the whole world. There, in the darkness of Calvary, He was forsaken before He gave up the Ghost [died]. He paid the penalty for sin by going to the second death [Hell] on that cursed tree and thereby, averted our appointment there. When He yelled out *"it is finished"* (St.

139

John 19:30), it had already happened; it was done—He had already fully experienced the nadir of Hell for us and freed us from that mandatory destiny.

On the Cross Jesus saved us from the second death[Hell] by going to it Himself. We are saved from eternal Hell because of His paying that price on the Cross. He did not die to save us from dying a physical death here in this life. If that were the case then we wouldn't have to die and go to the grave. On the Cross, Jesus saved us from going to hell eternally.

Relative to our thesis concerning the unique and eternal union; Jesus' experience on the Cross is referred to as the Nadir [the lowest point], the profundity [the depth]; i.e. the lowest Hell which is the epitome of His being with us who were destined to that Hell ourselves eternally. In the Hell experience of the Cross, Jesus showed just how deep the **anuEl [Imm/anuEl]** relationship is relative to God's commitment in Immanuel to never leave us or forsake us.

This is the fulfillment of the *anuEl* union at its most severe point. Jesus' consciously and willingly submitting to the Hell of the Cross proves that nothing can separate us from Him, not even Hell. For on the Cross, He answered the Hell question.

In this chapter, I present that:

(a) That the Cross-Hell experience was the work of Jesus-Immanuel only. That is the depths of the Hell of the Cross could only be endured by Jesus. It was His own private charge.

(b) I speak of Hell in terms of a nadir [very lowest point], *profoudis immenses*, humiliation.

(c) I speak of Heaven and the throne to which He ascended after this horrible Cross, with terms such as the zenith and supranomination , ad glorious in excelisis.

(d) Jesus consciously and willingly went to the Hell of the Cross, having full understanding.

(e) Immanuel Jesus experienced the judgment of the Cross fully and completely—it took Him being God to have fully experienced the measureless nadir of the Cross-Hell.

(f) He and He alone satisfied the heart of God—for human death was only a consequence for man's sins but does not and cannot qualify as the sacrifice for sins as Jesus' Hell experience did.

Jesus Experienced Hell to Its Fullest Extent

Relative to Jesus' going to Hell, He went into the jaws of suffering and death and was a victim of them to the furthest boundary of the damaging capability of each, except for corruption. He saw no corruption, for He lacked the seed of corruption.

Had Jesus not been God almighty, He could never have gone either to Nadir [lowest Hell] or zenith [highest point] to *profundis* or *in excelsis*, that is to say; to hell or the throne of God.

No Other Man could Go from the Lowest of Hell to the Highest of Heaven, Only Immanuel was Fit to Go to Both

"Immanuel, the only man to ever descend and ascend the numberless scale of God, *profundis immensis ad glorious in excelsis*. No other person could have taken such journeys! Nadir to Zenith. Humiliation to supranomination. Hell to Heaven. Jesus, our savior was *in profundis*—to suffer *de profundis*—for crying. *Ex profundis*—for raising, transcending exiting. Johnson's notes book II pages 62–63

Only God could Create the Low Things of Immanuel's Humiliation

God alone created the low side of these just-presented terms, for only He could know them. Neither Satan nor man could create, know or produce them. Satan and man were not in the bosom of the Father. They had not the sensitivity to His heart regarding the awfulness of sin or the glory of man's salvation. Only God the Father (could devise) the special hell of the Cross and appoint the extra splendor of His Throne.

No other mind could imagine it (the Hell). No other could permit/create it. No other person apart from Immanuel could descend to it; therefore, subsequently and consequently, no other person could rise to God's throne. No being in the kingdom of darkness (Satan's) or in the kingdom of men knew the glory, majesty, might, splendor, and greatness of God's throne. Lucifer at one time wanted to ascend to it and be like God, but was severely blunted in his attempt to accomplish this.

Lucifer and His Cohorts were not Privy to Heaven And Hell-Like Jesus Was

As Lucifer and his cohorts could not know the splendor of Heaven, neither were they permitted to know the depths of Hell.

Both *profundis immensis* and *gloria in excelsis infinitam* were of knowledge too high, too wonderful for the powers of the underworld. Heaven's God decided that only His Only Begotten Son, Immanuel, Jesus Christ Our Lord could be privy to both. His mind and His body were prepared for *profundis* while traveling through His earthly experience. He had a mind and body prepared for (*in exelsis*), His post-Calvarian administration in glory.

Daniel and the Hebrew Boys were Delivered from Their Light Hell-Like Experiences, but Jesus-Immanuel had to go All the Way through the Ultimate Hell

For Daniel's case with the lion's den, El shut the mouths of lions, **but** for Immanuel, El allowed Him to be killed, devoured by lions, (See Psalm 57:4—"My soul is among lions"); i.e., He went into the jaws of suffering and death and was a victim of them to the farthest boundary of the damaging capability of each, except for corruption. He saw no corruption, for He lacked the seed of corruption.

Shadrach, Meschach, and Abednego were Delivered from the Friary Furnace, but Immanuel Endured the *Profundis* of the Hell of the Cross

For Shadrach, Meschach, and Abednego, El caused the violence of fire to be quenched. *But* for Immanuel, El allowed a different and more powerful fire to burn on Him and caused Him to suffer all of it! For lions and fire, it was all part of His Immanuelness, to be WITH US. Jesus had to actually experience Hell in reality, unshelted, unprotected from it—he must pay the price.

Jesus, the Only Qualified Sacrifice—Which Satisfied the Heart of God by Going to Hell

Only Jesus Christ could go to Hell and satisfy the heart of God in going. For only He had the heart to feel all and understand all of the reasons—including what the penalty for being in Hell meant in relation to the hurt of the heart of God. Any sinner who goes to Hell will certainly be punished while there, but his going to Hell will never be an "Order Quietis Finalis," for the lost sinner will lack the heart that is necessary—as well as the capacity to satisfy the heart of God.

Jesus Christ Immanuel was the only human being ever with the dual capacity (mind and body) to fulfill all of the requirements of God for a damned soul. Only with His mind could He plumb all the depths of the ramifications of sin against God. No other person has had, has now, or ever will have the mind of Christ, which was necessary to fathom sin and Divine judgment.

Note "His grace, alone, can fathom sin and make my heart all white within." Jesus was the only one with the mind, required to do it.

The Mind Required to Go to Hell as Immanuel did Was put in No One Else but Immanuel

Only with this mind can a Hell-victim satisfy the heart of God—and God will never, never, not even once, give this feeling, knowing mind to another. God will not allow another human being in either time or eternity to have the mind to fully feel the depths of eternal judgment—not even those who go to Hell.

God will not give this unique mind to men. He will give them the mind of Christ to follow Christ and to eventually know eternal glory and joy, but never to "go to

Hell with"—to experience the joys of heaven and eternity—yes, Jesus Christ, Our Lord Immanuel.

Man Cannot Go to the Hell to which Jesus Went

God denies and isolates, for His own reasons, every man from the pangs of the depths of Hell. He'll allow us to share eternal joy and peace with Him, but not Hell,; not even sinners who eventually go to Hell.

They will go there alone, not with Jesus in mind or in body. No man accompanied—nor will accompany—Jesus to Hell. That was His unique province. He went alone. He'll take us to heaven with Him, but Hell is forever "His private experience. "He gives to men the mind and spirit by which to follow Him to glory, but never the mind by which He descended to Hell, the lower parts of the earth. In other words, we can know the joys of Christ in heaven, but never His sorrows of Hell, except in believing. Hence, no man can ever truly know hell as Jesus knows it—and knew it. "The psychology of Hell" will forever be hidden from men. Its depths of emotion will be private and unique to Jesus forever.

Hallelujah what a Savior who could take a poor lost sinner lift him from the miry clay and set him free. I will ever tell the story shouting glory! Glory! Glory! Hallelujah! Jesus ransomed me!
From the depths of sin and sadness to the heights of joy and gladness Jesus lifted me ... in mercy full and free ..."

Only Calvary Could Satisfy God's Judgment

Only Calvary was God's finished judgment. His only Odor Quietis Finalis –[satisfying sacrifice] all other judgments are "unfinished." Only the Messiah made an end to sin and brought in everlasting righteousness – an Odor Quietis Finalis this only because He made an end to sin. Only Calvary concludes the issue of sin with the heart of God. In hell sinners will simply be there suffering, but not to the "satisfaction" of God.

Jesus had the Only Mind Fit to be the Ultimate Sacrifice

The only mind that could wholly experience Hell and thus satisfy God's heart by the experience was the mind of (or in) Christ Jesus—the mind vested in Him of God. This mind had never before been vested in another. In the future, as long as God lives, it will never be vested in another for this unique purpose.

When holy scripture says "let this mind be in you which was also in Christ Jesus," it has nothing to do with the full and final experience of hell—*that is a mental and physical experience that includes the absolute human capacity and the absolute "divine capacity" to experience the event.*

Would God as a just judge spare Adam and his children the death of the Cross and give them the lighter sentence of Hell because of mental retardation due to the fall? ...and send Jesus to the "Cross-Hell" because of what He knew? States are slow to execute the mentally retarded because of their mental incapacity to understand their penalty.

But Jesus knew fully what the Cross and Hell meant. He had a perfect understanding as to the depth of all the pain and the guilt and the wedge that earned the penalty. He knew the pains that he must suffer to span the great gulf that separated God from man. No one else knew and thoroughly understood it like Jesus. Then, having that understanding, He still for the Love of God in Him willingly went to the Cross-Hell for us.

The scripture says, "never a man spoke like this man." Neither did a man feel and sense man and God as this man. Only because Jesus was God could He feel all God put in Hell for man and God. As God is with us (men), He felt both the hurt of man and God, absolutely—and He knew all of the reasons. The Father knew that the Son knew all the ramifications of death #1. From Adam, whose mind was retarded in the fall, to all men who died thereafter; none knew the full ramifications of death. Only Immanuel did.

Therefore, death was a punishment for man, but not a satisfaction to God of His wrath. In the case of death #2, none but the only begotten Son of God who was in the bosom of the Father and therefore experienced a spiritual osmosis of intelligence or wisdom could die death #2 and satisfy God. "Thou shalt see the travail of His soul (only) and be satisfied.

Jesus went to death #1 and death #2 willingly, submissively, knowingly. Men don't go to either death with all these characteristics. Sometimes willingly, as in war, as in a mother who seeks to save a child from a burning building, but never knowingly - for no man understand the God/death factor.

"By His knowledge shall my righteous servant justify many." Isaiah 53:10

> *Isa:53:10: Yet it pleased the LORD to bruise him; he hath put him to grief: when thou shalt <u>make his soul an offering for sin,</u> he shall see his seed, he shall prolong his*

days, and the pleasure of the LORD shall prosper in his hand.

11: He shall see of <u>the travail of his soul</u>, and shall be satisfied: by his knowledge shall my righteous servant justify many; for he shall bear their iniquities.

12: Therefore will I divide him a portion with the great, and he shall divide the spoil with the strong; because <u>he hath poured out his soul unto death:</u> and he was numbered with the transgressors; and he bare the sin of many, and made intercession for the transgressor

Conclusion: Our Lord Jesus Christ, Immanuel, the only man who has ever lived, or ever will live, who was both "Cross and Throne compatible." He was the only man who could qualifiedly be equal to both. Only because He was absolutely equal, or compatible with Hell, He also, compatible with God's Throne!

Terms Relative to Jesus' Humiliation and Exaltation that shall be used in the discussion in the next Three Chapters:

De profundus – out of the depth
Profundus – the depth
Profundus immensis – the vast fathomless depth of the Cross
Ex profundus – exiting *profundis*–relative to the resurrection
Gloria excelsis – glory to God in the highest
Gloriam in excelsis infinitam – glory to God in the highest-infinitely endless
Supranomination – the name above every name, which Jesus-Immanuel received in His exaltation
Adminsitration – His administration at and from His throne in His glorified state
Pre-Calverian – before the Cross, in Christ's life and the state before going to the Cross (Calvary)
Calverian – on the Cross, pertaining to the Cross. The situation of the Cross, the lowest hell, epitome of humiliation, what happened on the Cross, *profundis-immesis*, the cry my God, my God, why hast thou forsaken Me? (*de profundis*)
Post-Calverian – after the Cross-resurrection, ascension, glorification, enthronement, administration, *gloriam in excelsis infinitam*

Chapter 14

THE RISING UP OF IMMANUEL
The Union of God and Man—Seen in the Resurrection

"Whom God hath raised up having loosed the pains of death, because it was not possible that He should be holden of it." Acts 2:24

The resurrection of Jesus Christ was Immanuel exiting death and the grave. By His resurrection He transitioned from the things of His humiliation, to those of His exaltation. Through the entire process of His decent, His death and His grand resurrection He never stopped being fully man [us].He was simultaneously fully God.
This shows the inseparable union between God and man even down to the grave, in the resurrection. As He said and proved by His death, burial, and resurrection: "I will never leave you nor forsake you" Here the eternal and inseparable union is demonstrated relative to our going to the grave, by the resurrection.
Christ being raised from the dead dieth no more, death hath no more dominion over Him. - Romans 6:9.
He that raised up Christ from the dead shall raise us up also by Him.

Jesus Rose from the Suffering and Death of the Grave
He went into the jaws of suffering and death and was a victim of them to the-farthest boundary of the damaging capability of each except for corruption. He saw

no corruption, for He lacked the seed of corruption. From the grave, He rose.

Opposing Forces of Death and Hell were Negated by the Resurrection

Thus, God negates the power of opposing forces in the "raising up process," whether, as in the case of Jesus, He was raised in the presence of death to live forever. For God's "rising up" is powerful. In Acts 2:24, God raised Him up, having loosed the pains of death, because it was not possible that He should be holden of it.

The Resurrection Showed Victory over Death

According to I Corinthians 15:21, "For since by man [Adam] came death (the gulf) by man [Imm/**anu**/el] came the resurrection (the dissolution of the gulf) (I Corinthians15:22) For as in Adam, all die (basis of difference; the gulf); even so, in Christ [Immanuel]shall all be made alive (dissolution of the gulf). Hence, death was swallowed up in victory. That means He conquered death when Jesus rose, showing that "Death is swallowed up in victory—it was absolute abolition, dissolution of the difference, gulf, and all that separated us from the life of God. Acts 2:30-31, The scriptures teach that God would raise up Christ to sit on His throne ... He, seeing this, spoke of the resurrection of Christ that His soul was not left in neither his flesh did see corruption. This Jesus hath God raised up...

Immanuel's Resurrection Changed our Vocabulary on Death *by changing death's effect on us*

Immanuel's arrival on the scene *as far as death was concerned* added a new and different dimension factor to time's realm. Eternity had come [*Jesus' work in His death brought the work of eternity into time on the Cross and in His death*]. The impact was that Time's subjects would thereafter never be the same - i.e. the believing ones. He came to change the landscape of sin, Satan, sorrow, sighing, disease, **and death**. He came to blunt and/or ameliorate their previous effects. Thus, by the resurrection, Time, Satan and cohorts were all interrupted and intersected ***by the power of the resurrection.***

Only Immanuel could realistically change; i.e., in fact, our vocabulary on death, by changing what the grave is to the saints. It has been changed from a place of separation to the presence of God for saints. It has been changed from a horrible place of pain and separation to having no sting or causing harm to saints; all because of Jesus-Immanuel's Cross and glorious resurrection.

Even the Grave is Not the Same Since the Resurrection of Immanuel

Jesus was the man who made a difference everywhere He went - even the grave is not the same since Jesus went to it. In the resurrection Jesus answered our death by His life.

Immanuel being with us in the grave changed it forever. Naught of death can flow from Him who is life eternal. Man who was under sentence of death, condemned, doomed to die by divine verdict obtained eternal life as a gift. "The gift of God is eternal life through Jesus Christ, our Lord." Having died unto sin once, He will never die again.

Immanuel's Resurrection was a Confirmation of Our Coming Resurrection

Christ being raised from the dead dieth no more, death hath no more dominion over Him. Romans 6:9. He that raised up Christ from the dead shall **raise us up** also by Him I Corinthians 6:14; II Corinthians 4:14. Romans 6:4. ***Thus, Jesus' resurrection confirms ours to come. It also shows our power to walk in the newness of life as believers***. That just as Christ was raised up from the dead by the glory of the Father, **even so we should** walk in newness of life (i.e., by the glory of the Father).

As it says in Hebrews 11:19, James 5:15, He could be made sin for men, die on a Cross for them and in actuality, never stop living. To live while dying to die while living, etc., etc., etc., etc. (Immanuel is El with the illimitable etc.)

In Immanuel, He who is the shepherd whose rod and staff comfort us in Psalm 23 and removes the fear of the shadow of death, is with us, *in and out of the grave.*

As Henry Lyte wrote; "I fear no foe with Thy Hand near to bless. Ills have no weight; and tears no bitterness. Where is death's sting, and grave thy victory? I triumph still if thou abide with me" ... In Immanuel, God will abide.

Acts 3:26 - God having raised up His Son Jesus, sent Him to bless us (no empty purpose raising Jesus. He was raised to be sent, to bless). Acts 5:30 - The God of our Fathers raised up Jesus.

In the Resurrection God Shows Immanuel Off

According to Acts 10:40 - Him God raised up the third day, and showed Him openly. (God raised up—God showed off His dynamic work.) Yes, this was to His glory.

The Rising Up of Immanuel

As it is taught in Acts 13:23, God raised unto Israel a Savior, Jesus. In Acts 13:33-34, it is said that He hath raised up Jesus again.

The Resurrection is by the Glory of God
A Major Part of the Glory Plan of El was Fulfilled in the Resurrection.

In the glory of El is the glory of all of the stages and events of Immanuel's humiliation-exaltation. That glory is the glory of all of Immanuel's works. It is the glory of all that Immanuel must fulfill, high or low:
The glory of Immanuel's condescension
The glory of *His* ascension
The glory of *His* humiliation
The glory of exaltation
The exaltation of humiliation *of Immanuel*
The exaltation of glorification *of Immanuel*
The power of humiliation *of Immanuel*
The power of *the* exaltation *of Immanuel*
The divineness of condescension *in Immanuel's descent*
And most certainly, the glory of His grand resurrection from the dead

The Principles of Humiliation and Exaltation are Exemplified in the Resurrection

We can benefit from seeing Immanuel-Jesus' Cross and resulting resurrection. We should take note of the divineness of ascension and glorification to his enthronement after His powerful resurrection and be ready to say to each other, "Humble yourselves therefore under the mighty hand of God, that ye may be **also** exalted in due time" (See Ephesians 4:1; I Peter 5:6).

Here, we see humility in a process that is conducted by God's mighty power as well as the exaltation process. It was so in Jesus, Immanuel, *as seen in His victorious resurrection.*

After the Resurrection, Immanuel Ascended on High to His Session and Glory

It was in El's plan that He not stay in the grave but rather that He rise from the dead and ascend to His high place and be there eternally.

Thus, having ascended, Immanuel now reigns in "ex-less" glory. Now, never an "*ex*" (He will never leave His state of glorification and neither will the saints when they are glorified). He is in glory eternally.

In reference to *profundis immensis* [the depth of the Cross] relative to Immanuel, there was "*in*" " *de*," and "*ex*" "*ad*" "*via*". These are relative to His death and grave.

But, pertaining to *gloriam in excelsis infinitum*, [His resurrection and glorification] relative to Him, there is only "*ad*," "*in*," "*via*," "*de*" (for He blesses us out of this glory, while He abides in it) but - no "*ex*."[2] Pertaining to the profundis immensis *experienced on the Cross and the grave, Jesus conquered it and **exited** it [ex] via the resurrection, never to go there again. This is ex profoundis immensis. But in His glorious reign since the resurrection*

---

[2] *ex* is Latin for out of , in means in it , *via* means by the glory, *in* means in the glory, *ad* means at His glory.

*and by the resurrection He will never exit [ex] there.*That He will never be unglorified So for glorium *excelsis infinitum* [His state of glorification] there is no *"ex".* Hence *no exiting, no dethroning, no backsliding to hell and the Cross. Thus He our forerunner is glorified forever. This is significant because by this we know that once the church is glorified so shall we ever be because of Him.*

Jesus Christ, our Immanuel is *in gloriam in excelsis* infinitam. Immanuel in glory, giving glory, making glorious, sustaining in glory, infinitam. Only by *gloria in excelsis* could Immanuel go into *profundis immensis* **[the Cross, death and the grave]**, bear it unmoved and leave it with an eternal "*ex.*" [*the resurrection*]. This is the witness of the resurrection, only God could do such a thing. Only by *gloria in excelsis* [the glory of God that engaged the Cross] could He rise into *gloriam in excelsis* infinitam [state of exalted glorification].

Therefore, Out of God's Love and Determination to Save Us, He did all of this for Us, all of this in Immanuel; Thus Immanuel:

(1) died by the glory of The Father (*in excelsis*)

(2) rose by the glory of The Father

(3) was glorified by the glory of The Father

(4) administers and reigns by the glory of The Father

Immanuel was God in Christ. Immanuel was God with us.

He [El] wrought IN Christ-Immanuel.

He [El] raised Him up and gave Him glory.

The Resurrection should Increase our Faith to believe God for Victory in our Lives

In our human and individual spheres, with the quality of this *gloria in excelsis*, we too, just like Immanuel in His resurrection, can descend to our "lowest depths" and rise to our "highest heights," remembering always that our depths and heights are relative to His, but never equal to His. His descending and ascending are unique and exemplary!

Let this mind be in you which was also in Christ Jesus Philippians 2:5

Immanuel's Resurrection the Confirmation of Ours:
a. "The last enemy that shall be destroyed is death." Here is the testimony of God that man's most formidable foe is facing certain destruction by Imm/anu/el.

 "Jesus' ultimate testimony"
b   "I am come that they might have life and that more abundantly"
c.   "If a man die believing in me, I will raise him up at the last day"

        Jesus shall fashion our vile bodies to be like His glorious body - the body with the glory in it which He had (in God's purposing) before the world began. Philippians 3:21

Jesus-Immanuel Holds the Keys to Death and Hell—Rev 1:18
        Having in His hand the keys of Hell and death, He will never relinquish them till all be consummated (I Corinthians 15). Once New Testament believers and saints are made immortal, and glorified, they as their Master was, will never be uncrowned, (unglorified, mortalized (an Eng. word) again. Immanuel will be with us in the resurrection/rapture and forever thereafter.

Once clothed in incorruption and immortality, they will never be unfrocked or unclothed. When mortality is swallowed up of life, that will be the accomplishment Immanuel's main aim.

According to I Peter 1:18-21 ... God raised Him up from the dead and gave Him glory; that your faith and hope might be in God. It is a testimony to the glory of God and a hope for all who believe in the power of God to raise us up.

In our initial salvation, we have the glory of God in earthly vessels. ***That is now that we as saints are saved, but not glorified—still in our human bodies***. But in our ***coming*** eternally redemptive state, we will possess the glory of God in our glorified bodies—an altogether new and higher state, *all because Immanuel was with us in the resurrection.*

Conclusion: The resurrection of Jesus was God's own antiphonal response to His Son's death. He Himself decided that there was no other commensurate answer. So glorious was His work in Christ on the Cross that only Jesus' resurrection, ascension, glorification, session and supranomination could be correlatives thereto. Through the entire process, He never stopped being withusgod. Thus, the resurrection is a proof of His union with us.

Preliminary Essay

Preface to Chapter 15
"Immanuel, with Us in Glorification"

As we discuss the eternal union of God and man seen in the glorification of Jesus and His saints. It will help our understanding to know the milieu and the history of El's [God's] quest to have an eternal, inseparable union with man.

It started when God made Adam and placed him in the garden, an immortal being. God had planned to bring Adam close to Him by elevating him into a state of glorification and Godlikeness. God would have had an eternal and inseparable union with him back then.

But the fall came and wedged God from man. Death and Hell, the most formidable enemies of God and man, became the major separator. The earth would have been glorified into the same state as seen in the New Heaven and New Earth (Rev. 21) had it not been for the fall. Adam would have come into the eternal state of an immeasurable union with God automatically.

In this study, the eternal state is discussed referring to Heaven, the New Heaven and the New Earth, eternal communion with God in glorified bodies, Immortality, and man's eternal permanent state of Godlikeness. It is when man will be gloriously and eternally in God in an eternally indissolvable way. This was the vision of God from the beginning when He made

Adam. The coming eternal union will never end. There will never be another fall to cause the wedge again. Adam God's first son caused the fall which averted the union. But in the second Son, Jesus Immanuel, the plan for an eternal union is revived and fulfilled.

In Immanuel, the separating gulf is closed, and death, the most formidable enemy and component of the fallen world will be abolished. Man is brought into the eternal state that was at first intended *[Behold I[Immanuel] make All things New].*

Thus, the glorification of the saints in the eternal state is the answer to the wedge and disunion caused by the fall. It is the fulfillment of the original plan for man to be Godlike in an eternal union with God. It is the fulfillment of God's plan for the redemption of the Earth itself, which was damaged by the fall.

Thus, Immanuel came to bring man and God together in an immeasurably close eternal union. He leads us to glory upon His own journey there by being us in Immanuel. He /we are exalted to our/His seat(s) at the right hand of the throne of God where we will be eternally. He is there now, holding our eternal spot as the forerunner of man at the throne. Hereby, God finally brings Adam [us] to that first planned place of an immeasurably close union and glorification with Him.

CHAPTER 15

IMMANUEL, GOD WITH US IN GLORIFICATION

He that descended is the same also that ascended up far above all heavens, that he might fill all things. Ephesians 4:10

As it is the aim of this thesis to show the unique and eternal union between God and man in Jesus Christ as Immanuel; in this chapter, we show the **eternal aspect of the union** of God and man fulfilled in/via Immanuel.

Herein I discuss the eternal state of the union between God and man fulfilled in Immanuel's ascension, glorification and session, and its relationship to our glorification and eternality.

In the previous chapters of this book leading up to this point in our discussions, we saw how Jesus-Imm/anu/El [with us God] was with us in His incarnation, in His state as the God-man here on earth, and His being with us in the very low humiliation of the Cross-Hell and the grave.

However, in this chapter, His "withness" is illustrated by His/our immortality and eternal glorification.
In Immanuel, God did everything necessary to see to it that we would have eternal life and dwell with Him forever. This is also divinely expressed in the anuEl part of the name Imm/**anuel [usGod]**.

Immanuel, God With Us in Glorification

This commentary on the glorification of Jesus and the saints is different from others, because it discusses glorification in light of and in terms of the unique and eternal union between God and man in Immanuel.

Thesis Statement:

To show <u>the unique and eternal union between God</u> and man in Jesus Christ our Lord, the Son of God, as revealed to the prophet Isaiah in the name of Immanuel.

The glorification and session of Immanuel-Jesus has infinite and eternal implications for us. He left the Glory that He had before the world began and humbled Himself in His incarnation and ultimately in His death on the Cross-Hell. He, as our Immanuel, was with us in all of these lowly things of His humiliation. Thus, in this chapter we show His union with us in His exalted state of His glorification and His session.

I establish three main points that show the intent of God for an inseparable and eternal union between God and Man, which are/will be fulfilled by and/ or in Immanuel's glorification and session.

a. The entire process of His humiliation and exaltation [glorification] was for us.

b. The Entire Process of His Humiliation and Resulting Exaltation was for us.

C The ultimate Goal and Plan for our Immortality and Glorification is fulfilled in Immanuel's Glorification.

The Session and Glorification of Jesus and the Saints

The session of Jesus is His being seated at the right hand of the throne of God after His resurrection and ascension. It is a place of the highest honor of God. His session was not needed by Him who came from Glory, but rather for us who He brings to glory. This point is unique to this thesis. The session of Jesus is for us. In His session, He represents us. He is our forerunner to glory and to be seated on thrones in glory. There seated, He is man. It is the church. It is us [we] [the church] that God uses Immanuel to bring to eternal glorification.

The following scriptures speak of the session of Jesus:

> *The LORD says to my lord: "Sit at my right hand until I make your enemies a footstool for your feet." Psalm 110:1*

> *God exalted him to his own right hand Acts 5:31*

> *But this Man, after He had offered one sacrifice for sins forever, sat down at the right hand of God, Hebrews 10:12*

> *Which he wrought in Christ, when he raised him from the dead, and set him at his own right hand in the heavenly places, .. Ephesians 1:20*

Immanuel, God With Us in Glorification

Who is gone into heaven, and is on the right hand of God; angels and authorities and powers being made subject unto him... I Peter 3:22

Glorification of the saints is the future and final work of God in us, where He translates our mortal physical bodies to eternal, immortal bodies and puts us in Heaven where we will dwell forever with Him [Eternal, inseparable union].

and if children, heirs also, heirs of God and fellow heirs with Christ, if indeed we suffer with Him so that we may also be glorified with Him. Romans 8:17

when He comes to be glorified in His saints on that day, and to be marveled at among all who have believed--for our testimony to you was believed. 2 Thessalonians 1:10

When Christ, who is our life, is revealed, then you also will be revealed with Him in glory. Colossians 3:4

Therefore, I exhort the elders among you, as your fellow elder and witness of the sufferings of Christ, and a partaker also of the glory that is to be revealed, I Peter 5:1

> [0] *For our citizenship is in heaven, from which we also eagerly wait for the Savior, the Lord Jesus Christ,* [21] *who will transform our lowly body that it may be conformed to His glorious body, according to the working by which He is able even to subdue all things to Himself. Philippians 3:20-22*

> *In a moment, in the twinkling of an eye, at the last trump: for the trumpet shall sound, and the dead shall be raised incorruptible, and we shall be changed. 52*
> *For this corruptible must put on incorruption, and this mortal must put on immortality.53*
> *So when this corruptible shall have put on incorruption, and this mortal shall have put on immortality, then shall be brought to pass the saying that is written, Death is swallowed up in victory. 54 I Corinthians 15:52-54*

(a)Immanuel's Exaltation was/ is a Reward for His Humiliation

Immanuel's glorification discussed in this chapter, is the high exaltation explained by St. Paul in Philippians 2:5-10. His glorification is the result of His very low humiliation, epitomized in His death on the Cross.

> *Let this mind be in you, which was also in Christ Jesus v 5*

> *Who, being in the form of God, thought it not robbery to be equal with God v 6*

Immanuel, God With Us in Glorification

But made himself of no reputation, and took upon him the form of a servant, and was made in the likeness of men:

And being found in fashion as a man, he humbled himself, and became obedient unto death, even the death of the Cross.

Wherefore God also hath highly exalted him, and given him a name which is above every name:

That at the name of Jesus every knee should bow, of things in heaven, and things in earth, and things under the earth;

And that every tongue should confess that Jesus Christ is Lord, to the glory of God the Father.

Jesus, who left His mighty throne to be with us [anuEl] on Earth, just before His crucifixion prayed; "Father, give me the glory that I had with Thee before the world began" (i.e., was purposed). John 17:5

Jesus left His throne to come to us and is now awarded a place at the throne for us [standing at the right hand of the throne of God], holding our place until the rapture.

His major purpose for coming was/is to take us to Heaven with Him; that is, to bring us to glory, in an eternal and inseparable union Him; He'll take us to heaven with Him, ...He gives to men the mind and spirit by which to follow Him to glory......

In Immanuel, Everything Necessary to bring Us to Eternality was done in Immanuel

> *When He had by Himself purged our sins, set down on the right hand of the majesty on High Heb 1:3*

> *..When he ascended on high he led captivity captive and give gifts unto Men... Ephesians 4:8.*

> *But this man, after he had offered 'one' sacrifice for sins forever, sat down on the right hand of God; Hebrews 10:12*

He is Glorified because of His Humility
He humbled Himself to dwell with us, having
A. Poor birth conditions
B. Hostile, spiritual environment
C. Poor living circumstances
Then, He was destroyed on Calvary. Yet, He remained with us In His ascension and session!

Immanuel, From Humiliation-Incarnation to Glorification
In Immanuel, we behold a mighty manifestation of El, God as He takes a speechless babe being nourished with milk from its mother's breast through a hostile environment, and the Cross, then finally to the throne of God to form a church and reign over all as Lord and Master. Behold the Glory of God!
His exaltation is at the point of the 'wherefore' in Philippians 2:

Immanuel, God With Us in Glorification

" Wherefore God hath highly exalted him , giving him a name which is above every Name….."

In His humiliation He was with us in that He was made sin for us. He bore our sins—the sins of the whole world in His own body. He suffered the eternal judgment of sin for us and as us on the Cross.

Immanuel in Union with Us in Exaltation and Glorification

Because Immanuel was with us in the lowly state of His life and became the ultimate sacrifice—the Cross which is the epitome of His Humiliation. God hath highly exalted Him and given a name above every name. This is what is meant by supranomination.

(b) The Entire Process of His Humiliation and Resulting Exaltation was for Us

Question: How can one be given that which he already possesses? How can one enter a place he already occupies? This question is referring to the fact that God already had Glory before coming as Immanuel and needed not to earn it; but for us, He in Immanuel did everything for us to come to glorification with Him eternally.

His death, burial, resurrection, ascension and glorification are all part of His ultimate plan for an eternal union of God with man via Jesus Christ as Immanuel. This point is raised to show that His humiliation and humbling was for us. There is nothing He needed for Himself that required Him to leave His throne. It was what He planned for us that required this great humiliation.

He, our Immanuel, completed the entire process of His assigned Humiliation and Exaltation of which Culminates in His Final State of Glorification

He is at the right hand of God for us

He is at the right hand of His majesty for us.

 After Immanuel's grand resurrection He ascended on High. Jesus Christ, our Immanuel is now in *gloriam in* excellsis *infinitam*. That is to say Immanuel is in glory, giving glory, making glorious, sustaining in glory "*in, infinitam*.

Only by *gloria in excelsis* could Immanuel go in to *profundis immensis*, bear it unmoved and leave it with an eternal "*ex*."

Only by *gloria in excelsis* could He rise into *gloriam in excelsis infinitam*.

He died by the glory of The Father (*in excelsis*).

He rose by the glory of The Father.

He was glorified by the glory of The Father.

Exaltation, Glorification of the Saints will be Forever

His exaltation and glorification are a part of His post-Calvarian glory. What I mean by post-Calvarian is after Calvary—after the Cross. The effect of Calvary. It is what occurred because of and after Jesus' suffering and humiliation.

Now, after Calvary, Immanuel now reigns in "ex-less" glory. Now, never an "*ex*." In reference to *profundis immensis* relative Immanuel, there was "*in*," "*de*," and *ex* "*ad*" "*via*"

In reference to *gloriam in excelsis* relative to Him, there is "*ad*" "*in*," "*via*," "*de*" (for He blesses us out of this

169

glory, while He abides in it) but - no "*ex*."   Here 'never an ex means that Jesus will never be unglorified. He exited the Cross and the grave because they were only for a period but His glorification is infinite-eternal and unlimited.

(c)The ultimate Goal and Plan for Our Immortality and Glorification is Fulfilled in Immanuel's Glorification

We are Called to be Glorified Because of Him
We are called to Glorium excelsis infinitium *too. That is, we are called to be glorified like Him. Hence, we shall be glorified like He is.*

The God of all grace who hath called us unto His eternal glory (*ad gloriam in excelsis infinitam*) by Jesus Christ (Immanuel, who is the full spectrum and scale of Divine glory from *profundis immensis to gloriam in excelsis infinitum*), after that you have suffered a while (by that glory) make you perfect, stablish, strengthen, settle you by that same glory. Seeing Him glorified assures us that we shall be glorified too. We shall be like Him.
So then, after the Lord had spoken unto them, he was received up into heaven, and sat on the right hand of God. Mark 16: 19

In Immnauel, Is incorporated the Things of the Cross and the Throne—He went to Both for /as Us

Our Lord Jesus Christ, Immanuel, the only man who has ever lived, or ever will live, who was both "Cross and Throne compatible." He was the only man who could qualifiedly be equal to both. Only because He was absolutely equal, or compatible with hell was He, too, compatible with God's Throne! See Philippians 2. He went to God's appointed nadir. He went to God's appointed zenith. He that ascends is the same that descended first into the lower parts of the earth. He is, that is, the same being, character, person. He is not another another Son, Lord, Master, Servant, Saint, etc., etc., etc. He is the same being who was crucified.

> **Luke 9:51** *As the time approached for him to be taken up to heaven, Jesus resolutely set out for Jerusalem.*
> **Luke 22:69** *But from now on, the Son of Man will be seated at the right hand of the mighty God."*
> **Luke 24:51** *While he was blessing them, he left them and was taken up into heaven.*

Immanuel takes Us from the New birth [Initial Salvation] to Glorification

The ministry of Jesus, a sampling of His future tenderness, shepherdizing, etc., etc., etc. The Cross - of Jesus, The resurrection of Jesus, The glorification of Jesus,The supranomination of Jesus, The session of Jesus and The administration (post-Calvarian) priesthood and royal throne. *All of this is for us. It is our calling*, etc. (Romans 8), etc., etc., etc., etc. *His session is for* our session in the holy city in Jesus' presence on thrones, seats. i.e. Jesus from birth to enthronement. We from new birth to enthronement. He from a virgin's womb to a throne in glory. We from the dark night of sin to thrones, seats, in glory.

Our Second Glory—Glorified Bodies

Ought not Christ to have suffered and to enter into His Glory. Father, give me the glory that I had with Thee before the world began (i.e. was purposed)
The glory of power, authority. The glory of position, place. The glory of name.

He broke His union with The Father, left His glory to bring us to glory and an eternal union with God [El].

The union of Father and Son was broken on Calvary so that the union of Jesus and His saints, God and His saints, might be forever indissolvable. (Romans 8) Here, we have the great mystery of disunion and the great mystery of fellowship. Behold what was wrought (by) what was wrought! No mountain laboring to produce a mouse.

Apostle John said, "...and we beheld His glory as of the only begotten of the Father, full of grace and truth—this was the glory of Jesus as He dwelt among them as a mortal Son of God. This was glory incomparable and incomprehensible. The disciples said concerning the observation of this glory on one occasion, "what manner of man is this...?"

The glory which Jesus has entered into transcends His pre-Calvarian glory. Is the difference in Jesus' post-Calvarian glory quantitative and not qualitative, as set over against His pre-Calvarian glory? The glory of Jesus vested in Him as a creature begotten of a woman a son of man and His glory vested in Him sons Adam and Mary was his first/pre-calvarian glory. His first glory was that which accompanied Him, as "He was made under the law and made of a woman." In His second glory, He bypasses both.

Like Jesus, our first glory as saints is in our earthly bodies. We have this treasure in earthen vessels, but our second and eternal Glory will be in glorified eternal bodies. 2 Corinthians 4:7

In our initial salvation, we have the glory of God in earthly vessels. In our eternally redemptive state, we will possess the glory of God in glorified bodies—an altogether new and higher state.

Jesus shall fashion our vile bodies to be like His glorious body—the body with the glory in it which He had (in God's purposing) before the world *began.*

Immanuel is with us in His glorification. He is not exalted without us. His main mission was to exalt us to where He is [in glory] by bringing us to immortality.

Everlasting Glorification and Immortality
El being last in the name Immanuel is here indicative of his assuring us of a final glorification that will be final and will never be undone.

Once New Testament believers, saints are made immortal and glorified, they as their Master was, will never be uncrowned, (unglorified *mortalized* (an Eng. word) again. Once clothed in incorruption and immortality, they will never be unfrocked unclothed. When mortality is swallowed up of life, it will be another of Immanuel's final acts. He is man's everlasting "Barrier-Remover." He is man's everlasting "Union-Producer."

Finally, in our Glorification, Adam's Mortal Life will be Completely Abolished by El's Eternal Plan in Immanuel

Immanuel, God With Us in Glorification

It is seen in Jesus' session that the plan of El, through Immanuel was that Adam's life will be completely abolished and displaced by God's life; mortality will be displaced by Immortality. Immanuel is ultimately about immortality; i.e., "God-likeness" for man. Immanuel is about the abolition of death and all that is kindred to it, or bespeaks it. Immanuel has to do with life beyond life, uncaused life, transcendent life, the life that God is.

Do we get a glimpse of the purposes of El's intent in such terms as justification, peace, righteousness, reconciliation, communion, fellowship (power), and, most of all, immortality, etc., etc., etc.? Thus, The culmination of the "Immanuelness" of Jesus is one immortality. His "Imm" is for our "Imm"(ortality). His "with" for our "not.

God did Much in Immanuel to Bring Us to Eternal Life

"Why all of God's gigantic enterprise in Immanuel, including His grand resurrection, glorious ascension and infinite glorification, if we be not able to come to immortality; "If in this life only we have hope in Christ (Immanuel) we are of all men most miserable.

The ultimate cause for His "Imm" is our "Imm." "Imm" for "Imm." "He that hath wrought us for the selfsame thing is God" - that mortality might be swallowed up of LIFE! Even as we will forever be with Him at the rapture We will ever be with Him [eternal inseparable union].

Because of Immanuel, We shall be Glorified

The following passages show the planned glorification of the saints:

> *when He comes to be glorified in His saints on that day, and to be marveled at among all who have believed—for our testimony to you was believed in that day 2 Thessalonians 1:10.*

> *Who shall change our vile body, that it may be fashioned like unto his glorious body, according to the working whereby he is able even to subdue all things unto himself. Philippians 3:21*

> *Moreover whom he did predestinate, them he also called: and whom he called, them he also justified: and whom he justified, them he also glorified. Romans 8:30*

> *Beloved, now are we the sons of God, and it doth not yet appear what we shall be: but we know that, when he shall appear, we shall be like him; for we shall see him as he is.*
> *1 John 3:2-4*

Jesus' Ultimate Testimony, Immortality of the Saints

In Immanuel, God moved all of His "heavy" and "highly refined" salvational [eternal salvation] equipment into place for man's sake. The purpose hereof was to affect everything for man's temporal and <u>eternal</u> deliverance—up to and including immortality. What I mean is that God put His best forward in Immanuel, to bring us to eternal life.

175

Immanuel, God With Us in Glorification

("Imm" for "Imm"(ortality)) **Immanuel's ultimate and most glorious cause (raison d'etre) [reason to exist] was and is our immortality (see II Corinthians 5). This is expressed and demonstrated in "Jesus' Ultimate Testimony"**

A. "I am come that they might have life and that more abundantly"

B. "If a man die believing in me, I will raise him up at the last day"

Note: St. Paul's witness in I Corinthians 15,

"The last enemy that shall be destroyed is death." Here is the testimony of God that man's most formidable foe is facing certain destruction by Imm/anu/el. (Romans 5) "Where sin abounded, grace did much more abound. Sin and its consequences are overwhelmed by the power and wisdom of Immanuel. Hallelujah! All that Jesus Christ is bespeaks super victor(y) over all the forces of "the underworld." He is Christus Victor indeed [here: Christ the victor over death]. Nothing, absolutely nothing, about His Name means weakness, ignorance or defeat.

Conclusion: What is significant about the glorification and session of Immanuel? The glorification of Jesus Immanuel is not only a personal reward (as if it were something He earned for Himself alone) for His work on the Cross, but to bring us to an immeasurably close union with Him in eternal Glory. When God first gave the name Immanuel to Isaiah, He had the eternal unending closeness of God and man in The Eternal State in mind.

Chapter 16

THE TRANSFORMING GLORY OF IMMANUEL - Jesus Christ the Right Image

In this chapter I discuss Jesus-Immanuel as the image of God that the church should have as its sole model. The purpose of the church is to pursue the glory of God that was given to us in Jesus Christ, the Son of God.

Jesus-Immanuel is the only image given to us by God who is the exact likeness and express reflection of God in a man. He is the perfect example of what God wants to see in us. Therefore, we must continually behold Him.   As we behold Him, we will be transformed into His image. That is to say we will be changed, made more and more like Him.

When it comes to spiritual matters pertaining to our salvation Jesus Christ is the main goal of man's pursuits. He is to be the greatest end of all our strivings. He is our leading light. He is the one to emulate, the one to be like, the one to copy. He is The Image of the glory of God as it should be seen in the Church.

We are to behold Him, but how? We can behold Him as He is revealed to us through the enlightenment of the Holy Ghost. The knowledge of the gospel when He is preached to us. We must be filled with the Holy Ghost. He, the Holy Ghost, will lead us, guide us, and illuminate us. Through the Holy Ghost, Jesus removes all things that block our clear vision of The Image [Jesus Christ].

*" Mark the perfect man, and behold the upright: for the end of that man is peace. ".*Psalm 37:37

The Transforming Glory of Immanuel

I press toward the mark for the prize of the high calling of God in Christ Jesus. ... Philippians 3:14

The goal is to conform to the spiritual qualities, characteristics that are seen in Jesus Christ such things as His humility, His submission to His appointed suffering, His spirit of charity, His conquering sin and getting the victory over sin and death etc etc....

Paul described this by saying that the Glory of God is in the face of Jesus Christ. He is what God wants us to be. He is how we are supposed to live. He is an example of the reflection of God. God uses this image to show us what He wants to see in us:

In Relation to Jesus' Glorious Sonship;

1 . How He came to be
2 . How He wrought
3 . How He conquered sin and Satan
4 . How He humbled Himself to God
5 . How He submitted to Satan's cruelty
6 . How He serenely died
7 . How He victoriously rose again
8 . How He entered in to glory

We behold Him with open minds. We receive Him and as we receive Him, we are transformed into His image, which is the goal of God in Christ for us.

We are Foreordained to be in His Image

It is in the mind of God that the church be conformed to His image; *"For whom He did foreknow, He also did predestinate (long ago and stands yet unchanged) to be conformed to the image of His Son, that He might be the first born among many brethren"* [Romans 8:29].

II Corinthians 3:18

But we all, with open face beholding as in a glass the glory of the Lord, are changed into the same image from glory

to glory, even as by the Spirit of the Lord. The goal is that we will become more and more like Him, and so much so that when we behold Him, it will be like looking into a mirror. The glory of God seen in Him will be seen in us.
II Corinthians 4:4
"....Christ, who is the image of God."

The Glory of the Image is in the Face of Jesus Christ
Colossians 1:13-15 "...His dear Son: ...who is the image of The Invisible God." We have not seen God graphically or physically but we have a clear picture [image] of Him glory-wise in Jesus Christ. Until we get to heaven, Jesus is the only view [glory] of God that we can behold.
Note: The glory of God is in the face of Jesus.

Being Face-to-Face Transformation, Moses from the Mount Compared to Jesus
We are not to be like Moses and the children of Israel, in the case when Moses put a veil over his face when he came down from the presence of the Lord in Exodus 34:33. This he did, because there was such a glory upon his face, that the Israelites could not bear to look upon him; and also to take off that dread of him, which was upon them, for they were afraid to come nigh him; and that so they might be able to hearken and attend to the words of the Law, which he was to deliver to them. They just were not ready to receive or behold what God sent through Moses.
Two things must happen for transformation to occur: the face of Jesus must be exposed and reflected and the face of the believer must be unmasked, that is to say, fully open to receive and be transformed into His image.
Unlike Moses mentioned above who veiled his face because the people were not ready to receive the glory

that shined out from his face—we with open faces and Jesus with an unveiled face of the glory of God behold the glory of God in the image of Jesus Christ and are thereby transformed into His image.

In the Old Testament, they didn't have the Holy Ghost to enlighten them in Moses' day but we the believers who are born again have the Holy Ghost, which causes us to be able to see the glory of God in Jesus Christ. By having that image to behold, we are transformed into His likeness by, taking on the spiritual qualities and characteristics of the image [Jesus Christ]. Thus, we become like Him.

The Effect of Reading Moses
Focus Scripture:
15 But even unto this day, when Moses is read, the vail is upon their heart.
16 Nevertheless when it shall turn to the Lord, the vail shall be taken away.

Even if the people had received Moses' message it was a convicting and condemning message. It was depressing and magnified their condemnation and its connection to death. The Law did not offer the resolution of life that is offered in the New Testament's Image of Jesus Christ. What good would it have been for them to have read it?

The Effect of Reading Moses
"Moses is read..." What was in Moses?
St. Paul calls it "the ministration of death," a document glorious, but one of sub-glory. *It actually exposed their distance from God's image.*

What's contained in the literature we read? It cannot give us more than it contains. There are some things reading cannot do! To read and become a better person is not to be conformed to the Image; i.e., the image of God's Son. Jesus is the Image of God and the Image which He has appointed for believers. II Corinthians 3 is for the born-again ones.

Dr. M. L. King read Jesus and Ghandi. He studied and admired both—and became a dynamic and outstanding person, but that didn't transform him into their image by their spirits - though he was somewhat after their likeness - in passive resistance. For believers to behold the glory or image of Jesus in glory, brings us into a transformation process related to His likeness, by His Spirit, by His glory. Jesus' documents and glory are "sub" nothing! They transcend all! We are transformed by His Spirit.

Old Testament Mask

With uncovered, unmasked minds relating to identifying; believing/accepting. In Moses, the source of glory was masked (he himself) and the people had open eyes [Exodus 34:29-36]. The people were not ready for the glory from the presence of God that shined from Moses' face. And reading it would not have been the answer because that document did not have the transforming power to conform them to the image of the righteousness of God that the Law portrayed in its articles. They could have beheld the glory of God which was then reflected from the face of Moses but no transformation.

But in the New Testament we read the gospel, we behold the glory of God in the face of Jesus Christ and we are thereby transformed.

New Testament Openness

In the New Testament, the glory of the Lord is unmasked and so are our minds. **That is in relation to Jesus' Glorious Sonship;**

1 . How He came to be
2 . How He wrought
3 . How He conquered sin and Satan
4 . How He humbled Himself to God
5 . How He submitted to Satan's cruelty
6 . How He serenely died
7 . How He rose again
8 . How He entered into glory

What He will do with us futuristically is another aspect of His glory. This we see through a glass darkly. This, we know in part. These things are points of the gospel of Jesus Christ. Our beholding of Him is in the gospel. This is why preachers need to preach the gospel to the people; this is our means of exposing the face of Jesus so that the people can behold it and be transformed by it.

In the gospel there is a wisdom of God, there is power, there is great light, which are given to us by The Spirit.

The Lord Himself is the Mask-Cover, Remover

We with uncovered, unmasked minds, we are beholding those things that made Jesus such a glorious Son of God, the facts hereof are freely flowing from Him to us via the Spirit of God in revelation.

Note: "Shall be <u>taken</u> away"—The Lord Himself is the mask-cover remover. We don't remove our masks. They are part of our Satan-infected nature. It takes Jesus to open our eyes to Him and how we are to be like Him.

Reading Moses, but Still Veiled

Note: Moses is read (good), yet the veil is not taken away. Reading alone doesn't affect the veil, though reading is good. Yet reading is not a power itself.

The Ethiopian Eunuch was reading, but he was asked, "Understandest thou what thou readest?" He answered, "How can I except some man guide me" (to open my understanding). It took not only a well-read man, but an inspired man to open his understanding (remove the veil) from his mind. We are enlightened by the preaching of the gospel and the Holy Ghost, confirming all that He said and has modeled for us.

15 But even unto this day, when Moses is read, the vail is upon their heart.
16 Nevertheless when it shall turn to the Lord, the vail shall be taken away.

17 Now the Lord is that Spirit: and where the Spirit of the Lord is, there is liberty.

When the Mask is taken Away by the Light of Holy Ghost, We Have:

A. Clarity of mind, thought to isolate, to identify the arm, might, wisdom, excellence of God that is wrought in Christ from eternity to His throne in the Heavens.
B. Faith and acceptance to effectuate the truth of the Spirit into the mind, spirit, heart, and being.

This brings about transformation, metamorphosis even by The Spirit of The Lord. We can be transformed, but our faces must be open and we must believe/accept the sights of God's glory that we behold. The common denominator between God's glory and (us) our minds is OPENNESS.

Comparing the Glory of the Old Testament 'the Ministration of Death' to the New Testament's Transforming Power of Life

The Old Testament law which was presented by Moses to the Israelites is called by St. Paul"...the ministration of death written in stone; referring to the 10 commandments - "written death" or "death written" yet glorious. The ten commandments were then "written death, " not "written life." Exodus 24 and Exodus 34:28-35 ("...I will write..." - Chapter 34:1,28) Exodus 32:15-16 (19 broken).

The New Testament is glorious. It is a testament of The Spirit of Righteousness and Life. It exceeds the first [O.T.]in glory. The first was done away. Ours [the New Covenant] remains.

When we are beholding the glory of the Lord (Jesus), we are seeing the mighty arm of God, His matchless strength, His infinite wisdom at work. From before the foundation of the world. We are viewing incomprehensible, and uncomprehended light shining towards us (See St. John 1) - i.e. light or life invincible, forever unconquerable.

We too were thought of by God before the world began. We too will be guided by God through the world. Beholding the glory of God operating in Christ is the surest road to, of transformation for men.

What Happens when We Constantly Behold Other Things? We are Affected by what We Behold

What happens when we constantly behold human weakness? **Weakness!**

What happens when we constantly behold human failure? Failure!
What happens when we deny the glory?
No transformation.
We must behold, believe/accept it—then we'll surely be transformed ...into the same "glory-made" creature.

The Glory of God which Made Jesus Master Over All can cause Us to Master Whatever *We need to Master,* *especially* sin and Satan, pride, lust and demons. God required that Jesus qualify for the cross-eternity's super assignment. We aren't called upon to qualify for that. We're simply called upon to walk with Him now by which we qualify for heaven by way of Him (and His cross), etc., etc.

But we must behold and this is a work of faith? We cannot cease to behold. Note the present participle beholding ...as in a glass (i.e. clearly). Our minds are renewed, transformed, and transfigured in the beholding, reflecting process relating to the glory of Jesus.

We behold - we reflect, we see - we are seen, i.e. we behold Christ - Christ is beheld in and upon us. Beholding is believing, accepting, reflecting by which we are transformed, transfigured.

When I speak of a mask, I speak of any thoughts or darkness, ignorance, misconceptions, anything Satan uses to block our view of Jesus. These must be removed so that the glory of The Image can shine to us uninhibited and the process of transformation can happen. Jesus is the mask remover.

Barring All Others, Jesus Christ is the Only Image for the Born Again Believer to Pursue

In our world, we [the Church], in our quest for excellence seek models that replicate success in many fields of pursuit: philosophy, religion, education, science, entertainment; 'even popular ministry trends, popular preachers, and singers etc.

In the realm of the church world, over time man have made established church culture, traditions, philosophies, doctrines trends for the church world follow and conform to, emulate or practice. However, the main purpose of the church is to expose the image of God in Christ, through the preaching of Jesus Christ.

Many men have become, have been Made many things, but God has predestined men to be conformed to only One image, and that image, pattern, plan, etc., is the man who was, became and is all that He is by the glory of the Lord. He was, is and is to come only by the glory of the Lord.

There have been many great men, but only He who was planned by, born of, perfected by, guided by, strengthened by, exalted by and positioned by God's glory is God's image for man.

Men have many images they want us to take after, but God has only one, and that is Jesus Christ. To many, this is a stumbling block and rock of **offense** [they don't like this idea].
It flies into the face of human intelligence. It does not agree with most fathers, mothers, schools, and societies. For this is not their image for men. To many, the perfect image is a scientist, neurosurgeon, airplane pilot, orator, athlete, national leader, movie actor, rich man, college professor, doctor of medicine, T.V. commercial person, sports announcer, preacher, lawyer, politician, supreme court judge, etc. etc., etc., etc. all of which can never bring eternal life like only Jesus can.

Jesus the Only Image to be Transformed To

Jesus The Image of God is the only One-and it's permanent. It was given us in Jesus Christ before the world began. He's the light that lightens every man that cometh into the world.

To the church, which is the light of the world, God has predestined it to be conformed to The Image of His Son. This is life's highest goal—its ***summum bonum*** [the highest good] Its *ultima thule [the highest image]*.

To the church, which is the world's example, there is no other standard or image (the *Imago Dei* in Christ–***the image of God in Christ***). We behold the glory of God in The Image. As we continue to behold it with an unveiled face, we are transfigured in to the same image by the Spirit. Only the Holy Spirit can transform us into this image.

Men have self-made themselves, and yet are self-making themselves into many images—some of them are noble and good, yet they are not The Image which God has given and fixed for the church, the world's example; which transforms beholders to it by The Spirit.

There is One God, One Church, One Image, One Destiny! Only One!! Jesus Christ is "God's Glory Image " - He by glory and we by glory. We are brought into the likeness of God's Image of Glory by the Glory of The Image. By glory we behold The Glory. By Glory we come to glory . . . . . and by nothing else.

It is a great mistake to assume that we can come to the likeness of the glory of this great, glorious -being apart from the Glory of God i. e. The Holy Spirit. So Jesus said, ***"You must be born again of water and Spirit" or you cannot see or enter the Kingdom of God"***. The Kingdom of God has always been and is now a Kingdom of Glory. It is righteousness, peace, and joy in the Holy Ghost-and Jesus had it all by the Glory of The Father.

He was begotten and born by The Father's Glory.
He lived by The Father's Glory.
He died for us all by The Father's Glory.
He rose again from the dead by The Father's Glory.
He lives and reigns by The Father's Glory.
He saves the lost by The Father's Glory.
He will return and rapture His church by The Father's Glory.
He maintains His church by The Father's Glory.
He's God's glory creature! He's God's Image for all men who would live in glory and come at last to God's eternal glory.

The World's Images of Greatness and Success

The world's images of greatness and success can be:
Without God's wisdom
Without God's righteousness
Without God's power, glory
Without humility before God
Without service to God and man (*Pro Dei Et Homine*)
God's image of greatness and success includes each of these, for they were <u>all</u> <u>resident</u> in Jesus, <u>The Image of God.</u> God has said in Isaiah 55, "My thoughts are not your thoughts, neither are my ways your ways."
I. Thoughts by mind quality
II. Ways by nature

God's Image of Success

Jesus God's image, who is uniquely different from the world manifests to us through His life and character that success is based on humility and service to others-— "If any man will be great, let him be your servant."

Jesus Christ is the only person of the sacred pages designated which New Testament believers are TO BE (passive) conformed. There is NO OTHER, either in or out of the Bible.

We are not admonished to be conformed to the image of Abraham, Isaac, Jacob, David, Isaiah, Daniel, Paul, Peter, or even John the Revelator - George Washington, Abraham Lincoln, John Kennedy, Martin Luther King, our father, our mother, our husband, wife, sister, brother, lawyer, doctor, pastor or friend.

We, as preachers, are to highlight The Image in our preaching. We are to preach the words of, and about, the other great Biblical characters to establish and strengthen faith towards The Main Person Jesus Christ the Righteous **The Image of God.**

I write this to the Church, concerning how we deal with Jesus Christ, The Image. Today the church is bombarded with many proposed images; ideas, trends, programs, that vie for our attention. In these may be offered what we see as innovative approaches to ministry and the administration of the church. There is much, right in the realm of the Church world, to draw our attention away from the image. There is; programming, business concerns, and many other matters of the Church's dealings that can occupy our thoughts and drive our agendas and the source of our pursuits.

However, we must remember that for the church Jesus Christ and His Gospel is the only image and goal for the church to conform to. We must preach Him, Teach Him, and magnify Him in our worship.

The church should pursue the knowledge of the gospel of Jesus Christ, 'The Image' and preach it. For it is called by St. Paul 'the light' *"the light of the glorious gospel"* If we preach it, it will shine. If it shines and man receive it they will be transformed into the image of the glorious Son of God.

II Corinthians 4:1-5

Therefore seeing we have this ministry, as we have received mercy, we faint not;

[2] But have renounced the hidden things of dishonesty, not walking in craftiness, nor handling the word of God deceitfully; but by manifestation of the truth commending ourselves to every man's conscience in the sight of God.

[3] But if our gospel be hid, it is hid to them that are lost:

[4] In whom the god of this world hath blinded the minds of them which believe not, lest the light of the glorious gospel of Christ, who is the image of God, should shine unto them.

[5] For we preach not ourselves, but Christ Jesus the Lord; and ourselves your servants for Jesus' sake.

Conclusion The church has a sole image to which to be conformed - examples, yes, but only one Image—our LORD JESUS CHRIST, and He is so appointed by God!

Index of Manuscript Notes Pages
By Chapter
These are the pages of the original manuscript
notes that make-up the content of the Chapters:
They are identified by their Manuscript Search
Numbers and are noted as MS # in the chapters.

Appendix of Essays

The following Essays are included in this appendix : 76,86,97,98,99,113,125,126,127, 137,139,140,153

Manuscript notes page numbers are the Essay Numbers:
Essay 1a ,

You are Immanuel, the Christ,
The Messiah
The one destined for "The" Cross
The one to be the world's sin-heaven assigned to take away—away the sin (s) of the world
The one appointed to a unique resurrection, ascension and session (seating) on Heaven's throne. The only one chosen to found and administer and glorify the church!
Thou art the Christ! You are the one appointed by heaven to inherit a Name above every name—not only in this world, but in the world to come.
Look at: Things unique to Jesus!!!
His cross
His resurrection
His ascension
His session and Glory
His post –resurrection church
His coming rapture of saints

Essay 76

Immanuel's arrival added a new and different dimension, factor to time's realm. Eternity had come. Time's subjects would thereafter never be the same - i.e. the believing ones. He came to change the landscape of sin, satan, sorrow, sighing, disease, and death. He came to blunt and/or ameliorate their previous effects.

Time, satan and cohorts were all interrupted and intersected, as they dashed across human history, by the King of the ages, Immanuel.

Song: "Arise and shine for the light has come at last and Jesus is here (Immanuel) and the cloudy day is past. What a joy in my soul since The Comforter has come. He's brighter than the morning star. He's sweeter than the honey comb."

Only Immanuel could realistically change - i.e. in fact, our vocabulary on death.

Essay 85

"The High Ground of Humility"
God speaks above the mercy seat to find inanis, there, is to be on high ground.

Song: Lead Me to Calvary

Calvary, the ultimate "Inanis." In Genesis 1, darkness was indescribable. However, the Spirit of the Lord

moved upon the face of the deep darkness. On
Calvary, in Jesus' deep darkness, He was forsaken.
Psalm 138:2 - Magnified Thy word above all thy name.
MS 85

Essay 86
"The High Ground of Humility"
God speaks above the mercy seat to find inanis, there,
is to be on high ground.
Song: Lead Me to Calvary
Calvary, the ultimate "Inanis." In Genesis 1, darkness
was indescribable. However, the Spirit of the Lord
moved upon the face of the deep darkness. On
calvary, in Jesus' deep darkness, He was forsaken.
Psalm 138:2 - Magnified Thy word above all thy name.
MS86
"In search of inanis et vacua in order to find Dixitque
Deus." Humble yourself under the mighty hand of
God, that He may exalt you in due season. MS 87
This is recommended to read with Chapter 15
Immanuel from Humiliation to Exaltation

Essay 97-98
I Immanuel, everything about El's relationship to man
is expanded - and beyond measure. Everything moves
outside the boundaries of thought and language, e.g.
Immanuel's love passeth understanding. Immanuel's
peace passeth knowledge. I.e. is "thrown beyond..."

Appendix of Essays, Book I

In Immanuel, the apostle exclaims, "0, the depth of the riches both of the wisdom and knowledge of God, how unsearchable are His judgments and His ways past finding out!"

Only in Immanuel are the unsearchable riches of God super abundantly unsearchable.

In Immanuel, God's thoughts and ways not being our thoughts and ways take on a new, a different degree of immeasurableness. Never the disparateness so immeasurably pronounced as in Immanuel. (Yet union! Yet union!)

In Immanuel, God breaks all His past, previous records for greatness, for wisdom, for might, prudence, judgment, etc., etc., etc.

Eternity, time and eternity to come are composite in Immanuel. All that could or can ever be known of God is composite in Immanuel.

No wonder Saint Paul declared, Jesus Christ, the power of God and the wisdom of God - I Corinthians 1:24. He's not chiseled in stone on the libraries, but He ought to be.

Christ Jesus is the wisdom of God, INTO (poised) and out of (poured out). In Eum et Ex Eum.   MS 97
Jesus Immanuel read with humialtion chapter

Essay Page 98

God makes foolish the wisdom of the wise by producing a superior means for man's righteousness, holiness, power and peace. He destroys it, not by demolition, but by giving man something so superior to it that what man has to do the work of man is overshadowed by what God does (See II Corinthians 3). E.g. the agency of salvation in a man's heart transcends self-effort as day transcends night in glory. Mankind didn't condemn and destroy, per se, crank-starting cars, he simply made them foolish with an electric starter. Other examples: Electric irons; automatic washers and dryers; the automobile made traveling long distances by horseback foolish, e.g. gas furnaces, electric air-conditioning set over against hand fans, etc., etc., etc. For wisdom, sanctification, righteousness and redemption, nothing supersedes Christ. He makes all else obsolete!

The world by self-revelation, by self-discovery could never come upon and know Jesus Christ, a superior means to everything godly which man sought after. God has made foolish the wisdom of the world by the introduction to it of His wisdom and power, which is Christ, Immanuel.

The introduction of the incandescent lamp has made dressing by candlelight obsolete, foolish.

79 80 81 82

Essay 99

According to Colossians 2:3, "All the treasures of wisdom and knowledge are hidden in Immanuel. El has accumulated, stored, His wisdom/wealth for us in Him.

He, Immanuel, who has been for us, in His cross, blotted what was against us even the law of commandments contained in ordinances (Ephesians 2:15). He has broken down the middle wall of partition. He has slain the enmity, even the law. He has blotted out the handwriting (Colossians 2:14) and took it out of the way (way to perfect unions between God and man).

In the nature of the case of His name, Immanuel has/will remove everything that is contrary to us, against us being like God - one with Him. MS 99

Essay 113
Immanuel the great
"The greatest preposition; the greatest pronoun; the greatest power = Immanuel, **The Eternal Word.**

The greatest bridge, from two eternities it spans time. The greatest Jacob's ladder.

Immanuel is truly DeProfundis because its origin is God's bosom. Nothing is so (more) profound. Nothing provides a human being with such an exalted, immeasurable range of thought. In the thought world, Immanuel is all - transcending. It eclipses all areas of human philosophy. See Colossians. This is because Immanuel, Jesus Christ, is the wisdom of God and the power of God.

In God using "with" and "us" in His name, both the preposition and we, like Mary being chosen for Immanuel's mother; were highly favored. Mary became blessed among women, to be perpetually cited for her faith and humility, In Immanuel, God sanctified both "with" and "us" by His joining Himself with both." "With" greatest non-personal word in human language because it is used by God to relate

Him and His persons in the most unique way of all relationships. In Immanuel, God sanctified a small word "with," "cum," "anec," etc. - and earthen creatures by His eternal, unmeasured and forever measureless -presence. Short word - earthen creatures - eternal God. Here is Immanuel-what a person!
What a word! God could have used a long word and joined Himself in an angelic relationship and produced a longer, complex word - but not so "with" + "us" + God. MS113

The angels' tongues have no words so great, for Immanuel is greater than angels' tongues (See I Corinthians 13:1-2). Nothing in angels' vocabulary compares to Him, Jesus Christ, our Lord, Immanuel.

Man, first soil only, breath added.

Virgin, without a man to get his Son (by God's power).

Rib, without a chest to get a woman (by God's power).

Preposition, a relational word. Pronoun, not a noun - and with a pervious reference to a noun, pronoun without a sentence. With God "added" - by God's power, the greatest name.

A helping word + sons of the soil + El = The greatest name ever!

No wonder the late Bishop R. C. Lawson worshipped Jesus with the exclamation, "Bless His Matchless Name!" MS114
Recommended reading with chapters 1, 3, 4, 5, sign chapter

Appendix of Essays, Book I

Essay 125-126

Beyond Tenebrae(s)

Depthless beyond light-years and here are the deeps (depths) of God's emotions in Immanuel. There are depths conceived as downward. There are heights so high that they too are conceived as depths. God in Christ, in Immanuel, moves in both directions in His "withness" with men. He moves down to the fathomless depths of mercy, pity, sorrow, shame, suffering, pain, "ragedy," darkness, etc., etc., etc.

He moves upward in (Himself) in love, joy, etc., etc., etc., to depths of defying expression. E.g. "For the joy that was set before Him, He endured the cross - here is an undescribable joy (beyond light-years, measureless) conjoined with matchless endurance of humiliation, sorrow, pain, darkness, etc., etc., etc. Here the word "cross" is a metonym for everything, absolutely everything, that divine wrath could mean for time and eternity manward.

Only when God takes on the name Immanuel and saves man by the cross does He move this far in this downward (to) direction in His Godness, and gives us the revelation of scripture therefor. He moves to this unbounded depth only when He is with us. The only boundary of the cross is God's own infinity.

No one else can know this boundary.

The job awaiting God in Christ at the rapture of the church and the subsequent bestowal of eternal glory upon her, again is bounded only by God's infinity and none else knows this boundary.

Immanuel, then, is God manifesting His emotions towards man in ***ad infinitum*** both up and down ("that is if in God there is an "up" and "down") C.F. The astronaut's remark about "looking up" at the moon.

David's shepherd, Psalm 23; David's light, Psalm 27; Habakkuk's 3;17 assurance, - these all reach exponential proportion in Immanuel. They are all magnified by El in Immanuel. (Song: O Sweet Rest) What a rest is here in Immanuel! He said, "Come unto me...and I will give you rest." Immanuel's rest is an exceeding, transcending rest. It is the final rest of man. God will offer no rest to exceed it.

In Immanuel, we are brought face to face with incalculable incomprehensible distances respecting the heart of God in the depths - "up" and "down."

Immanuel has to do with El, God in the maximum exercise and revelation of His: Prudence, Precision, Passion, Power, towards His people.   MS125-126

Essay 127
"O the depths of the wisdom and knowledge of God. How unsearchable are His judgments and His ways past finding out" - Romans 11.

"Such knowledge is too wonderful for me, it is high and I cannot attain unto it" - Psalm 139:6.

Heights are depths and depths are heights. The Old Testament reference is to heights. The New Testament reference is to depths. .Would this be because that in Immanuel, the Old Testament "heights" are exceeded, become exceedingly high, and so become "depths" - depthless?

Immanuel is about the unsearchableness of God. His incomparability, His measurelessness comprehended in a Man with men. God never related to men by a man as He does in Immanuel. In Immanuel, the heights of love, peace, power, etc., etc., which saints in the Old Testament experienced with El, Elohim, Yahweh, Jehovah, became "depths of the riches" (Psalm 1 39 :6) in the New Testament.

What is "unattainable" in the Old Testament is "unsearchable" in the New . Testament . Synonyms ? Unattainable - see but can not reach ? Unsearchable - don't know where to look, cannot see?

Does what was unattainable, unsearchable, unmeasurable in the Old Testament become yet glorious in the Old Testament become more expansive, more glorious in the New Testament in Immanuel - and yet nearer, more personal? MS 127

Essay 129

St. Paul's visceral exclamations of Romans 11:33 concern Immanuel's work! Not:

1. The craft of spiders weaving webs

2. The hibernation of bears

3. The migration of birds and salmon (fish)

4. The honey - making of bees

5. The singing of whales (which change songs annually)

6. There production of man

7. The changing of seasons

But:

Immanuel's love, mercy, and work.

Essay 137

12-26-90

Immanuel's rest, Immanuel's Peace

Song: 0, Sweet Rest

"There remaineth therefore a rest to the people of God" - Heb. Immanuel's rest is a unique, powerful and glorious rest. It includes the

peace which passeth all understanding - it continues (in every age) to pass (all) understanding. The peace of Immanuel transcends the understanding of men in every era, no matter what their mental states, capacities, glories, etc., etc., etc. MS137

Essay 139

12-28-90 (2:15 a.m.)

Immanuel as the "Freedom of God" could turn water to wine. He could see through darkness. He could command wind and water - and walk on it. He could make fish and bread grow in His hands. He could eat and drink with sinners - and contrary to agnostic belief, He could inhabit the flesh while doing all of these things.

He could be made sin for men, die on a cross for them and in actuality, never stop living. To live while dying - to die while living, etc., etc., etc., etc. (Immanuel is El with the illimitable etc.)

To study Immanuel is to study God in the boundless reaches of His freedom - in His height - depths thereof - God manifests Himself as never so free as in Immanuel! (Though He was always absolutely free.) In Immanuel, God ultimately manifests His prerogative to be God, The Eternally Boundless .Free One. Only when we're glorified will we see into El's freedom which was exercised in Immanuel. We must remember He was " With Us God . " Two unequal, disparate entities, inextricably joined - joined for the transfer of God's Godness to us - not our humanity to God. He needed nothing from us to assist, help, enrich His Godness.

It was our fallen humanity which needed everything from "good sense" (wisdom) to immortality. We were fallen - not God. He was always the same. He was problem-free and problems' master. We were problem-laden and problem-victimized. He came, to be with us. Behold this glory! We didn't — and couldn't go to be with Him. So He came where we were, that Some day we could be like Him and be where He is.

Essay 153
Jesus Immanuel
Man, the dying living, living one - (wasn't able to cause this, and was).
Wasn't born this way, and was (by a new birth).
Page 172
Jesus Immanuel

3-23-91 (Seattle, WA) In St. John 3:16

God said it, then unsaid it, while leaving it said, so that only the voice of revelation could say what was being said and only the ears of faith could hear what was (then) being said.

God said it, cancelled it, while leaving it standing for the operation of revelation and faith to effect any further saying and hearing.

Only God's voice of revelation is speaking here. Only faith can hear the speech. Here God truly speaks with a various language. Clarity then befogging, only made clear by revelation - to which alone all is clear.

Terms pertaining to Immanuel's Humiliation and exaltation

I.   A. NADIRAL   B. ZENITHAL
II. A. ABYSMAL   B. THRONAL
III. A. PROFUNDITY   B. PROCERITY

The Name of Jesus Christ
As
Immanuel

Books II

The Complete Anthology
From the Original Manuscripts Notes

By Bishop James A. Johnson, D.D., M.Th.

Introduction

In this two book series on the name of Jesus Christ as Immanuel, the author, Bishop Johnson points out some commonly overlooked perspectives of the Gospel which were only fulfilled in Jesus Christ as Immanuel.

The points of revelation he shares in this series, though over looked by a large number of Bible students, are supremely significant to understanding the Gospel from the perspective of Jesus Christ as Immanuel.

In book I of the series, he breaks down the word-name Immanuel in its original divinely given syllable arrangement Imm/anu/El and shows that God intentionally arranged the syllables in their sequence on purpose. In the syllable arrangement of the name Imm/anu/El, God spelled out the entire spectrum of the Gospel of Jesus Christ; from His birth in Bethlehem to His enthronement in glory. In his expositions Dr. Johnson proves this from every side and clearly establishes how Immanuel's name confirms the Gospel and the Gospel confirms the name Immanuel.

Here in book II, he continues the discussion of Jesus Christ as Immanuel where he shares insight from the original manuscript notes [book II]. This book is a complete anthology of the writings Dr. Johnson on Immanuel which are in his manuscript notes in titled "The Name of Jesus Christ as Immanuel, book II". The revelations shared in the dated notes were received by the author in different settings and on different dates and were all entered into the manuscript. The entry dates for the notes are in the upper left of the passage. All of the notes from the manuscript notes book II are in this anthological book.

The common theme of the anthology is apparently centered on "**What God did in Immanuel Only".** Even though this edition of the two book series discusses many different works of Jesus Christ, all of the chapters and the note passages in this anthology are showing something that could **only be done in Immanuel.**

The author brings out the uniqueness of the life and the works of Jesus-Christ as Immanuel. He shows the specialness of Jesus by pointing out those **things that were and could only be fulfilled in Jesus Christ as Immanuel.**

He discusses the unique life and purpose of Jesus Christ by comparing Jesus' life to Adam's life and comparing Jesus 'world of things' to Adam's' world of things'. He sets forth that Jesus' main purpose was that we would have life and that more abundantly. In here Bishop

Johnson explains how *"He came to give us life by negating that which negates life"*.

He exposes in his discussion the specialness of Jesus-Immanuel in His works— Included in the discussion of Jesus' works is an insightful explanation of how Jesus was the only qualified sacrifice to die on the Cross and to go to Hell in our stead—the author shows us how His (Jesus') going to Hell on the Cross satisfied God's required penalty for us. By this the author shows us that only Jesus could satisfy the heart of God as a Hell victim.

The author shares a clear comparison between Moses' Old Testament sacerdotal system and that of Jesus Christ the Lamb of God, as Immanuel—showing that God's final and ultimate satisfaction was/and is in the Cross of Jesus Christ-Immanuel 'the Lamb of God' who takes away the sin of the world.

Here in book II, Dr. Johnson opens to us by discourse how God in Christ provided righteousness for us by His own blood. In Jesus Christ God made us something we were not 'RIGHTEOUS' by making Himself something He was not and had no bases for being; 'SIN'. *He who knew no sin became sin for us...*

He discusses how Christ's humiliation was an example for us and is very relevant to us in that the low things in Christ are really high things.

He discusses the greatness of Jesus compared to all of the Old Testament's things— the angels, Solomon, and Jonas. Hence, nothing superseded Jesus-Immanuel.

In here is an enlightening discussion on the purpose of the grace of God in Jesus Christ as Immanuel.

In the last chapter the author delves again as he did in book I into discussion of the transforming glory of Jesus Christ as Immanuel and gives more insight on the effects and *impact* of beholding Jesus Christ the image of the glory of God. In the face of Jesus Christ is the transforming glory of God.

All of what is included in this book is unique to ***Immanuel Only.***

Manuscript Editor Lawrence E. Brown, Jr.

Editor's Preface

    I thank God, Lady Juana J. Johnson (Editor and Chief) and Bishop James A. Johnson (author) for including me in this most precious project as Manuscript Editor. I have had a sense of awe from the beginning of the project and even up to now; the first edition of book II.

    In book I, The Name of Jesus Christ as Immanuel I had tried diligently to structure and transfer all of the information from the original manuscript notes which were so well written into chapters in that book. In transferring the contents of those notes and essays, I sought to keep the exact contextual meanings in every chapter that were in the notes. I structured the chapters from notes of like topics which were on different pages and different sections of the original manuscript notes. That process was very appropriate for book I.

    However, in this second volume of Johnson's thesis on the Name of Jesus Christ as Immanuel, Book II I present the unedited notes in the same order they are in the manuscript notes binder. They were presented good enough to be placed directly in the book without the tampering of an editor's input. I feared that tampering with their original presentation by writing chapter introductions or summing them up with editorial chapter conclusions was unnecessary.

As manuscript editor, I don't feel that any one of us, his students, could say what he is saying in his notes any better than he says it in his own words. Therefore, prudence led to this approach. By this procedure I safely present this book assuring that the exact content of the author is conveyed to the reader; because I only present his own words. By doing this, there are few or no editorial comments in the chapters. The reader gets the original thoughts of this great Apostolic Father.

I only sectioned the manuscript notes into chapters by dividing the notes at what seem to identify good dividing points.

The chapters are in the order as they came in the manuscript notes. This was done using the same approach to making chapters and verse that the translators of the King James Bible used when they took the original text in its original order and divided it into chapters and verses.

This book is structured like the book of Ecclesiasts wherein Solomon speaks his mind about wisdom, the passages are not all in order as in a thesis book but they are in the order that they come. That is the nature and order of this book it is ordered as presented by this great Apostolic Father Bishop James A. Johnson in his notes manuscript. It is a collection of his notes and thoughts.

It is important to know that this book is presented with very little editorial thought injections. I did not try to change the indenting, punctuation, grammar nor the wording of the notes. I think you will agree with me as you read that the notes are good enough to explain the concepts. They don't need to be tampered with.

I only put the meanings of some of the Latin terms that might be unfamiliar to readers in the margins to the right of the text and or in footnotes. I also defined certain words in a glossary-appendix [Appendix A] in the back of this book. I have put study questions in each chapter, as a guide and interactive component for the reader.

Book Features

This book is a complete collection of the notes of Dr. James Johnson which are in his manuscript; " Notes on The Name of Jesus Christ as Immanuel Book II" It is a theological anthology of notes from the mind of a Great Apostolic father, whom God has given a keen insight into the Gospel of Jesus Christ from the perspective of Immanuel.

Dates: in the chapters usually in the upper right hand of the passage is the date that the notes were entered into the original manuscript.

Editors Input: are in black italics.

Hand written fonts: are notes added by the author in to the manuscript in his own handwriting—write-ins by the author.

Study Questions: are in the front of each chapter. The answers to the study questions are somewhere in the chapter in bold. The questions and their answers are also in the back of the book.

Definitions of words and meanings of phrases: the definitions of commonly unfamiliar words are written in the right margin of the page and or in parentheses immediately following the word or phrase or in footnotes.

Appendix A defines and explains special words pertaining to Immanuel's humiliation and exaltation. It especially includes those words and terms from the Latin which are used by the author, a number of times throughout the entire work [Book I and Book II].

Literary Composition This book is like the book of **Ecclesiastes** in that both books are a collection of passages (anthology) received by the authors over time and in different settings. All of the passages are put into a book with chapters and passages. As Ecclesiastes presents rich clusters of wisdom about life under the sun, here in this book, Bishop Johnson presents rich clusters of insight concerning Jesus Christ as Immanuel.

**Here in Book II, Dr. Johnson Insightfully
Presents
Divinely Extraordinary things God Did**

'In Immanuel Only'

As Solomon [the preacher] speaks of wisdom in the 'The
Book of Ecclesiastes; so dose Bishop Johnson [the preacher]
in this book, speak (write) of
"The Name of Jesus Christ as Immanuel"
As *Solomon imparts wisdom verse by verse, in the book of
Ecclesiastes, So does Dr. Johnson in this anthology, chapter
by chapter, impart insight into the Gospel from the
perspective of Jesus Christ as
Immanuel*
**In Here are the original Notes from the Mind of a
Modern Apostolic Father**

Chapter 1

THE LIFE AND PURPOSE OF JESUS CHRIST

Study Question: *Relative to El's [God's] relationship to Immanuel, Him being in the thought of God and thus in the bosom of the father; what word does the author use to describe the relationship of El to Jesus Christ that brought us our salvation?*

4-1-90
Jesus Christ spent His life for and gave His life for the LIFE of man. "I am come that they ...."
"The Son of Man is come not to be served but to serve and give His life a ransom for many."
What if, with Jesus' unmeasured breadth of mental capacity and boundless physical energy, would have been a scientist, mathematician, doctor, lawyer, engineer, etc., what would He have done to change "the world" for His interests? Rather He came to revolutionize man's relationship to living and LIFE EVERLASTING. His mission was not money or might or earthly majesty - but LIFE or mental giantism for man - and that more abundantly. He was the greatest!
Jesus was smart enough to have been anything - merchant, banker, manufacturer, farmer, lawyer, doctor, teacher, coach, jeweler, corporate executive, etc., etc., etc., yes anything! Yet, He, the greatest man who ever lived or would live, lived for, was committed totally to, LIFE. History's ideal person was the Son' • of God, a servant, a minister, a supreme sacrificer, yes, a man whose mission was LIFE
We cannot be equal to Jesus, but we can follow Him. Our greatest concern in life can be LIFE. We can support, i.e. be committed to LIFE. Jesus lived for life. He died for LIFE! He said, "My kingdom is not of this world...." (to Pilate, the governor)

"Then would my children fight that I ... but now is my kingdom not from hence..."

We cannot die on His cross. We cannot be the Lamb of God, but our greatest purpose for living can be LIFE ETERNAL Our first consideration for existing can be LIFE - yes and not the last consideration!

The Glory of God is in the face of Jesus!

"God raised Him up and gave Him glory that our faith and hope might be in God."

The Effects of Beholding the Glory of God
2-11-91

"We beholding the glory of God ..." - II Corinthians 3

"The glory of God is in the face of Jesus Christ?

Here we see that the glory of God, full-orbit, full circle, full-scale, full-spectrum all across, up and down is in Immanuel. To see the fullest revelation of the operation of God's glory manwards, we must, for we can only, behold it in Christ Jesus, Our Lord, Immanuel!

From profundis to in excelsis ad gloriam infmitam immensis Emmanuhel Solus.

The glory of God is in Christ!

From Humility to Exaltation
2-19-91

"Humble yourselves therefore under the mighty hand of God that you might be exalted in due season."

Note the word "exalted."

How can one be exalted from a state of humility unless humility is itself a high place?

In Christ Jesus all places are high places. The low places are high and the high places are high.

The Spirit which directs to and sustains in humility is the same Spirit which promotes to glory. One glory is the glory in the depths and the glory in the depths and the glory in the heights.

Low ground is high ground. High ground is high ground. Gloria in excelsis is everywhere in Christ Jesus.

"From mountain tops of humility to high plains of glory."

Apostle John did not see the Holy City from a valley, but from an exceeding high mountain. He was on high when, in glory he saw the city having the glory of God. John was on Patmos, in The Spirit, on The Lord's Day, on an exceeding high mountain when he saw the Holy City.

"Exalted to God's Ground Level" in order to exalted to His sunlit summits of ever-expanding glory.

Faith is God's first high place, plateau for us. When God engenders faith in a man, this puts him, at once, on high ground - no matter where he goes from thence - and it can only be somewhere higher, i.e. to gloria expanded; from faith to faith; from grace to grace; strength to strength; light to light; glory to glory.

Song: "Is Not This The Land of Beulah
Blessed, Blessed, Land of Light?"

God giveth grace to the humble - those on a high place.

Religion with Man Compared to the Eternal Things of Hope in God

    A.   Old birth and old direction
    B.   Attempt at: Old birth and new direction
    C.   New birth and new direction
    D.   New birth and old direction

Here is religion with men or non-religion.

Hope - External life and its related eternalities. These save us. These are all invisibilities. These do not in any wise belong to Adam's domain. They are wholly other.

A world of ever-abiding, eternal, never-fading (fadeless) glory; glory all-transcendent! A world ethereal, unmatched and forever matchless. Indescribably beautiful. Too marvelous for words.

Justification and Salvation Only through Him
4-9-91

In Romans 5th chapter, we see God in Christ, Immanuel addressing our depravity in His absolute power and supra absolute power.

vs. 8 We were sinners, our absolute slavery. Immanuel addressed this in His absolute freedom to die for us. His freedom to be, to choose, to do.

vs. 6 We were without strength (dead weight, helpless, limp). This was addressed by Immanuel's absolute strength to bear pain, suffering, death and divine judgment Here His absolute knowledge was brought to bear upon our situation. We were absolutely ignorant as to how to affect a way of deliverance for ourselves. We didn't have standing to execute salvation. We didn't have knowledge of anything, including God to bring about our deliverance from sin, so 'by His knowledge, He justified us."

We were without strength - so Immanuel's strong arm brought salvation - His absolute strength.

We were sinners - so Immanuel's absolute righteousness, obedience, holiness came to bear.

We were enemies - so Immanuel's absolute sonship, relationship, fellowship, union with the Father, His **_bosomness"_** with the Father was what heaven recognized and so by which full salvation came to us - by One Man.

Now, much more - Here is Immanuel's supra-absolutism. Only Immanuel can know this realm of His greatness. It is too wonderful for us. It is high, we cannot attain unto it. We can only accept the revelation by faith - and so live.

We cannot truly know what precedes "much more" - how can we then know beyond "much more"? vss. 9, 10

Note: "Much more we shall be." "It does not yet appear what we shall be." Note: "Being now justified...we shall be" "being reconciled...we shall be." Justified by blood (His). Reconciled by death (of His Son).

220

Only Jesus can Give Life and Negate the Negation of Life

11-13-87 (K.C., MO)

The gift of life and the negation or the annulment of life inhere in human conception. Only Jesus Christ, who bestows pure life can negate the negation of life. Our human hope is a deathful hope, life mixed, mingled with death. "In the midst of life we ARE in death." Jesus begets us unto a deathless hope! - A lively hope.

5-14-91 St. Louis

Note: **Our parents' Copulation which Produced Us:**

Was both a pleasurable act and the propagation of death simultaneously - both the pleasure of the flesh and a death sentencing process together. Pleasure for them - death in the end for us. It gave existence and guaranteed the destruction of existence which it gave at the same time. The act transferred both life and death. Because of corruptible seed (see Rev. D. Jordan). In the incarnation, God bypassed the pleasurable act of both male and female in order to produce a being who by His act of birthing men into eternal life would start an ultimately
deathless "race."

Jesus begets us unto an untainted, uncorrupted and incorruptible hope. He alone! He who alone is Immanuel.

Immanuel's Healing and Life

11-14-87 (ICC., MO)

"Man's hurt; God's Heart; Immanuel's Healing (All are great) -

God the greater!

"Man's misery; God's mercy; Immanuel's might.

Grace greater than sin

Medicine greater than disease Physician greater than patient

Grace greater than disgrace

Our first birth after the first man could not give us permanent glory. Neither could it transcend death. Therefore God in His unbounded mercy gave us a second birth by the Spirit of a man through whom it was proven by witnesses and many infallible proofs that He had mastered death and possessed permanent (eternal) glory. (approved)

God proved His purpose (man) before He set the world-work in motion. He put the first man to death, buried him and left him dead to prove that eternal life and eternal glory were not in him. He raised the new and second man up and gave Him glory in the presence of many witnesses to say to distressed mankind, "Your only hope is in this man."

The negative evidence of weakness and incapability is in Adam - He does not exist. The positive evidence of power and capability is in Jesus Christ! He ever lives. Hence there are two roots:

A.   The root of our first birth, Adam which is now dead and gone.

B.   The root of our second birth which is Jesus Christ, alive, gone away, yet eternally active.

Ecclesiastes is Adam's book.

Ephesians is Jesus' book.

We do not need faith at all to be affected by Adam's realm of vanity and death - i.e. nothing alive or dead is mentally needed. The whole enterprise is essentially dead anyway.

Not so with Jesus! To be a part of His living realm, something must be done. To enjoy the living benefits of this living man (one), one must have a living faith - a mind alive with Spirit-induced life. To die in Adam we need nothing, need do nothing. To live in Christ, we must have the faith of or from the Living One, The Son of God.

Adam's Life Compared to Eternal Life

In Adam, "the grass withereth, and flower fadeth, and the fashion thereof falleth away because the Spirit of The Lord bloweth upon it."

In Jesus Christ, one goes "from glory to glory."

In Adam, the outward man perisheth.

In Christ, the inward man is renewed day by day.

Jesus Christ, our Lord, is man's only "non-witherant," "non-fadant" agent. "0, come, come, come Immanuel and ransom captive Israel."

Chapter 2

JESUS, GREATER THAN ANYTHING ELSE

Study Questions: *1. How is Jesus' might mightier than that of angels? 2. What does Jesus have that angels do not have?*

He is greater than anything He is compared to
Jesus Immanuel's Might Compared to that of Angel's Might
Jesus' Might after the resurrection far supersedes angles Might.
The Blood of Jesus Speaks better things than the Blood of Abel and is much more powerful than Satan's opposing forces.
Jesus Supersedes all that was prior to Him[OT]

Post-Calvarian Is after the cross and resurrection

6-26-91
Angelic might and Jesus' Post-Calvarian Might Contrasted

6-25-91
   Angelic might - created might contrasted with the might available to saints by the blood of Jesus.
   Angelic might is the might beings, of divine direction exercised without God's blood, i.e. without God's life given up.
   The might saints exercise by Jesus' blood is the life energy vouchsafed to men by the life God in Christ gave up. It is life by life - given up. It is blood-might. Angelic power is bloodless might.

In Daniel, Michael fought 21 days with the Prince of Greece and Persia and prevailed - with bloodless might. We can surely prevail over demons and devil power with the might vouchsafed to us by Immanuel's blood - blood might.

We have a salvation that angels desire to look into (I Peter 1:12. The glory of which we are a part in Jesus Christ is the zenith, pinnacle, the ultimo. Thule of all of God's manifested glory. It is post-calvarian or post-sacrifice, post-blood glory. There is no glory to compare to this glory!

We all come to the blood which speaketh better things than the blood of Abel (i.e. the blood of his which was shed by his brother). Abel's blood called for justice, vengeance, reprisal. Jesus' blood calls for power, fellowship, glory, rest, peace, eternal life, etc., etc.

Note: "The Speech of Jesus' Blood"

'The Speech of Abel's Blood"

'They that are with us are more than they who are with them." In Hebrews 12 the final thing mentioned is the "blood of sprinkling." Nothing in this text supersedes the blood. It is final even to the innumerable company of angels.

In this text nothing exceeds the blood of Jesus! In the blood all the meaning of Christian religion culminates, summates, is made final. Consummatum est is only *at* The Cross!

The ultimate power, glory, might and meaning for man as decided by God is finalized in the Cross, the blood of Jesus. Nothing comes to man from God in grander fashion than comes from Jesus' blood - e.g. God's ultimate name (Philippians 2:9) rests on His blood!

"His oath, His covenant, His Blood support me in the whelming flood. I Peter 1:12

Angels' ministry is a "preliminary," a "fringe benefit" to believers. Jesus' activities are the "main attraction" to our Christian existence, glorious, incomparable.

Angelic Might - Christian Might contrasted.

The cross is the ultima thule of all of God's planning, willing, purposing, manifesting, naming. It is His final "therefore," His ultimate "wherefore" and "because." There is no Divine causation which exceeds or transcends the cross! Anything which God vouchsafes to mankind by or i.e. because of the cross towers immeasurably beyond whatever He vouchsafed to man without the cross. Hence none of God's Old Testament, pre-calvarian names are as fraught with meaning as His post-calvarian name, Jesus! Post-calvarian Jesus is God's ultimate name, for by Him (His cross) He gave Himself His ultimate cause for benefitting man!

Now, then, in reference to our war weapons, the apostle says, 'The weapons of our warfare are not carnal, but are mighty through God (through God's work via the cross)..." Our weapons are Cross-related. Satan had no cross. He shed no blood. He amasses no cross-artillery. This is the unique province of Christian believers. Our weapons are new and incomparable weapons.

"I fear no foe with Thy hand near to bless" - i.e. Thy post-calvarian hand. So, the fathers song, "Lord, keep my soul from day to day under the blood ....
The cross is God's ultimate "via," means by which, channel, medium, cause for anything.

The ultimate why, wherefore, because and therefore; the ultimate "where upon," "for this cause"; the ultimate and eternal "show cause."

Jesus Christ, the Wisdom of God

Jesus Christ, the wisdom of God is made unto us wisdom, righteousness, sanctification and redemption.

There is none so great in any realm - not even Satan's. Jesus Christ, Lord is the wisdom of God and the power of God. These are the "core" of any living being - wisdom and power, wisdom and strength. These are the glory of the living creature. Song: "All I Need." Satan cannot match these. Jesus is not these things to angels via a cross, for He did not die for them.

We've been reconciled to God by the cross. O' what a friendship! Anything by the cross is "out of sight."

Jesus' post-calvarian wings are incomparable ... "Healing in His wings." The wings of Jesus:
Pre-calvarian
Post-calvarian

Nothing Previously Given by God, Even in the Old Testament, Supersedes the Power of the Blood
6-28-91

Anything "By Him" or "By His Blood," in the nature of the case is unprecedented. Nothing like it precedes it. Nothing like it succeeds. What is by Him cannot be found in the Old Testament. What is by Him will not be transcended in the New Testament.

St. Paul? (The Hebrews' writer) exhorted us or made reference to those who come unto God "by Him." Here then, is a "new breed" of comers. Here are comers with some kind of super advantage over all prior comers. Note the "By Hims" of the book of Hebrews. St. Peter in I Peter Chapter 5 makes reference to our being called unto God's eternal glory "by Him." Here too, is access to some new "dimension" for believers in God's glory, not previously available.

No wonder the angels desire to look into it. It is a "new dimension" of glory; an unprecedented gift; a new area - an aspect of glory the angels were not familiar with before Jesus came and became man's divine "via" into the riches of God. The Hebrews' writer said, "God having provided some better thing" for us. We are indeed "Kings and priests unto God, having been made so, "By Him." No precedent - no succession!

"By Him" is the term of the Bible which has to do with God's ultimate. IT is a signpost to incomparable glory! Jesus, Immanuel, was heaven's ultimate man. Only He could bring us to ultimate benefits. He, alone, is heaven's ultimate benefactor!

6-29-91

Has God, as He did with Adam, barred us from the "tree of life" of miracles, and mighty acts of His in the near-end of the twentieth century? If so, why would He bar us?
Jesus Christ is the same yesterday, today and forever! Does this have a present and relevant meaning to us modern saints?

Chapter 3

JESUS-IMMANUEL THE SAME BEING, FROM
HUMILIATED TO EXALTATION

Study Question: *Sin reached it maximum in Christ, how did He respond to it?*

The Lord Jesus is both cross and throne He is the same being who is like a caterpillar being transformed into a butterfly, He went through the Cross, through the grave and to glory 'the same being'

This chapter answers the study question "Where is Jesus Now"?
The Same being-Jesus
6-10-91

Our Lord Jesus Christ, Immanuel, **the only man** who has ever lived, or ever will live, who was both "Cross and Throne compatible." He was the only man who could qualifiedly be equal to both. Only because He was absolutely equal, or compatible with hell was He too, compatible with God's Throne! See Philippians 2. He went to God's appointed nadir. He went to God's appointed zenith. He that ascends is the same that descended first into the lower parts of the earth. He is, that is, the same being, character, person. He is not another - another Son, Lord, Master, Servant, Saint, etc., etc., etc. He is the same being who was crucified, dead and buried.

A caterpillar which experiences metamorphosis in the cocoon is the same creature which weaves (spins) the cocoon but he (it) experiences a change. It's not a matter that one creature goes into the cocoon and a wholly other creature emerges. There is a single life which moves through the entire process with the being encased in the cocoon. However at the end of the metamorphosis days, a "new" creature, different" creature emerges, but the same being. The mode of movement is different, color may be different, its glory is different It has been transformed by the process of metamorphosis, yet the same fundamental creature.

Jesus' World –An Exceeding World
6-12-91

Jesus' world of things is "an exceeding world," a world beyond the thoughts and acts of men. It is a world upon which, as author and finisher, everything is inherently "copyrighted." It cannot be copied or reproduced. It is a unique world. In His kingdom, the righteousness of the citizens must exceed the righteousness of the scribes and Pharisees (with all of their laws for producing righteousness). He makes promises to His adherents which are exceeding great_ He Himself has ascended up far above all heavens. Jesus is not competing with men, for He has no qualified competitors. Actually, the field of life where Jesus operates is not a level field - everything is highly tilted in His favor.

A key word in Jesus' Kingdom is "exceed." Jesus is not attempting to make mere "better Adams," but "new" ones. He's not competing with Adam's line of rich men to give His Sons more of the world's riches than Adam, but to give them "true riches," eternal riches, incomparable riches, unique riches.

"Behold I make all things new."

St. Paul makes reference to "newness of life" in Romans 6:4. Newness of-life here is not equivalent to Adam's "good religion." Peace with God through Jesus is an incomparable peace.

Our justification, based (Chapter 4) on His resurrection is a unique justification. It has nothing at all to do with self-attainment. Our justification is absolutely new! Our peace is absolutely new! Our access is absolutely new! (new wisdom; New strength).

Since our access is by Him, it cannot be like any other access (and now by faith I have access to Him All through His precious <u>blood</u> (the unique blood could not provide a common or unusual access - but uncommon, unusual). We cannot imagine or explain the scope hereof! It is great, however!

Our rejoicing of hope is also unique.

....and not one(ly) so, but we glory in tribulations also, knowing.

Note: Jesus`blood was shed before He was glorified - then we were justified by Jesus' "natural blood," but we shall be saved by His glorified life - which is Heaven's own degree(s) beyond. Jesus' blood was incomparable, though unglorified. It contained all it needed to contain in its natural, holy, precious state. *The shedding thereof qualified Jesus to go into His super glorious, eternal administrative state - where He now, saves, sanctifies, exalts, glorifies and makes His saints immortal. (Saves from wrath, too.)*

Grace much More

Note the term "much more."

vs. 9 "through Him," the exalted glorified supranominated Christ. vs. 10 "by His life," the exalted, glorified supranominated Christ. Note vs. 3, "and not one(ly) so, but we glory ... also.

Note vs. 11, "and not one(ly) so, but we also joy in God through our Lord Jesus Christ, <u>by</u> whom we have received the atonement (the unique one's action is the figure).

Note St. Paul says ... But not as the offense ... much more the grace of God, and the gift of grace, which is by one man, Jesus Christ .... Here is Immanuel!

What is in Christ must always exceed. It must always be new and different! In Adam - death.

In Christ - abounding grace and God's gift.

Adam right or wrong, obeying or failing was limited in what He could give of good, blessings, life or death.

Immanuel, exalted is with limits of neither power, blessings or life. New creature - Galatians 6:15; See also 5:6.

Where Sin Abounded Grace did Much More Abound

7-11-91

"Where sin abounded Grace did much more abound"

The fact of sin and the consequence of death abounded unto the necessity of a "Handler" for both. That Handler was by necessity Immanuel. He, who was wiser and stronger than both disposed of both by His own body on the tree. "Thou hast laid help upon One who is mighty? Note, 'The Mighty Immanuel." More mighty to handle the abundance of sin and death than these two were to eventuate into His death, by either cause or volume.

"The Answer of Immanuel to the question of sin and death was far greater than the "question" itself. The glories vouchsafed by Him are more abundant than the "causes" of sin and death. **Sin reached its "max" of abundance in Jesus. He responded to it by His person and His work more abundantly. This is how Immanuel was Christus Victor; by His person and His work, He gave back for sin and death more than both brought to Him. And he accepted the "max" of what they brought to Him!**

Chapter 4

JESUS THE ONLY QUALIFIED SACRIFICE
Immanuel only was Fit to Satisfy God's Demands for Hell and Blood Atonement
Study Questions: *1. Did Jesus go to hell?*
2. If so what happened to Jesus in hell?

> St. John 1:29
> 'The next day John seeth Jesus coming unto him, and saith, Behold the Lamb of God (Adonai), which taketh away (beareth) the sin of the world. *What strength?*
> And looking upon Jesus as He walked, he (John Baptist) saith, Behold the Lamb of God! (Adonai)

Jesus the Lamb of God Takes Away our Sins
>> ***The whole sordid mess***
>> ***The entire Volume***

A Lamb, both WISE AND MIGHTY! RIGHTEOUS, LOVING OBEDIENT MS 29

Our Sins
They can't go up.
They can't go down.
They can't go East, West, North, South.
They can't go to the land fill.
They can't go to any other land area.
They can't go into the air.
They can't go into the seas.
They can't go into the planets.
They can't be placed on the stars.
They can't go to inner space nor outer space.

The whole sordid mess
The entire Volume

Referring to our sins

Where did they go?

By the body that bore them they must be taken away. The body that was taken away! Where is it? Find the body - find our sins.

Isaiah 53:10
..., and the pleasure of the LORD (Jehovah) shall prosper in His hand.

Isaiah 53:11
He shall see the travail of His soul, and shall be satisfied: by His knowledge shall my righteous servant justify man; for he shall bear (*one that is mighty*) their iniquities.

Jesus Christ the Only Qualified Sacrifice
7-29-91 (New Orleans, LA)

Only Jesus Christ could go to hell and satisfy the heart of God by going. For only He had the heart to feel all, understand all the reasons - including what the penalty for being in hell meant in relationship to the hurt of the heart of God. Any sinner who goes to hell will definitely be punished while being there, but his going to hell will never be an "Quietist Finalis," for the lost sinner will lack the heart which is necessary - as well as the kodil - capacity to satisfy the heart of God. **Jesus Christ Immanuel was the only human being ever, who had the dual capacity (mind and body) to fulfill all of the requirements of God for a damned soul. Only with His mind could He plumb all the depths of the ramifications of sin against God**. No other person has had, has now, or ever will have the mind of Christ which was necessary to fathom sin and Divine judgment.

Immanuel's Decent into Hell-Only One Qualified to Go

Note: "His grace, alone, can fathom sin and make my heart all white within."

235

Only with this mind could a hell - victim satisfy the heart of God - and God will never, never, not even once give this feeling, knowing mind to another. God will not allow another human being in either time or eternity to have the mind to fully feel the depths of eternal judgment - not even those who go to hell. God will not give this unique mind to men. He will give them the mind of Christ to follow Christ and to eventually know eternal glory and joy, but never to "go to hell with" - to experience the joys of heaven and eternity - yes, but not hell. This mind began and ended with Jesus Christ, Our Lord Immanuel.

The Experience of Death and Hell Which Was for Jesus-Only

God denies and isolates, for His own reasons, every man, from the pangs of the depths of hell. He'll allow us to share eternal joy and peace with Him, but not *so with* hell, not even sinners who eventually go to hell. They will go there alone, not with Jesus either in mind or in body. No man accompanied/ nor-will accompany-Jesus to hell. That was His unique province. He went alone. He'll take us to heaven with Him, but hell is forever "His private experience." He gives to men the mind and spirit by which to follow Him to glory, but never the mind by which He descended to hell, the lower parts of the earth. In other words, we can know the joys of Christ in heaven, but never His sorrows of hell, except in believing. Hence, no man can ever truly know hell as Jesus knows it - and knew it. "The psychology of hell" will forever be hidden from men. It's depths of emotion will be private, unique to Jesus forever. Hallelujah what a Savior who could take a poor lost sinner lift him from the miry clay and set him free. I will ever tell the

236

> *It story shouting glory! Glory! Glory! Hallelujah! Jesus ransomed me!*
> *From the depths of sin and sadness to the heights of joy and gladness Jesus lifted me ... in mercy full and free ..."*

Only Calvary was God's finished judgment. His only Odor Quietis Finalis - all other judgments are "unfinished." Only the Messiah made an end to sin and brought in everlasting righteousness - and this only because He made an end to sin. Only Calvary concludes the issue of sin with the heart of God. In hell sinners will simply be there suffering, but not to the "satisfaction" of God.

> As sinners burn in hell for eternity, God will only look back to the cross when He seeks His own heart-satisfaction for the punishment of sin.

Jesus-Immanuel had the Only Mind Capable to Go to Hell and Satisfy God's Demands for It
7-30-91

The only mind which could wholly experience hell and thus satisfy God's heart by the experience, was the mind of or (in) Christ Jesus - the mind vested in Him of God. This mind had never before been vested in another. In the future, as long as God lives, it will never be vested in another for this unique purpose. When holy scripture says "let this mind be in you which was also in Christ Jesus," it has nothing to do with the <u>full and final</u> experience of hell - that is a mental and physical experience which includes the absolute human capacity and the absolute "divine capacity" to experience the event.

> Would God as a just judge spare Adam and his children the death of the Cross and give them the lighter sentence of hell because of mental retardation due to the fall? ... and send Jesus to the "cross-hell" because of what He knew? States are slow to execute the mentally retarded.

The scripture says, "never a man spoke like this man." Neither did ever a man feel and sense man and God as this man. **ONLY BECAUSE JESUS WAS GOD** -* could He feel all God put in hell for man and God. As God with us (men) He felt both the hurt of man and God absolutely - and He knew all of the reasons.

The Father knew that the Son knew all the ramifications of death #1. From Adam, whose mind was retarded in the fall, to all men who died thereafter, none knew the full ramifications of death. Only Immanuel did. Therefore, death was a punishment for man, but not a satisfaction to God of His wrath. In the case of death #2, none but the only begotten Son of God who was in the bosom of the Father and therefore experienced a spiritual osmosis of intelligence or wisdom could die death #2 and satisfy God. "Thou shalt see the travail of His soul (only) and be satisfied.

Jesus went to death #1 and death #2 willingly, submissively, knowingly.

Men don't go to either death with all these characteristics. Sometimes willingly, as in war, as in a mother who seeks to save a child from a burning building, but never knowingly - for no man understand the God/death factor.

"By His knowledge shall my righteous servant justify many."

Only because Immanuel had a most perfect understanding of all the ramifications of death, and willingly experienced it, did He fulfill God's righteousness thereby and thus satisfy the heart of God. The death of every other man therefore, is simply a judgment, a punishment, but not a "satisfaction." He Himself finds this only in Immanuel's cross. From time throughout the boundless reaches of eternity, God finds only one "satisfaction" for man's sins - i.e. Immanuel's cross. God's (Odor Quietis Finalis - in fact!) Not death #1, not death#2, but the Cross! The Cross!

> ...but the dear Lamb of God left His glory above to bear it to dark Calvary.

Jesus, the only Perfectly Qualified Sacrifice fo the Sins of the World

Jesus Christ, Immanuel had to have absolutely perfec knowledge before He could justify us from all things fron which we could not be justified by the law of Moses.

Had He been in the least bit ignorant of the salvationa process from 1-2 (death 1 & 2), He could never have come to "consumtnatum Est." E.G. He had to know:

I. Of whom - God who commanded (the authority or demand)

Odor Quietis Finalis: final and satisfying sacrifice.

"consumtnatum Est.": The finished complete sacrifice –it is finished St. John 29:10

II. To whom - God who would perfectly receive only what was perfectly perfect - He who sought an "Odor Quietis Finalis "

III. Why - Sin as a curative agent as well as the profundity of God's hurt. Note: Mercy as "healing by nurturing."

IV. For whom - us in totality.

V. What (of the why) The depths of the character of sin.

VI. Unto which - deaths 1 and 2 in total character.

VII. By whom - the character of His own holiness as a qualifier for sacrifice faultlessness, holiness, perfect obedience, i.e. the position of the sacrifice in relationship to God. E.G. "Father, I know that thou hearest me for I always do those things that are pleasing in thy sight."

VIII.   Where, whereunto ("a whereless" where for the sin to go).

IX. Wherefore - the result, life eternal.

In Jesus' sacerdotal System, He:

I.   Was the sacrifice being brought to the priest.

ii.   Was the man who brought it to the priest.

Iii   Was the Priest who offered the sacrifice on the altar.

IV.   As God, was the One who received the sacrifice in Glory.

The whyness

The whatness

The whoness

If a man told me to remove something from one place to another, I'd have to have some idea as to where the other place was. What if he gave a what and a how to do it, but no where? What could I do? The lack of "a where" would immobilize me.

Jesus was commanded, charged, authorized, directed and equipped to take our sins away, after bearing them in His own body on the tree - after the tree - where?

He could not deposit them in heaven and contaminate it. He could not deposit them on earth and thus leave the earth as it previously was, i.e. full of sins. He could not "dump" them in the sea or release them into the atmosphere. They had to be removed from the presence of God, angels and men. Where, had He not been God, and under such conditions, would He have placed them? Yet Jesus took our sins away. No preposition. No object of preposition.

Only Immanuel could take away the sins of the world. Only the Lamb of God (who came from God) Only by Him could a super day of Atonement have been effected! Jesus' blood is precisely as He said, "the blood of a NEW testament."

Moses' Sacerdotal System Contrasted with Jesus' Sacerdotal System

On the day of atonement, two goats - kids, symbols of weakness and ignorance - insufficiency. They didn't know they had blood, much less its worth - or how shedding it related to man. "With sacrifices and offering thou was not well pleased, but a body hast thou prepared me."

8-21-91

Moses' sacerdotal system contrasted with Jesus' sacerdotal system contrast the ignorance and dimensional place where the scapegoat went with Jesus- The animal whose blood was sprinkled on the mercy seat. He knew nothing about sin and mercy - nor did he understand death. Jesus understood all three - "ally." (Even the fit man who conducted the scapegoat into the uninhabited wilderness was not actually "fit" for what he was dealing with. Neither he nor the goat understood sin, abandonment and death. The priest who put his hands on the goat really did not understand the seriousness and weight of the "passing sins." The scapegoat was neither mentally nor physically able to carry the Israelites' sins The fit man wasn't fit. The animal wasn't fit. The wilderness wasn't fit. The helpless animal standing isolated and abandoned in the wilderness didn't understand his ignorance and lostness. A lost animal for sinful men - a picture of insufficiency. Moses' sacredotal system was a system fraught with incapacity and ignorance in priest, worshipper and victim. These sacrifices could never take away, sins because:

1. They lacked mental and physical capacities to carry such heavy loads.
2. They didn't know why they were victims (no consciences).
3. They, being ignorant of the whole scheme, didn't know where to put them.
4. They had no "whereless" where, no "placeless" place to put them. To take them away this had to be a factor.

Only the caring One, Immanuel could do this! "Behold the Lamb of God that taketh away the sin of the world." 'Thou has placed help upon One who is mighty."

With reference to a man's sins, how could he think past a poor, bleeding, helpless, ignorant, speechless lamb, bull, heifer, or goat to God? Only Immanuel was capable enough and wise enough to make the sacerdotal system for man really "work."

Jesus the Only Qualified Sacrifice

7-15-91

The Emotions of Jesus (on our behalf) as He anticipated and experienced the nadir of the cross and the zenith of the throne of God.

The *patripassianism* of the Father as He anticipated and experienced His Son's descent to the nadir of sorrow, anguish, pain and humiliation of the cross and His subsequent, consequent glorification and accent to the throne of God.

In, Profundis immensis, de profundis immensis, and ex 'profundis to ad gloriam in excelsis infinitam.

0' what a journey! 0 what emotions of both the Father and the Son - all accomplished - all that is by Immanuel, God in Christ, God with us.

From an Unplottable Nadir to an Unplottable Zenith

7-16-91 (Indianapolis, IN)

"An unplottable nadir," Jesus took us to, to bring us to "an unplottable zenith." Only God's mind can know and contain both. Here again, is profundis immensis and gloria in excelsis, with an untraceable gift along the way.

The cross was a place, a nadir so low that only Jesus Christ could know it and go to it. The Throne of God, a place, a zenith so high that only Jesus Christ could ascend to it.

Only Immanuel could know the depths and go there, and only He could know the heights and go there. Only Immanuel could truly identify with the depth of the depths (profundis immensis), or the height of the heights (gloria in excelsis). Jesus Christ, while fully conscious, took us unconsciously to profundis immensis. We can go there only by faith, not by feeling or experience. He alone did

243

this experientially. As to gloria in excelsis, He will conduct us there, fully conscious, experientially, in a new realm of feeling and knowing - not by faith, but in a new actuality.

Jesus Christ in His loving, caring and unique capacity spared us all of the agony and pain of profundis immensis which He experienced in order for us to experientially enjoy all the glory of in excelsis *infinitum.* Hallelujah! What a Savior!

7-17-91

The Savior of the world (men) had Himself to be a man accredited enough to certify other men, or qualify other men to ascend to and enter the Holy City where the throne of The Thrice Holy God is. As Brother Jude says, "Faultless before the presence of His glory - " He had to qualify to do this ALONE. He also, prior to this, had to qualify to do everything salvational for man on the cross, in one place, at one time - ALONE. Hence, He had to qualify men - alone and conduct them, immortal, eternally young and eternally righteous, into the presence of God!

Who, but Immanuel, God in Christ could do these things?

Yes, indeed, Jesus was God and is God, without question!

In qualifying men for the absolutely darknessless presence of God, the man-Savior had to be wise enough and strong enough to die for every man after having carried every man's sins in His own body - and after having done away with those sins until they were absolutely unfindable, abolished in absolute and final disposal.

8-21-91

On the day of atonement, a young bullock was chosen (Leviticus 16:3) and two kids of the goats. All "young things." This bespeaks ignorance, immaturity and weakness, and insufficiency. What could these animals really carry? What did they really know? As to blood, they didn't know they had any. They didn't know God, man, sin or death - or why they should die.

9-2-91

Only because God has a "cross of record" can His soul be satisfied. In Immanuel's cross He has a full penalty to satisfy His anger against sin. Only in Immanuel's cross does He consequently have man's passage into the realms of eternal glory."Of Penalty and Passage."

Chapter 5

JESUS-IMMANUEL, THE GREATEST OF ALL

Study Questions: 1. *Comparing Immanuel to Solomon, what are the things about Him[Immanuel]which makes Him greater than Solomon? 2. Comparing Immanuel to Jonas, what are the things about Him [Immanuel]which makes Him greater than Jonas?*

Immanuel, Greater than Solomon, Jonas for in Immanuel God was in Christ

12-9-91

Behold, a greater than Solomon is here. Immanuel was greater in knowledge, holiness and power.

Solomon was wise enough, and was certified by heaven to practice law on earth, but he was not certified and knew nothing about practicing law for a universal clientele before the tribunal, bench of heaven. He made an historic decision concerning the two disputing women respecting the ownership of the(a) child. However, he was not qualified to determine the destinies of men respecting life and death before the "King of the Ages."

Immanuel Greater than Jonas

Only Immanuel was qualified and certified here. He was greater than Jonas. **Jonas was a persuasive preacher. Possibly a great orator, but eternal redemption required much more than this.**

Solomon was an organizer, builder, procurer, administrator and judge, but not a redeemer.

His wisdom was reflected in all of his great works (see Ecclesiastes 1:3), but redemption's plan and execution required a super brilliance which, while Solomon was the wisest man in all of human history, yet he did not possess redemption knowledge. This was unique to Immanuel. MS50

11-29-91

"God was in Christ, reconciling the world unto Himself, not imputing their trespasses unto them." II Cor. 5

The Gospel is glorious in its uniqueness, its unthinkableness; in its paradoxes. E.g. God, Elohim, El, the boundless One with a locus, a place. God, Elohim, El, the timeless One with a tense (was). The tenseless One was a tense.

Reconciling unto Himself, El, the thrice-holy One making friendship between Himself and those who were conceived in sin and shapen in iniquity.

Not imputing He who knew all and could count all, and knew where to place or put all - yet not imputing.

"Deus Erat In Christo ...." [God was In Christ]

The tenseless One in time, with a tense. The spaceless One with a location. The ageless One with a birthday. The sinless One making Himself at one with sinners. *Only in Immanuel*

Seeming contradictions, opposites in perfect harmony.

God took on a tense in Christ to make us forever tenseless.

God took on our mortality to make us forever immortal.

God took on our sins to make us eternally holy.

God took on a location to make us forever boundless, unbounded.

Only in Christ does God be born and die to make us birthless, deathless and eternally young. Adam was not born of a woman. His children were. He was made a full man. In the resurrection, the rapture, we'll not be born, but we who have been born again, will be made fully immortal and eternally whole - instantly!

Immanuel was born and died so that in the day of redemption eternally one bodies, we'll be fully made - not born to grow into perfect manhood.

Jesus was born into another world. For Him this was when He appeared the first time. When He went to the next world, He was made glorious instantaneously. We were born into the Kingdom of God, another world for us. When we go to the next world, we'll be made fit for it instantaneously. Jesus was born into this - made ready for that. We were born into the church, we'll be made ready (ready-made) for the Holy City.

Reconciling - not imputing. 0 what mighty works were going on in Jesus simultaneously!

Look at El's super massive thought - Behold His mind! Notice how He, in His infinite wisdom could be reconciling us, not imputing our trespasses unto us who were known by Him to be absolutely guilty of everything He saw through His all-seeing eyes - and affecting these dynamics by Immanuel He was absolute roughness and absolute smoothness perfectly coordinated. Immanuel, what a LOCUS! Immanuel, what unthinkable actions, occurrences, events, operations went on within Him!

Reconciliation by Immanuel

Since we were El's objects of reconciliation, we couldn't be the objects of imputation. We couldn't be both. We had to be one or the other. Jesus was the object of imputation so He couldn't be the object of reconciliation. He had to die as The Sinful One. Neither could He be both!

God in Christ *in Immanuel* took the man who was absolutely friendly, made Him the object of His unfriendliness, victimized Him as such that we who were absolutely unfriendly might escape the victimization of the unfriendly in order to be made His friends.

0 Thou great Jehovah, El! How marvelous are thy works, 0 LORD! For us who deserved imputing, El would not input. To Him against whom He could not by dessert input, He imputed, to save us. All by His own holiness. He who was all right, El made wrong (to be sin), so that we who never had (born wrong) been right (always wrong) might be made right before Him. These are facts of the matter, not idle theories, Christ did verily

die for the ungodly! He was delivered for our offenses. He was raised again for our justification.

Chapter 6

IMMANUEL, FROM THE DEPTH OF HUMILITY TO THE HEIGHT OF GLORIFICATION

Study Question: *How does the author describe 'Immanuel' in terms of Him being the 'thought of God'?*
The Profoundity of God to :
1.Create the Idea of the Cross and the Decent, the Resurrection and Glorification
2.To MaKe Himself Sin for Us
3.To Make Us the Righteousness of God in Him
12-1-91
Profundis Immensis - Gloria in Excelsis
Nadir and Zenith
Cross and Throne Glorification
Hell and Throne

   God alone created the low side of these terms, for only He could know them. Neither Satan nor man could create, know or produce them. Satan and man were not in the bosom of the Father. They had not the sensitivity to His heart regarding the awfulness of sin or the glory of man's salvation. Only God the Father(could devise)the special hell of the cross End appoint to the extra splendor of His Throne. No other mind could imagine it (the hell). No other word could permit *or* create it. No other person apart from Immanuel could descend to it, and therefore subsequently, consequently no other person could rise to God's throne. No being in the kingdom of darkness (satan's) or in the kingdom of men knew the glory, majesty, might, splendor, greatness of God's throne. Lucifer at one time
wanted to ascend to it and be like God, but was severely blunted in his attempt to accomplish this. As Lucifer and his cohorts could not know the splendor of heaven, neither were

they permitted to know the depths of hell. Both profundis immensis and gloria in excelsis infinitam were of knowledge too high, too wonderful for the powers of the underworld. Heaven's God decided that only His Only Begotten Son, Immanuel, Jesus Christ Our Lord could be privy to both. His mind and His body were prepared for profundis while traveling through His earthly experiences. He had a mind and body prepared for in excelsis for His post-calvarian administration in glory.

Had Jesus not been God almighty, He could never have gone either to Nadir or Zenith, to profundis or in excelsis, to hell or the Throne of God. (N.B.)

The Planner   )
)
The Promise   )
)
The Performer   )
)
The Perfecter of our salvation
)

12-1-91
Why does the SPIRIT help our infirmities?
A.   The greatness of the Spirit's power.
B.   "Immeasurable expansiveness of the Spirit's knowledge.
C.   The Uniqueness of The Spirit's love.
D.   The depth of our infirmity.
E.   The depth of our ignorance to self-help ourselves.
The president of the U.S. doesn't come to plead a person's cause in traffic court. He may be called upon to pardon an impeached president. Big problems demand big men. We don't need a neurosurgeon to remove a simply-placed brown straw splinter. Big men for big things We can't heal all diseases with cough syrup ....!

Immanuel's Decent Into Hell for Us

Immanuel, the only man to ever descend and ascend the numberless scale of God, profundis immensis ad glorious in excelsis. No other person could have taken such journeys! Nadir to Zenith. Humiliation to supranomination. Hell to Heaven. Jesus, our Immanuel was in profundis - to suffer de profundis - for crying. Ex profundis - for raising, transcending exiting.

Once He reached ad gloriam in excelsis - never an "Ex"! Our "ad," and "in," but never an "ex," as with profundis immensis.

Immanuel cried de profundis "My God, my God, etc. while in profundis. When He rise it was ex profundis. The profundis immensis, He cried out of for it as by nature different from Him. Now He only operates in gloriam in excelsis because that which He speaks of which He acts by is of His same glorious substance - no more "ex."

12-18-91

The exaltation of (in) humility, humiliation.

The exaltation of (in) glorification, glory.

In Emmanuhel, the condescension be not God's if it be not immensis. The ascension be not God's if it be not infinitam. Profundis, in the nature of the case must be immensis. Likewise gloria in excelsis must be infinitam.

Only if the nadir be immensis can the zenith be inifinitam. Hence the cross and the throne are correlatives. Only Emmanuhel could go to both!

Ex profundis immensis ad gloriam in excelsis infinitam
Emmanuhel solus.

Ad gloriam reciprocates in profoundis to which jesus went 12/12/2002
The depth was so low that only the measureless height of God's throne was au equal in just compensation in reciprocation. Both Jesus' hell and Jesus' throne are equal in rival respectively
.

Descender, one who or that which descends.
Ascender, he who or that which ascends
(See Ephesians 4)

1-13-92

Made us Righteous and Made Him Sin

Immanuel (cont'd)

In II Corinthians 5, where St. Paul says God hath made Him to be sin for us who knew no sin that we might be made the righteousness of God in Him - there is a dual "creatio ex nihilo" God had no pre-existing basis in Jesus out of which to make (manufacture) sin, yet He made Him i.e. the whole of Him to be sin FOR us that we might be made, i.e. we who had no basis to be made God righteousness in Him. We were neither righteous nor in Him Immanuel.

Jesus *wasn't* sin. We weren't righteousness. God made both opposites by His own unique process. He made Jesus sin without a basis for His becoming and (thereby created His own basis'for our becoming, righteous. For Jesus - no basis. Then God manufactured His own basis for our becoming/ in Immanuel alone! In ourselves, there was no basis for our becoming righteous or being placed in Him. He alone became our basis. He was the original creation without a basis for)being made sin. We had no intrinsic, inward basis for being righteous. God created our basis, in, by, and through Jesus. Jesus first - then us! We had no substantial reason (for becoming).

Jesus alone was our somethingness, for becoming righteous, otherwise all of us was nothingness. We ourselves were without form and void until Immanuel the word came and "addressed" us. Now we are by Him, Apart from Jesus Christ, Immanuel, we have NO basis for being God's righteousness. What brother, sister Christian do you have to say about your present state? How did it happen? Out of what does it come? Answer: God made (manufactured) Him to be sin for me, and out of this we were made righteous. He made us something out of His own "material" alone. we had nothing for Him to work with. We had no place, no person, no power in which, by which or through which to be. He made us righteous in Himself.

Jesus Christ alone is our. original substance by which we have become. Note: The earth was made from God's word. Man was made from earth. No earth - no man. Immanuel was God's fundamental "creatio ex nihilo" when He was manufactured "sin for us." We are "creatio ex et in Immanuel" when we are made the righteousness of God "in Him." In Immanuel God created a basis for our being or becoming righteous. Jesus was the original. He had no basis, absolutely no basis for being, or out of which He was made sin.

Make Himself the Qualified Sacrifice for Us
1-14-92

We needed a sacrifice, substitute, One to be made sin for us. We had a need - a great need, but we could not supply or produce it. We lacked:
A. The Knowledge
B. The Right (Authority)
C. The Power
D. The Substance

So God made (manufactured) Jesus to be SIN for us. What a feat! 0, Immanuel, How precious, How unique You are!

Immanuel, From the Depth of Humility to the Height of Glorification

The Old Testament text "0 Lord, how great is the sum of thy thoughts towards me" (Psalm 139:17) (*Psalm 40:5) reach their zenith, are culminated, and chapter consummated in Immanuel. God's super(lative) thoughts are manifested in Him! E.G. His origin, His work, His Cross, His resurrection, His glorification, His session, His supranomination, His church, His church's glorification, His church's future existence.

Jesus is so much of the thought of God until Apostle John calls Him, "The Word" - Logos.

Jesus, Immanuel, the Thought of God enfleshed, made visible. 0, how self-exalted is God's thought in Christ! God manifested the ultimate of His thought power in Jesus (i.e. as far as He would make revelatory to us).

Created Something Out of Nothing

He had no sin and we had no righteousness he was made both for us

1-15-92

.

Only one ***inamis et vacua***. Emmanuhel, a true Creatio Ex Nihilo. Once El, God made Immanuel, He had a new, all-glorious, boundless, unmatched, and eternally matchless universe out of which, through which, by which, in which, because of which He, Jehovah, El Elyon, El Shaddai, Elohim could make (manufacture) anything. Through this "universe" He willed to make men righteous with His "highest class" of righteousness; i.e. "righteous by Jesus"; the church, immortal men in myriads - anything! anything! etc., etc., etc.! Here is Creatio Ex et in Emmanuhel. God took the quality of Immanuel's righteousness

inamis et vacua.

Something from nothing

(obedience *unto* death even the death of the cross), and thereby made ungodly men the righteousness of God in this wholly Righteous One.

Chapter 7

IMMANUEL'S MOST EXCELLENT NAME

Study Question: *What was Christ made that caused us to be made the righteousness of God?*

1-15-92

In Immanuel, God self-exalted His own name beyond any height previously revealed or manifested to men. Likewise in Immanuel, El, God provided a quality of righteousness of His own in Jesus' obedience unto death, even the death of the Cross (a unique cross) never previously manifested. Then He took that calibre, quality, degree of righteousness manifested in Jesus and bestowed it upon us, in making us His righteousness in Jesus. God had never before manifested to men this degree of His exalted, excellent, intrinsic - this character of His righteousness as He here exhibited in Jesus. God's righteousness was here by our Lord Jesus Christ

Hence, it is here the most exalted degree of God's righteousness ever bestowed upon men. Anything from God vouchsafed by Immanuel/Jesus has, as Jesus' Name by the Cross, new dimensions. Immanuel becomes exponential to anything coming to men from God by Him. Note: "When a man is exalted he doesn't remain the same."

Our righteousness of God is the One Jesus used in Gethsemane and on Calvary - the one which was exercised in death-obedience. No scripture says that Jesus was ever "counted righteous." He was the righteousness of God embodied. As Immanuel, and especially on the cross, He ranged in the exalted realms of God's righteousness where men had never trod. Abraham, our father, was counted righteous.

Made Sin for Us that We Might be Righteous in Him

Immanuel was God's righteousness manifested, and He soared as high in it as the mind of God willed. He reached His own zenith hereof in the Cross, and from this zenith He opened the way for us to be made the righteousness (same quality) (degree?) of God in Him. i.e. having the same high, exalted quality of God's righteousness beyond which none of God's revealed righteousness exceeds. The righteousness of God in Christ, Immanuel is the ultimate of God's righteousness. We come to the ultimate of Divine things only BY Jesus Immanuel.

1-16-92

When Immanuel, as only He could have been was made sin for us, He became God's New Creation, His super act to produce a new and super result(s). We have been made the righteousness of God in the super man who had been exalted and supranominated. Immanuel is God's New Being. Immanuel has a New Name. Immanuel manifested and bestowed a new degree of God's Righteousness.

Note: He is made unto us wisdom, righteousness, sanctification and redemption. 0, what degree, what quality is here!

Chapter 8

WE ARE MADE RIGHTEOUS IN IMMANUEL

Study Question: *How is Immanuel's ascending and descending compared to that of Solomon and all other men?*

1-16-92

God made a son, Isaac for Abraham and Sarah to come out of a death background. He made us sons from a death background. God put life in Abraham and Sarah and He put sin and death in Jesus. Abraham and Sarah had no life for procreation in them. Jesus had no sin and death in Him. In Holy Scripture we are to look for God's righteousness and glory.

1-16-92

For Abraham, the father of us all, and us, as New Testament believers, there was a difference in the basis of righteousness, hence a very significant difference in the seals which followed.

Abraham believed in God, in hope against hope, that he, a dead man would have a child by a dead woman - and he did. We believe in Jesus Christ, who being an absolutely sinless One was made to be sin (for us). Abraham and Sarah were respectively man and woman, and though physically dead were human nevertheless. Jesus Christ positively, definitely, absolutely was NOT sin, hadn't been sin, had no propensity for sin, never would be, or by nature, even could be sin. Abraham was restored to life, Sarah was enlivened with life. Jesus could not be restored to what He never had been. Neither could He be enlivened with that which was natural for Him. Hence God "had" to do a new thing, absolutely new thing with Jesus, God had to MAKE HIM to be sin. It is by faith in this One that we obtain God's righteousness and the subsequent seal of eternal life. Abraham's seal was circumcision. So the seals are different because the faith-bases are so vastly different. Is God's "operational righteousness" in these incidences of a different degree, of different involvement, of a different quantity? etc., etc.

1-16-91
"Thou hast loved righteousness and hated iniquity, therefore God, even thy God both anointed Thee with the oil of gladness ABOVE thy fellows. "The anointing above" - The above anointing must have been the consequent of a somehow "above righteousness."
The aboveness of Jesus' Name is now the consequent of the aboveness of His sacrifice. Calibers to righteousness?

1-16-91
Only superlative, ultimates and absolutes are befitting Immanuel.

1-17-92
    "Immanuel, The Self-Evolution and Self-Revelation of God"
    E.g. "God hath glorified His son, Jesus"
    "God raised Him up and gave Him glory"
    "God hath highly exalted Him and given Him a Name" etc., etc., etc.
    When God self-made Immanuel to be sin for us, He made Him the worst for He made Him to be sin for all of us sinners. Then He caused Him, while self-prepared for it, to

die the worst death - He died for all. He tasted death for every man. Herein He went to the lowest of ALL hells, the deepest nadir, the profundis immensis. Out of this, from this He ascended to the throne of God - the highest of heights, in eternal splendor. To this glorious place He will "one day" conduct His glorified church.

God the Father manifests the ultimate glory of His divinity in Immanuel. No revelation like it prior to Immanuel, none after. God as Benefactor to man does not pull out all the stops of His benefits to mankind until He manifests Himself in Immanuel. Man reaches the maximum, the ultimate of his becoming in Immanuel. Only when God becomes ALL that He self-wills to be towards man can man become all that he can possibly become. Fallen men, stained by sin and under perpetual sentence of death can only become supremely righteous in standing and state and eventually become immortal in eternal glory by

Immanuel - God with us - as most to man. Men can only become most as God will be The Most to him.

Only by Him! One-ly by Him! One-ly by Him! (Junction City, KS)

Immanuel is God's Most (by self-appointment).
Immanuel is God's Ultimate (by self-appointment).
Immanuel is God's Superlative (by self-appointment).
Immanuel is God's Absolute (by self-appointment).
Note: Ultimate men only by the Ultimate Man (One).
Superlative men only by the Superlative Man (One).
Absolute men only by the Absolute Man (One).

There is no evolution, no revelation of God beyond Immanuel. He is the first and the last. We are privileged with the maximum sight of God, here and throughout the endless ages of eternity in Immanuel.

Scripturally, our first glimpse, view, sight of God is in relation to Immanuel. Our last view has to do with Immanuel. We are introduced to God in Genesis, but further reading of the sacred texts inform us that the church was chosen "in Him BEFORE the foundation of the world."

He went to the deepest, descended to the deepest depth, ascended to the highest height, so we could be the most - no one, and nothing else is capable of bringing us to ultimate potential. Only He who planned the heights for man, provided for our passage to the heights, can conduct us thither (there).

Emmanuhel Solus! "Of Nadir and Zeniths In Immanuel." The essence of His name is all excellence from eternity to eternity, from thought to everlasting action.

Whether in eternity, in time, in its actions "flat," or in descending, or ascending actions, or in eternity to come, Immanuel has to do with a name, being, power, work of super excellence. *If He descends, He descends deeper than all. If He ascends, He ascends higher than all. He has no equals, a greater than   a greater than Solomon is here! If He lives, He lives more! If He dies, He dies more! If He lives again, He lives beyond!*

In Immanuel, God is not with us, He is not for us. He is not in us as, but beyond! In Immanuel, God makes all things new. The prophets had the Spirit of Christ, but not as He is in His church as Immanuel, hence, while they had the Spirit, they did not speak in tongues or have the full insight into the structure of the church as the Immanuel - filled Apostles.

1-17-92

The big thing of the Psalmists and the prophets was not that a new star was aborning or that a new galaxy was dawning or forming, but rather that Immanuel was coming. The universe and science was not the most glorious thing in their vision, but the sight of The Coming One, The Messiah, Immanuel. He who would save His people from their sins, establish righteousness and usher in endless ages of peace.

1-17-92 (A New Thought)
Note: The Sweep of The Text - "Textual Sweep" A Eternity Past - The Plan
B.   Time Past - The Promise
C.   Present Age - Temporal Fulfillment
D.   Eternity to Come - Future Fulfillment
Textual Sweep, i.e. what is the range or extent of the text? This is a good theological consideration for any text.

I Corinthians 5

16   Wherefore, henceforth know we no man after the flesh; though we have known Christ after the flesh, yet now, henceforth know we Him no more. (The self-evolution and self-revelation of God in Inunanuel.)

Creatio Ex Nihilo Making something out of nothing

17   Therefore, if any man be in Christ, he is a new creature(ion); old things are
passed away; behold, all things are become new.
18   And all things are of God, who hath reconciled us TO HIMSELF BY Jesus
Christ, (Immanuel) and hath given to us the ministry of reconciliation; (what a ministry!).
19   To wit, that God was in Christ
A reconciling the world unto Himself,
B. not imputing their trespasses unto them, and hath committed unto us the word of reconciliation. (what a word!)
"Without Him became nothing which became"

20   Now, then, we are ambassadors for Christ, as though God did beseech you -by us; we beg you in Christ's stead, be ye reconciled to God.

21 FOR HE (EL) HATH MADE HIM, WHO KNEW NO SIN (THE NIHIL0), TO BE SIN FOR US, THAT WE MIGHT BE MADE (THE SUBSTANCE) THE RIGHTEOUSNESS OF GOD IN HIM.

The Creatio Ex Nihilo

The Creatio (See Ephesians 2:10, 4:24) Ex et (de?) in Emmanuhel (Ex is OK - See II Corinthians 5:18

What is the sweep of this most glorious text?

If St. John 3:16 is "the Golden Text" of the Bible, then II Corinthians 5 must be the silver, diamond or platinum text of the Bible.

Chapter 9

THE SWALLOWING UP

Study Questions:1.*Where are our sins that Jesus bore on the Cross? 2. What happened on the Cross?*

1-31-92

Immanuel (Solus)

Emmanhuel (<u>God's Resource Person for Man</u> 1-31-92)
Only He can swallow up death in victory.
Only He can Swallow up mortality in Immortality (life).
Compare War: How outposts (satellites) of the enemy fall before the central place of government falls. E.g. the small places in France, Belgium, and Germany fell before Berlin did. The small places of the Pacific, even Nagasaki and Hiroshima fell before Tokyo collapsed - so even now God (Immanuel) giveth us the victory by Jesus Christ. God causeth us always to triumph in Christ until the collapse of the "Big One(s)," sin and death.

Jesus Christ, Immanuel is a - and our conqueror, a mighty victor, a mighty victory.

'Thou hast laid help upon One that is mighty." Behold the strength of His Arm, the Wisdom of His mind, The Glory of His Presence, The Beauty of His Name, The Rest in His Words, The eternality of His life, The fullness of His Redemption.

The Rest of His Peace
The Comfort of His Words
The Joy of His fellowship

Now the outposts, the forward positions, the satellites are falling, i.e. are being destroyed, being rendered ineffective - until the day that Immanuel comes and totally demolishes, swallows up sin and death. It may take a protracted campaign, but He'll bring Satan and all of his forces to "the deck of The Missouri" - they'll all come to the armistice table - they'll all "stack their arms and study war NO MORE Emmanuhel Solus!!!

Until then, He gjveth us the Victory!

0, LORD, LET NOTHING DARKEN OUR VIEW OF THAT GREAT DAY!

He causeth us to triumph! - always

i.e. continuous victory until that glorious moment!

2-1-92

Both Immanuel's body which bore our sins, and the sins which were borne in it are unfindable.

"Unfindable Things"

Where did they go? Was there a where strong enough to hold either. They were unified in the cross. They became fetus, embryo-like, inseparable. Both vanished? Heaven decided, "there is NO WHERE" for them, earth, heaven, the sea, hell, outer space - NO WHERE for them. Only God could prepare the body of Immanuel - only God could prepare its sin-laden destiny.

1.   Mary bore Jesus and did not lose her virginity.

2.   Immanuel bore our sins, took them away and never left His holiness nor His Locus. He didn't leave the cross or the grave until He got another body. So, Immanuel took our sins to "an uninhabited land" and didn't leave the altar of burnt offering. With an unchanged and mortal body, He laid in the grave, with our sins having been taken away by His blood, i.e. His sacrifice.

3.   God will dispose of the bodies of glorified Saints in 'The Change" of the rapture. These bodies too, will be eternally unfindable. Oh, the glory of the:

A.   Conception/Incarnation

B.   Crucifixion

C.   (Jesus') Resurrection

D.   Justification of Men

E.   Sanctification of believers

F.   Glorification of Saints

The Swallowing Up

The Old Testament says as far as East is from West, so far hast thou removed ... East and West are relatively findable - but where are our sins and Immanuel's sin-bearing body?

2-1-92

Only Immanuel's Victoriousness can swallow up death! Only Immanuel's life can swallow up our mortality.
None other! None other! None other! Hence we shall only be saved by "HIS LIFE" (Romans 5). See Obadiah 1:16. Death dies perishes.

Swallow up, to make away with or destroy completely: to cause to disappear utterly (as if by absorption): cause to vanish (as if by devouring or absorption into itself).

Immanuel is able to subdue all things unto Himself. Manward or usward there is NOTHING excepted - Emmanuhel Solus!

Immanuel is the only MAN who has this power - and only because He's God! Were He less than God, He'd lack the wisdom and power to subdue all, i.e. make everything subject to Him - at will.

Immanuel shared the dishonor of men in being buried in the heart of the earth "with us." Note the dishonor (the Prince of life in a grave), the King of The
Ages, buried, incarcerated in a lowly tomb. The greatest, the highest in the lowest place - 'borrowed' at that. He made His grave with the rich (who were in death brought to inglory like the rest of men) in His death. So here the richest of all was entombed. The Highest of all was brought low, lowest of all - for He went down farther, descended deeper than all. Here was the starkest humiliation of all the rich! From thence He ascended on high - to "gloriam excelsis infinitam."

Graves for the rich are the most degrading, humiliating. Jesus made his grave with the wicked and the rich in His death - i.e. an absolute identity with both. N.B., N.B.

The disparateness of the grave and everyday life was not as great for Lazarus as it was for the rich man Lazarus left.

"Nothing to go to nothing." The rich man went from everything to nothing. For Lazarus, the descent was not as steep.

With the wicked, i.e. as being where one deserved to be - after all Jesus was a victim of capital punishment

Men expect wicked men to be executed, cut off from life and buried in "Potter's Fields," graves for "the indigent" Jesus made, His grave with the wicked and the rich.

He was a rich man who carried Himself as poor. He was a righteous man who died as though He were wicked. "Though He was rich, yet for our sakes He became poor that we through His poverty might be rich."

1-31-92 (See Page 90)

Swallowed Up
What is Swallowed Up?

A.   Decomposes
B.   Suffers constitutional destruction
C.   Vanishes away
D.   Loses its character
E.   Loses its identity
F.   Sustains a brokenness of its force
Sustains a brokenness of its strength
G.   Can never return to its former state.

See Jonah 1:17, "Now the LORD had prepared a great fish to swallow up Jonah. And Jonah was in the belly of the fish three days and three nights. (Matthew 12:40)

Why wasn't Jonah swallowed up? Why wasn't Jesus corrupted in the grave? What God did with both counteracted against what was ordinary - something in Jonah. Something in Jesus.

Behold the might of Immanuel! "With us God" (to exercise His might) on hunger, fear, demons, disease, temptations, the flesh, the devil - and yes even death and all mortality. What advantage would it have been to God to have been with us and then not exhibit or display His powerful "stuff."

2-1-92

We don't like to see a great life or a young life "cut off," yet Jesus' was the greatest life ever cut off, and that while Jesus was in the "prime of life." He was the holiest man ever executed by "the state." The holiest capital punishment victim - and the richest man ever buried.

2-1-92

God sent His Son to be the propitiation for our sins. Immanuel accomplished this mission absolutely. He fulfilled it to "Consummatum Est." In all of Jesus' assignments, we must be aware of Psalm 89, 'Thou has laid help upon One that is mighty." This pertains to all of man's salvational needs from calling to glorification. The total manifestation of Immanuel's might - wherever found has to do with the revelation of a bare, glorious and single, unaided Arm of Jehovah (God). For instance, there is no reconciliation of men-**sans**- "God was in Christ.

sans- only no other than

1-27-92
Henry Cleaners, St. Louis, Creve Coeur, MO
This tag was on three pair of pants I had sent to this cleaner. This was my full order. For each it was the same notice.

We've tried and tried but we find that the stains on this garment cannot be removed without possible injury to the color or fabric.
This has been called to your attention so that you will know it has not been overlooked.

Printed in U.S.A. ±HB-16

Jesus Compared to Jonah

2-2-92 (See Page 86)

The character of Jonah and Jesus were similar as they approached their respective places of enclosure. Jonah knew the promises of God respecting the glory of the temple. Jesus knew the power of the Father's hand. Hence, Jonah said, "I will look towards the temple." Jesus said, "Into Thy hand I commend my spirit." Jonah believed God and cried in trouble. Jesus believed God and cried in trouble, but before He went into the grave. Jonah cried out of the belly of hell. Jesus was silent in the hell of the grave but He cried out of the belly of hell of the cross, "My God, my God, etc...."

Ordinarily, men are swallowed up by fish, and the fish which swallowed Jonah was prepared by God to "swallow up" Jonah, but God denied this because Jonah knew the temple and cried out of the swallowing up condition.

The Swallowing Up

The grave is ordinarily a place of corruption, but because of the nature of Immanuel and His faith, the grave with all of its attendant corruption, mortification was denied concerning Him.

2-3-92

Emmanuhel Solus
"Immanuel, On the Cross and In the Courtroom"

"He sat down ... having obtained ETERNAL REDEMPTION FOR US. *On the cross, an absolutely perfect, and the final sacrifice. The only sacrifice ever offered to God, or that could be offered accompanied by the "Consummatum Est."*

In the courtroom, an absolute and finally satisfying presentation of credentials and case. He the only "right man" with the sole case (and cause) for our redemption. *Immanuel as Martin Luther sangs in a mighty fortress; was "the might man on our side"*

No man and no sacrifice before Him nor since Him could have satisfied God as He and His did.

We don't have to fight for the man's work if we can only have the man. To properly have Immanuel is to have His work. To really have faith in His Name is to have His work.

Peter spoke of "God has glorified His Son Jesus (now) His Name through faith in His Name has made this man strong." Not by our power or holiness, but His Name through faith in His Name has done the WORK. I.e. the wisdom, the might to accomplish the miracle was released by Immanuel. Ours was only to believe. As it was in this case, so it is now and evermore shall be. We do not, cannot, and will not release the wisdom and energies, power of victory over the underworld and yes, even our mortality. This is Immanuel's work, appropriated to and for us by simple faith, confidence in Him. He is the Mighty Wisdom House and Energy Machine of God. Yes, we will become immortal and obtain our glorified bodies by the POWER which He has to SUBDUE ALL things unto Himself.

In St. Peter 1:3, we should note, the Apostle does not use the preposition"towards" a lively hope, but rather "unto" a lively hope, by the resurrection of Christ Jesus from the dead. "Unto," denoting MOTION TOWARDS AND REACHING.

How does El "back-pedal" on His redemption for man in Immanuel? How does El reverse, negate, "unfmalize" what He has made final in Immanuel? How does El (God) dismantle, dissolve, negate Consummatum Est?

Does He want to? Why would He want to? We must note that neither Immanuel nor His work is of man's devising. Man did not cause either. Therefore, can man "uncaused" Him and His work?

Chapter 10

THE GLORIFICATION OF THE SAINTS VIA IMMANUEL

Study Question: *What was God's Darkest Night?*

2-3-92

God having named Himself Immanuel and having manifested the eternal greatness (glory) of the name in absolute profundity and absolute exalted glory in Jesus Christ, how does He now "unname," "dename," "disname" or "rename" Himself?

How does El now efface His planned, promised, prophesied, all-powerful all-glorious glory? How does El deprogram all that He has programmed, set in motion in Immanuel?

1-4-91

The Might of Immanuel
(His Dual Redemption)

A. O f Spirit/Soul

B. Of Body

Great might was, is and will be necessary to affect the two redemptions. Colossians 2:20 to be dead is to be dead TO, or dead FROM something. In the New Testament, men are simply DEAD, DEAD. Death implies away from and unto. Christians are to be dead from sin but alive unto God. Immanuel engineered and accomplished both. The house which Jesus bought for me (i.e.) the new body, while yet unseen, is a GLORIOUS house - it is like Immanuel's present glorious body.

It is so glorious and so expensive a "house" or body that I could never have purchased it! Our efforts at purchasing either phase of redemption would at our best, be so meager, until it would compare to the now District Elder Ellis' effort to buy a Cadillac car by giving the salesman a quarter (of a dollar) down payment.

We are bought by God for God to use us. Even men don't buy things out of stores "to remain in the stores." We buy merchandise to use it. So did God! Redemption scriptures:

Romans 3:24
Romans 8:23
I Corinthians 6:20
Galatians 3:13 Galatians 6:14 Ephesians 1:7, 14 Ephesians 4:30 Philippians 3:20, 21
Colossians 2:20
Correlate Romans 8:23, Ephesians 1:14 and Ephesians 4:30

Redemption of Body and Spirit

0, what a new creature, new creation, 0 what a day, when Immanuel conjoins our absolutely sinless spirits (blood-redeemed) which He shall have redeemed with His own blood and death, with our deathless, all glorious bodies which He shall have redeemed by His blood and super power.

0, what glory! What un-imaginable and eternal glory! 0 what a new day that will be - and Emmanuel Solus!

9-16-91 (At Prayer)
In Philippians 3
His resurrection
His sufferings
His death have no other objectives, no other qualifiers.
Immanuel's resurrection, Immanuel sufferings, Immanuel's death "says it all."

The program "His," like His Name Jesus needs not adjectives to help it. Nothing assists Jesus in being great. He helps others while nothing helps Him.
"The arm of the Lord" is another expression which needs examination as to adjectives.
The New Testament refers to "His glorious body." However, this is done to distinguish between Jesus' two bodies - one glorious, an "inglorious." So the church would clearly understand that God is not going to fashion us anew according to an "old pattern" - but after the "new pattern," i.e. Jesus' glorious body. So the adjective "His life" also is non-adjectional in the New Testament.

9-15-91 (Note)
    The prize of 'The High Calling" are through lower callings and lower grade prizes of God in Christ - i.e. blessings beneath immortality and the out-resurrection that lifts one away from the rest of the dead? See II Corinthians 5:4,
Note: St. Paul says: The Mark; The Prize; The High Calling of God. (God's purpose and grace given us in Jesus!)

2-7-91
"Christ (in) You, the Hope of Glory, i.e. Glorification."
    Only by the glory within us (Christ, the eternal glorious One) can we go to or come to the glory which is to come - being gloria in excelsis infinitam. In Christ Jesus, or through and in Christ Jesus this is the glory which is here and now as the Holy Spirit. Only by, in gloria in excelsis which is where we are can we expect, hope to go to gloria in excelsis where we are not.
    Note by comparison, The glory of Jesus' cross and The glory of His Throne is one gloria in excelsis. What was the glory of God in the lowest was what was also the glory of

275

God in the highest. The glory which took Jesus to the lowest hell was the same glory which exalted Him ad gloriam in excelsis infinitam - and crowned Him in supranomination. One glory! We have tasted here, the powers of the world to come. We have tasted e'en here the eternal bless of our eternal home (glory).

Image and Superscription

In placing an image and superscription on coinage inheres a call by government for national (universal, extra-national) recognition and honor for the person(s) so presented.

A person's image and name on a coin is a true "status symbol." By this, i.e. images and superscriptions on coinage, we designate persons for honor. It is a manner of sealing their honor "in stone."

However, God, who is above all coin-honored personages, has inscribed His Name in the heavens. His signature inscription is in day, night, the mountains, rives, oceans, seas, and man.

He who has the greatest image and inscription deserves the greatest honor. Immanuel is the ultima thule of Divine images and superscriptions. He is the image of God with the name "Jesus." On coins are likenesses. Christ Jesus is the express image of God and bearing His Name.

Death In and by Adam, Riches Life and Victory In Jesus

1-16-91

"The unsearchable riches of Christ" - Ephesians 3:8

"In whom are hid all of the treasurers of wisdom and knowledge (of God) - Colossians 2:3

3-7-91

See Romans 5

Begotten by Adam, born from Adam, born into death. Adam, by disobedience became the source-person, fountain head for all of our dying.

Begotten by Jesus and (by the Word born from Jesus) we are born into the resurrection and the life. Jesus by obedience as Adam by disobedience, became the source-person, fountain head for living.

In Adam life is unthinkable, i.e. eternal.

In Christ death is unthinkable, i.e. eternal.

We cannot live eternally in Adam.

We cannot die eternally in Christ.

We cannot live eternally outside of Christ for outside of Him for us there is only Adam, and Adam's only end is death. For so it is mandated of God!

We must be born again into life. We must be born into Christ to have everlasting life.

Our first is absolutely insufficient for immortality. Christ only hath immortality - and dwells in inapproachable life. Heaven has mandated His exclusion from all mortals (when it comes to entering His dwelling place). So before we can go where He is we must be changed!

"As in Adam all die even so also in Christ shall all be made alive." Jesus Christ is a supra-universal presence, a boundless expanse, an unbordered territory ethereal, a Name above every name both in and beyond time.

He Was Made Sin for Us, We were Made Righteous in Him

3-9-91

Fact, Fiction, Figment of Mind or Final Truth?

I.   He was made (by God) sin for us (can't explain it)

II.   We made (by God) the righteousness of God in Him (can't explain it) Can't explain that - can't explain this. We can believe it, though! Behold the power, the manifestation of God's glory! He made both! God made Him what He wasn't in order to make us what we weren't. God made Jesus sin for a "moment" to make us righteous forever! God compressed eternal judgment into that "moment" to extract out of it
eternal release from judgment and consequently eternal rest for us.

The Cross "Jesus and God's Eternal Moment"

Here he tasted eternal death for every man from the 6th to the 9th hour - i.e. eternity in a moment.

God was making everything. He who created the universe creatis ex nihilo, could certainly compress eternity into Jesus' moment. Is there anything too hard for God?

Jesus' Eternal Moment was God's ultima Thule manufacturing event. That is, we have no revelation of anything beyond it. There is nothing we can find in Holy scripture which transcends it. Whatever God's night is which exceeds the cross, God doesn't want us to know it yet.

The Resurrection and Glorification

The resurrection of Jesus was God's own antiphonal response to His Son's death. He Himself decided that there was no other commensurate answer.

So glorious was His work in Christ on the cross that only Jesus' resurrection, ascension, glorification, session and supranoraination could be correlatives thereto. With these, The Father put His own equation in balance - that is, hereby He created His own equation. Immanuel 4- His Life + His Death = His resurrection, glorification, ascension, session, supranomination, etc.

278

Chapter 11

THE PURPOSE OF THE GRACE OF GOD, GIVEN TO US IN JESUS CHRIST

Study Question: *What did Jesus-Immanuel do with death*?

II Timothy 1 :6-11
God's Purpose and Grace given to us,
the Church, in Jesus Christ

Jesus Christ, Christ Jesus, our Lord, the locus of God's purpose and grace, given to us before the world began. This which has been given to us and given only, will remain ageless. The purpose of God and the grace of God will abide or endure throughout the ages of time and go into eternity. Neither can be eroded, altered nor annulled by the ages - by the ignorance and weakness of men.

"What God has abolished and established in and by the cross of Christ Jesus will never be respectively re-established or disannulled by Him. What has been disestablished will never be erected, supported, etc., by God.

If a house has a purpose to protect from the elements, provide comfort and beauty; and otherwise be functional for human occupants - there, of necessity, must be wisdom and strength applied. Otherwise, too many negative factors will render it useless. If the purpose for an automobile is to provide conveyance for passengers under year-round, comfortable and safe conditions, wisdom and strength must be evident in its production. Otherwise ..... etc., etc., etc.

For God to have given a purpose to men of living holily and unblamably through life and finally to become immortal, He decided a mighty grace (wisdom and strength) had to be provided. Because of:
A Wise and powerful foes in the spirit world

B. The character of natural forces, e.g. (time, weakness, sin, and death). Note: "His own (not another's) purpose and grace" C.F. Bishop S. N. Hancock on a tailored suit or dress, "made by and for

The One in whom alone the purpose and grace was given has appeared - what did He do?

I.   Abolished death

II.   Brought life and immortality to light through, via the Gospel

Jesus Christ brought the wisdom and strength for life and for immortality. Only the purpose and grace of God IN HIM could or can accomplish these super great factors in men. Jesus Christ is totally unique! There is no other source of the purpose and grace of God for the New Testament age apart for Him!

Jesus Christ's singular abolition of death singularly attests that there is no other source for LIFE and Immortality. Only He who abolished death can author Life and Immortality for men. He only has it!!!

What does life mean to men where there is no awareness that God has given a purpose - and given grace? They live beneath and apart from their privilege.

The purpose of preaching is to inform men of the purpose and grace for God for them - as given in Jesus Christ - which is for different from the purpose and "grace" given in Adam.

In Adam is purpose and (little) grace. It does not compare to the higher purpose and grace given in Christ - Immanuel.

A child has to be taught the purposes and capability (strength) of his body's members.

"Stop, look, and listen before you cross the street. Use your eyes, use your ears, and then use your feet."

Eyes for seeing, ears for hearing, feet for walking.

Purpose (3) The object for which anything is done or made, or for which it exists; the result or effect intended or sought; ends, aim.

The Purpose of the Grace of God, Given to Us in Jesus Christ

Provocative Love of Immanuel

2-6-92

Immanuel's love to me evokes my love towards Him I love Him because of His:

1. Crucifixion
2. Resurrection/glorification (subjectionally)
3. Supranomination/Session
4. Representation/justification before Heaven's Tribunal
5. Benefaction (i.e. His outpouring of The Holy Ghost)
6. Sanctification (of ms)/Intercession (for us)
7. Coming Glorification/Translation (of us) (objectively)

Songs:

A. I'll Live for Him Who Died for Me
B. I want to love Him better

"I see my Savior hanging on a bloody tree...."

2-6-92

"The High Place of Immanuel's Humility"

Philippians 2:8-9

...He humbled Himself, and became obedient unto death, even the death of the cross.

"WHEREFORE God ALSO hath highly exalted Him, and given Him a name which is above every name:

Behold the wisdom, might, grace and glory in, upon Jesus in His garden and cross experiences!

Immanuel, God's Super Power

2-17-92

Immanuel, God's super manifestation of His Power, Might.

...The Glory of God in the face of Jesus Christ. Jesus Christ is God's new creation, His super world.

Jesus is God's greater Sun, i.e. "The Sun of Righteousness." He is the Super Sun.

Jesus is God's Super Tree (of life)

Jesus is God's Super Wisdom

The Name of Jesus Christ as Immanuel, Book II

Jesus is God's Super Son (Fils Unique)
Jesus is God's Super Father (Bringing many sons to glory)
Jesus is God's Super Water (of life)
Jesus is God's Super Kernel of Grain Jesus is God's Super River
Jesus is God's Super Light
Jesus is God's Super Sabbath (7th day, rest)
Jesus is God's Super air breathing creature (made of flesh and Holy Spirit)" (conjoined, not simply spoken)
Jesus has God's super and final Name. "The heavens do declare the glory of God in fact, but not like Jesus, His Unique Son. No adjective used with the Name "Jesus." No adjective used with "His" Name. ie. no adjectives are used preceding "Jesus."

None is used after "His." E.g. His Righteousness, His Name, His Throne. God declares or manifests the profundity (procerity - height) of His thought in Jesus Christ, Immanuel as He does in NOTHING else!!

Chapter 12

THE TRANSFORMING GLORY OF JESUS CHRIST AS IMMANUEL

Study Question: *What did the first century Saints under the dynamic ministry of the apostles behold when they beheld Jesus?*

2-17-92
See II Corinthians 4:6 (full of Jesus)
Before the face of Immanuel, St. Paul cried, "0, the depth of the riches both of the wisdom and the knowledge of God, how unsearchable are His judgments and His ways past finding out!" - Romans 11:33.
In Immanuel is the super revelation/manifestation of His Glory.
In Romans 11:33, we have the "Bellow of the human soul" in the presence of Immanuel.
Note: II Corinthians 3:18 - "We beholding ... the glory of The Lord (in the face of Jesus; in Immanuel), are changed into the same image from glory to glory, even as by The Spirit of The Lord."
The greatest revelation of manifestation of God's glory is in Jesus. Note the super glory of I Timothy 3:16.
Note: What holy scripture says of the impermanence of the sun in Psalm 19.
Note: Jesus Christ is God - blessed forever.
Note in II Corinthians 3:10 - "... the glory that excelleth ... much more that which remaineth."

A. Minds blinded to the glory of the law.
B.   Unto you who believe (in the revealed glory) He is precious.
When Moses is read, the veil IS ....
"The Glory of Beholding The Glory"

From the Lowest Nadir to the Highest Zenith

Zenithal, adj. pertaining or relating to, situated or occurring at the zenith; also fig. supreme; culminating. 1891 Thomas Hardy, "Tess XXV, A zenithal paradise, a nadiral hell in

'Tess of The D'Urbervilles" Here was Immanuel! A Nadiral Hell – Profundity [*depth*]

A Zenithal Paradise – Procerity *[height]*

From: Nadiral suffering, death (the ultimate)

To: Zenithal glory (the ultimate)

From: Nadiral gloom

To: Zenithal glory

Nadir-nadiral relative to the lowest point

Zenith-zenithal Relative to the highest point

No star glory like the glory of Immanuel, The Bright, morning star See Acts 26:13

2-18-92
Psalm 8 and Psalm 19 (Show and Tell - To declare and to show. I have manifested Thy Name.) (Color has time, music has color.)
'Two Universes"
A.	The World
B.	The World's Word
A.	Man of The Word
B.	The Word-Man
I Corinthians 15:39 - All flesh is not the same flesh: but there is one kind of flesh of men, another flesh of beasts, another of fishes, and another of birds.
40 There are also celestial bodies, and bodies terrestrial: but the GLORY of the celestial is one, and the GLORY of the terrestrial is another.
41 There is one GLORY of the sun, and another GLORY of the moon, and another GLORY of the stars: for one star differeth from another star in GLORY.

St. Paul accounts in Acts 26:13 that the light he saw on the Damascan Road was ABOVE the brightness of the sun ... and voice saying ... "I am Jesus." The Glory of Jesus differs from the glory of the sun! The Glory of the sun's maker is greater than the glory of the sun which He made.
"But we see Jesus" - what did the Apostles see when they saw Jesus?

B.   "We all beholding as in a glass the glory of the Lord" - what did the first century Saints under the dynamic ministry of the apostles behold when they beheld Jesus?
A. "...and the Word was made flesh and dwelt among us and we beheld His glory as of the only begotten of the Father full of grace and truth." What a sight! What a glorious sight! i.e. The Sight of Glory Divine. This had to be for mankind the incomparable sight to behold, Divine glory! Christ Jesus, Our Lord, Immanuel, the Wisdom of God and The Power of God Immanuel was God's Word Incarnate Immanuel was God's Glory Incarnate Immanuel was full of Grace and Truth, hence He was the Grace of God and The Truth of God incarnate.
("And we beheld the 'glow' of the Word came to me early on AM. of 2-17- 92. Sans dictionary.) See I John 1:1
    Immanuel, the revelation of the scope and scale of God's Glory, God's Word. In the first creation it (i.e. The Word) made ocean floors and stars and " planets (other than earth). In Immanuel, God's glory made His Cross and placed Him on El's Throne. **Immanuel, the ultimate and final revelation/manifestation of God's Word/God's Glory.**
In Immanuel, we can behold El's Glory in profundity and procerity - in the Nadiral and in the Zenithal - the whole spectrum. These at their clearest - "and we beheld His glory."

"We were with Him in the holy mount when there came a voice from the excellent glory..."

St. Paul, by faith in the Words of Immanuel, i.e. the Word of the Word, learned how to be full and suffer need, how to abound and suffer need. How to be elevated and abased. Here was the glory of Immanuel, The Glory of God incarnate.

Tone has color. Color has tone.

Glory, brilliant distinction (for God it would be extremely brilliant distinction - my note.)

What happens when Saints see or behold God's glory? E.g.
1.   Moses at the burning bush (I will now turn aside, and see this great sight, why the bush is not burnt, C.F. Jesus on Calvary. ...and Moses hid his face; for he was afraid to look upon God.)
2.   Isaiah at The Temple
3.   Ezekiel at Chebar (1:1-28). (This was the likeness of the Glory of the Lord.)
4.   Daniel 8:15-27; 10:1-21**
5.   Peter, James & John on Transfiguration Mountain (Matthew 17:6).
6.   Paul on the Damascan Road (Acts 9:4, 6; Acts 22:6, 7; Acts 26:13, 14).
7.   John on Patmos (Revelation 1:17-18).

To truly behold is to be TRANSFORMED!

What happens to us when we truly see Jesus, the ultimate manifestation of God's Glory?

2-19-92

Song, *"...He is our light and glory.*

Note: The Holy City having the glory of God. Her light is like a stone most precious. The Lamb is

the light thereof. The Glory of God did lighten it."
See "light and glory in the Holy City.

2-19-92
    Note: In meditation we behold God's glory. In beholding the glory of God, we are transformed.
    Note: "And He shall be like a tree planted.... I.e. transformed into "tree-likeness."
    What Immanuel brought to man was as real and great as what He took Away

/

Appendix A-Book II
Words and Terms Pertaining to Jesus' Humiliation and Exaltation

In order to provide clear meaning for readers, I first present concept definitions for Latin words that are used often throughout this thesis. These words relate to Christ's Humiliation and Exaltation; some are in the Latin Vulgate. The words in this glossary are used by the author to explain the humiliation and exaltation of Jesus Christ as Immanuel and to reveal a more precise definition pertaining to the cross and the depth of its meaning. Therefore, we define each of the Latin words used by the author, thereby explaining their relevance to Immanuel's humiliation and exaltation.

Definitions of key Latin words and Terms Related to the Thesis:

The difference between *ad glorium excelsis and ad glorium in excelsis infinitam:*

Both of these phrases mean "to the glory of God in the highest," but the virgin birth is the glory of His miraculous incarnation into the bounds of humanity. The cross is to the glory of God, such that, in Christ, God humbled Himself to the bounds of death on the cross. All of this is within the bounds of his state of humiliation.

However, things change infinitely in the resurrection and in His glorification which came after Calvary [*postcaverian*]. His state is now glorious without the bounds required for His humiliation, i.e., His stay in the world as a man, His death and suffering on the cross and His stay in the grave. This is what is meant by the word *infinitum* or *infinitam*. *Infinitam* is without the bounds of His pre-Calvary humiliation and confinement.

The following four terms pertain to Christ' Humiliation, His cross, His death and His descent into Hell: *In profundis emensis, de profundis, ad profundis,* and *ex profundis*.

On the "just read list" of four words, there is one word, *ex profundis*, which describes the transitions from *profundis to glorium in excelsis*.

Glorium in Excelsis—Things pertaining to Jesus' resurrection, ascension and exaltation

The next four words pertain to Christ's resurrection, ascension, and His exaltation: *glorium in excelsis, ad glorium, in excelsis, de glorium in excelsis*; there is no *ex glorium in excelsis.*

After reading this appendix, you will be able to explain the following Latin sentence with clarity:

Ex profundis ad glorium in excelsis infinitam Emmanuhel solus.

Meanings of Related Words:

The following words: Nadir; zenith; abyss; thronal; profundity, and procerity are terms that are prerequisite to understanding this thesis.

Defining Words Related to the Study:

Nadir is the root of the word *nadiral* (opposite of zenith), the lowest point, bottom of the pit, depth of despair, lowest of the lowest hell. In this thesis, Christ's death and cross/hell are *nadiral* and pertain to the cross and Christ's descent into Hell, the lowest hell possible, into which only Immanuel-Jesus could go, and did go for us. Hence, when Jesus was in that situation, it is referred to as *profundis emensis* in this book. This describes the Humiliation of Christ spoken of in Philippians 2.

Zenith is the root of the word *Zenithal*, which means peak, apex, highest point, pinnacle, highest spot, and glory to God in the highest (opposite of nadir). Therefore, in this book, the zenith of Christ's resurrection and ascension into glory is the highest point that He will ever attain; thus, it is called the highest glory of God and in this book it is referred to by the Latin term: ***ad glorium in excelsis infinitam***, which means "to the glory of God in the highest."

Abyss is the root of the word ***abysmal*** and is almost synonymous with ***nadir***, a deep hole, gulf, void, chasm (opposite of the throne). In this writing, it pertains to the lowest, basest, bottomless hell, the farthest thing from the throne of Glory, a place of dishonor where only Immanuel could go. And surely He must have needed to go there on the cross and in His death in order to conquer it, and then to exit from there upwards to His throne, which is ***in glorium in excelsis*** (the glory of God in the Highest). The throne is Christ's exalted place, that which He earned by His descent into the lowest parts of the earth, going to a low, very low hell to achieve His victory over death and hell. Therefore, for this reason, God hath exalted Him highly to a throne with *a name that is above all names*. The name above all names is one that supersedes every name; therefore, it is called the *supra* (superseding) name (nomination). It is from this word that we get the word supranomination of Jesus in this thesis, which basically means the name above every name.

Throne is the root word for ***thronal***, (absolute opposite of abyss). This is the high place of Jesus, to which He has been exalted in glory, and which is referred to in this writing as ***in glorium in excelsis*** because Christ is there. Further, because He is there it is to the glory of God. Thus, it is described by the Latin preposition ***ad*** to mean; to or for, from which we derive the Latin term ***ad glorium in excelsis***, which means ***ad*** (to the glory of God). Thus, He is there "to the glory of God" or "for the glory of God." There in His exalted throne, He is administering from the glory of God in the highest. Thus, we use the term *de glorium in excelsis*, which means "out from within His glorious place" because He is in glory and ministering from within it to the church out of glory, in glory administering His plan from glory. His exaltation and being seated on His throne in Glory is referred to as His session. Session is Him being seated on His throne to administer.

Profundity is the opposite of *procerity*, deep and profound, and it describes the deep things of God pertaining to the cross and Christ's abasement on it. It is from the depth of the mind and counsel of God, which is referred to in this thesis as the bosom of the father. This word is related to *profoundis emensis* which describes the depth of Jesus-Immanuel's suffering on the cross. Hence, it was profound and it was *emensis*! This term includes the concept of the profundity of God's hurt, which was dealt with in Immanuel on His cross.

Procerity is the opposite of profundity.

Latin Terms Defined Relative to *Glorium in Excelsis*:

Ad glorium in excelsis, to or for the glory of God in the Highest.

In glorium in excelsis, in glory of God to the Highest.

De glorium in excelsis, out from within the place of the glory of God in the highest.

Caveat: There is no *ex glorium in excelsis*, because once Christ/we are glorified, we will never exit His glory. Also, Christ will never be dethroned or exit His place of glory. It is a final place to which we are headed, called *ad glorium in excelsis infinitam*, which means Christ is in glory eternally and infinitely (*infinitam*), having no end nor limit. Thus, there will never be *ex glorium*—no exit from glory.

Profundis Pertaining to Jesus' Cross:

My God, My God why hast thou forsaken me?

In Profundis Emensis

In profundis emensis is Jesus *being* in the situation of the cross, thus, *on* the cross, where He experiences all the pangs of the gulf that separated man from God.

It is referred to as ***profundis,*** because of the deep and profound suffering that Christ endured: only He could die such a death. It was there that the deep hurt and emotion of God was expressed and demonstrated. It was so immense that it is referred to as ***profundis emensis***.

De Profundis Emensis:

In about the ninth hour, Jesus cried out with a loud voice, saying, 'Eli, Eli, lema sabachthani?' that is, 'My God, my God, why have You forsaken me?'": Matthew 27:45–46.

De means out from within.

Profundis is the depth of the pangs and suffering of God in Christ.

Emensis was the range and extent of the pain, separation, and gulf.

De profundis emensis: An out-cry from ***within the depths of the lowest hell, while suffering the Judgment of God for the sins of the world. This is the nadiral, the abysmal and the profound experience of the cross of Jesus-Immanuel.***

Oh, what a death! What a gulf! What a pit! This is *profundis* in its *emensis* lowness. This is the humiliation of Christ mentioned by Paul when he said in Philippians 2; He humbled himself to the death of the cross.

'Eli, Eli, lema sabachthani?'
De profundis emensis

Thus, *de profundis* is the crying of Jesus who was in it, crying out from within it while being in it. Thus, the paraphrase is the out-cry of Jesus on the cross.

He descended to the lowest and tasted death for every man: this is a nadir, an abyss, the lowest of the low. It was *emensis*. It was the most profound judgment and pain, the worst separation of God from man. It was the gulf that separated God from man and had to be spanned. It too was the corollary, the opposite of the glory to God in the highest that resulted from it in Jesus' resurrection and exaltation to *glorium in excelsis infinitam.*

Ex Profundis Emensis:

After dying such a death and descending to the lowest hell, tasting death for every man, and conquering death and hell, Jesus-Immanuel was raised from the dead to ascend on High. Coming out of the grave in all power, He exited the grave. This is *ex profundis* [the exiting] and was exalted to *glorium in excelsis infinitam* (glory to God in the Highest), which is the final state of His work as Immanuel. This is where He is now, *in glorium in excelsis* infinitely, boundlessly. In the glory of God in the Highest place is [the zenith] of Immanuel.

Thus, He goes from the lowest pit of hell to the glory of God [*glorium*] in [*excelsis*], the highest.

When he had ascended on High.

Wherefore God hath highly exalted Him.

He that descended is the same as he that ascended.

Emmanuhel Solus means Immanuel only.

In Glorium in Excelsis.

Since Christ's resurrection and exaltation, He is now exalted, having been given the name above every name [this is supranomination]. God gave Him [Jesus-Immanuel] a name that supersedes all names. To supersede is supra and to name is to nominate. Thus, God supranominated Christ in His High state of Glory to God in the Highest. This is referred to as the supranomination of Jesus Christ. Therefore, He is in Glory which is *in glorium in excelsis*. He [Jesus] is now in glory, administering to the church from within glory. He is in glory infinitely and eternally, never to exit there. He has yet to bring us [the church] there at the rapture.

Ad glorium in excelsis:

Ad means 'to or for' the Glory of God and in the case of Jesus' exaltation it is 'by' the Glory of God in the Highest.

Thus, He is there to the glory of God in the highest.

De glorium in excelsis:

This is the meaning of the Latin phrase:

Ex profundis ad gloriam in excelsis infinitam Emmanuhel solus.

It is to be read: Immanuel alone has gone from the cross and the grave to glorification and exaltation without limits or bounds.

Study Questions and Answers

Chapter 1.

Study Question: Relative to El's [God's] relationship to Immanuel, Him being in the thought of God and thus in the bosom of the father, what word does the author use to describe this relationship of El to Jesus Christ that brought us our salvation?

Answer: We were enemies—so Immanuel's absolute sonship, relationship, fellowship, union with the Father, His *"bosomness"* with the Father was what heaven recognized and so, by which full salvation came to us—by One Man.

Chapter 2.

Study Questions:

1. How is Jesus' might mightier than that of the angels?

2. What does Jesus have that angels do not have?

Answer 1: Angelic might is the might beings of divine direction exercised without God's blood, i.e., **without** God's life given up.

Answer 2. The might saints exercise by Jesus' blood is the life energy vouchsafed to men by the life God in Christ gave up. It is life by life given up. It is blood-might. Angelic power is bloodless might.

Chapter 3.

Study Question: Sin reached its maximum in Christ. How did He respond to it?

Answer: Sin reached its "max" of abundance in Jesus. He responded to it by His person and His work **more abundantly.** This is how Immanuel was *Christus Victor*; by His person and His work, He gave back for sin and death more than both brought to Him. And he accepted the "max" of what they brought to Him!

Chapter 4.

Study Question: Did Jesus go to hell? If so, what happened to Jesus in hell?

Answer: Jesus Christ Immanuel was the only human being ever who had the dual capacity (mind and body) to fulfill all of **the** requirements of God for a damned soul. Only with His mind could He plumb all the depths of the ramifications of sin against God.

Chapter 5.

Study Question 1: Comparing Immanuel to Solomon, what are the things about Him[Immanuel] that make Him greater than Solomon?

Study Question 2: Comparing Immanuel to Jonas, what are the things about Him[Immanuel] that make Him greater than Jonas?

Answer 1: Solomon was wise enough, and was certified by heaven to practice law on earth, but he was not certified and knew nothing about practicing law for a universal clientele before the tribunal bench of heaven. He made an historic decision concerning the two disputing women **respecting** the ownership of a child. However, he was not qualified to determine the destinies of men with respect to life and death before the "King of the Ages."

Answer 2: Jonas was a persuasive preacher and possibly a great orator, but eternal redemption required much more than this.

Chapter 6.

Study Question: How does the author describe 'Immanuel' in terms of Him being the 'thought of God?'

Study Questions and Answers

Answer: Jesus is so much of the thought of God that the Apostle John calls Him, "The Word"—Logos.

Jesus, Immanuel, the Thought of God incarnate, made visible. How self-exalted is God's thought in Christ! God manifested the ultimate of His thought power in Jesus (i.e., as far as He would reveal to us).

Chapter 7.

Study Question: What was Christ made that caused us to be made the righteousness of God?

Answer: *When Immanuel, as only He could have been was made sin for us, He became God's New Creation, His super act to produce a new and super result(s). We have been made the righteousness of God in the super man who had been exalted and supranominated*.

Chapter 8.

Study Question: *How is Immanuel's ascending and descending compared to that of Solomon and all other men?*

Answer: *If He descends, He descends deeper than all. If He ascends, He ascends higher than all. He has no equals, a greater than   a greater than Solomon is here! If He lives, He lives more! If He dies, He dies more! If He lives again, He lives beyond!*

Chapter 9.

Study Questions:

1. Where are our sins that Jesus bore on the Cross?

2. What happened on the Cross?

Answer 1: Both Immanuel's body, which bore our sins, and the sins that were borne in it, are unfindable: "Unfindable Things."

2: On the cross, an absolutely perfect and final sacrifice was made. The only sacrifice ever offered to God, or that could be offered, was accompanied by the "*Consummatum Est.*"

Chapter 10

Study Question: What was God's Darkest Night?

Answer: Jesus' Eternal Moment was God's *ultima thule* manufacturing event. That is, we have no revelation of anything beyond it. There is nothing we can find in Holy Scripture that transcends it. Whatever God's night is that exceeds *the cross*, God does not want us to know it yet.

Chapter 11

Study Question: What did Jesus-Immanuel do with death?

Answer: **Jesus Christ's singular abolition of death singularly attests that there is no other source for LIFE and Immortality. Only He who abolished death can author Life and Immortality for men. He only has it!**

Chapter 12

Study Question: What did the first century Saints under the dynamic ministry of the apostles behold when they beheld Jesus?

Answer: "...and the Word was made flesh and dwelt among us and we beheld His glory as of the only begotten of the Father full of grace and truth." What a sight! What a glorious sight! i.e., the sight of Glory Divine...

Special Reference for Chapter 16, "Transforming Glory"

Note: ". . . by the Spirit of the Lord"

Let's compare our focus passage as it is read in different versions of the Scriptures:

New English Bible

"And because for us there is no veil over the face, we all reflect as in a mirror the splendor of the Lord; thus we are transfigured into His likeness, from splendor to splendor."

R. A. Knox

"It is given to us, all alike, to catch the glory of the Lord as in a mirror, with faces unveiled; and so we become transfigured into the same likeness, borrowing glory from that glory, as the Spirit of the Lord enables us."

C. B. Williams

"And all of us, with faces uncovered, because we continue to reflect like mirrors the splendor of the Lord, are being transformed into likeness to Him, from one degree of splendor to another, since it comes from the Lord who is Spirit."

Kenneth Wuest

Now, as for us, we all, with uncovered face, reflecting as in a mirror the glory of the Lord, are having our outward expressions changed into the same image from one degree of glory to another according as this change of   expression proceeds from the Lord, the Spirit, this out ward expression coming from the being

truly representative of our Lord
Changed 3339, metamorphoo; to transform (lit, or fig.
"metamorphose"): change, transfigure, transform.
Same vs. Mt. 17:9; Mk. 9:2 on Jesus' transfiguration
and also Romans 12:2, ". . .be ye transformed by the
renewing of your mind."

Special Reference: Latin Vulgate, by
St. Jerome used for Latin terms in thesis.

Bibliography

Albright, W. F. "The Names Shaddai and Abram".
Journal of Biblical Literature, 1935

Alfred, J., Kolatch, Jonathan. *The Jewish Book of
Why*. David Publishers, Inc. 1995

Barker, Margaret. "Isaiah". In Dunn, James D. G.,
Rogerson, John. *Eerdmans Commentary on the Bible*.
Eerdmans, 2001.

Bible Review: "Why God has so Many Names" by
Bernhard Lang (Old Testament and religious
studies, University of St. Andrews, Scotland &
Professor of Catholic Theology, University of
Paderborn, Germany), 2003.

Black, Henry. *Black's Law Dictionary,* 6th ed. West
Publishing, 1990

Special References and Bibliography

Brown, Raymond E., Fitzmyer, Joseph A., Donfried, Karl Paul. "Gospel of Matthew". *Mary in the New Testament*. Paulist Press, 1978

Burkett, Delbert. *An Introduction to the New Testament and the Origins of Christianity.* Cambridge University Press, 2002.

Childs, Brevard S. *Isaiah.* Westminster John Knox Press, 1996

Dictionary of the Bible, John L McKenzie (editor). Simon & Schuster, 1995.

Driver, S.R. "Recent theories on the origin and nature of the tetragrammaton". *Studia Biblica*, vol. i, Oxford, 1885.

Duling, Dennis C. "The Gospel of Matthew". In Aune, David E, *The Blackwell Companion to the New Testament*. Wiley-Blackwell, 2010.

Finlay, Timothy D. *The Birth Report Genre in the Hebrew Bible*. Mohr Siebeck, e, 2005.

France, R. T. "The Gospel of Matthew". Eerdmans, 2007.

Harris, Laird, Archer, Gleason, Jr. & Waltke, Bruce K. (eds.) *Theological Wordbook of the Old Testament*, 2 vol. Moody Press, Chicago, 1980.

Hoffman, Joel M. *In the Beginning: A Short History of the Hebrew Language*. NYU Press 2004

Joffe, Laura, "The Elohistic Pslater: What, how and why?", _Scandinavian Journal of the Old Testament_. Taylor & Francis, 2001.

Keener, Craig S. *A Commentary on the Gospel of Matthew*. Eerdmans, 1999.

Kretzmann, Paul E., *Popular Commentary of the Bible, The Old Testament*, Vol. 1. Concordia Publishing House, St. Louis, Mo. 1923.

Lightner, Robert. *The God of the Bible, An Introduction to the Doctrine of God*. Baker Book House, Grand Rapids, 1973.

Shaller, John, *The Hidden God, The Wauwatosa Theology*. Northwestern Publishing House, Milwaukee, Wisconsin, 1997.

Stern, David. *Jewish New Testament Commentary*. Jewish New Testament Publications, Inc., Clarksville, Maryland, 1996.

Strong, James, *The Exhaustive Concordance of the Bible*. Abingdon-Cokesbury Press, New York and Nashville, 1890.

Swart, Jacobus G. *The Book of Sacred Names*. Sangreal Sodality Press, Johannesburg, 2011.

Special References and Bibliography

Ancient References to the Harrowing [Jesus' decent into Hell]

Tertullian (A treatise on Christ and Anti-Christ 500/55)

Hippolytus (Treatise on Christ and Anti-Christ)
Origen (Against Celsus, 2:43)
St. Ambrose

Gospel of Nicodemus–Acts of Pilate
3rd Century A.D. chapter 17-27
Decensus Christi ad interos

Internet Articles and Sources

Merriam-Webster online dictionary [accessed 4/10/13]

http://grammar.about.com/od/il/g/juxtaposition [accessed 4/10/13]

http://www urban dictionary.com/define.php?term=juxataposition [accessed 4/3/13]

http://yahoo.com/question/index
http://dictionaryreference.com/browse/juxtaposition [accessed 4/9/13]

http://www Vocabulary.com/dictionary/juxtaposition [accessed 4/8/13]

The Name of Jesus Christ as Immanuel, Book II

http://thesaurus.com/browse/juxtaposition [accessed 4/11/13]

http://mathworld.wolframe.com/concentriccircles.html [accessed 3/4/13]

Latin Vulgate . Com: Helping You Understand Difficult Verses, http://latinvulgate.com [accessed 4/11/13]